DANGEROUS WATERS

Dangerous Waters

The Life and Death of Erskine Childers

Leonard Piper

Hambledon and London

London and New York

Hambledon and London
102 Gloucester Avenue
London, NW1 8HX

175 Fifth Avenue
New York
NY 10010

First Published 2003

ISBN 1 85285 392 1

A description of this book is available from the
British Library and from the Library of Congress.

Typeset by Carnegie Publishing, Lancaster,
and printed in Great Britain
by the Bath Press.

Distributed in the United States and Canada exclusively
by Palgrave Macmillan, a division of St Martin's Press.

Contents

Illustrations   vii

Introduction   ix

1   Young Erskine   1

2   Sea Fever   19

3   Soldier   39

4   Author   61

5   Marriage   81

6   New Interests   99

7   Gun-Runner   121

8   The Cuxhaven Raid   139

9   The Dardanelles   157

10   Sea and Sky   173

11   Sinn Fein   193

12   Civil War   215

13   The Tragedy of Erskine Childers   231

Notes   243

Bibliography   249

Index   251

Illustrations

1 Erskine Childers with his brother Henry
   (*Courtesy of the Board of Trinity College Dublin*)

2 Erskine Childers
   (*Courtesy of the Board of Trinity College Dublin*)

3 Erskine and Molly Childers, Flensburg 1906
   (*Courtesy of the Board of Trinity College Dublin*)

4 Aboard the *Sunbeam*, with his sisters Constance
   and Dulcibella and others
   (*Courtesy of the Board of Trinity College Dublin*)

5 Molly Childers, with rifle, and Mary Spring Rice aboard
   the *Asgard*
   (*Courtesy of the Board of Trinity College Dublin*)

6 Glendalough House, Annamoe, County Wicklow
   (*Courtesy of the Board of Trinity College Dublin*)

7 Molly Childers with her son Erskine
   (*Courtesy of the Board of Trinity College Dublin*)

8 Erskine Childers talking to Eamon de Valera
   (*Courtesy of the Board of Trinity College Dublin*)

9 Under Irish arrest
   (*Courtesy of the Board of Trinity College Dublin*)

Introduction

When I was a small boy, a tide-table hung upon our kitchen wall, dog-eared with constant use. Also subject to frequent inspection was the weathercock in the shape of a sailing barge which perched high on the barge's topmast holding up the washing-line in the garden. For, although our home in Colchester was five miles from the sea, the sea dominated our lives. There was also always the same question in need of an answer: whether my father would get home that day. He was the skipper of a Thames sailing barge, the *Saltcote Bel.* Upon her, in more peaceful times, he had roamed the English coastal waters from Cornwall to the Tyne, carrying wheat or timber, sugar and cement. But now, with the country at war, he was employed in carrying Canadian wheat from the London docks to a mill in Colchester and returning with flour for the capital.

It was from my father that I first heard the name Erskine Childers. My father read only two kinds of books. First, there were westerns, which he devoured at great speed and then discarded entirely without comment. Secondly, there were any book dealing with ships and the sea. Unlike the westerns, these were taken seriously, read slowly, carefully digested and the slightest error ruthlessly exposed. Very few met with his approval – but one that did was *The Riddle of the Sands.* It seemed to set the standard against which all the others were tested and frequently found wanting.

As for my own experiences of the book, there is somewhere, tucked away amongst my childhood memories, a recollection of *The Riddle of the Sands* as one of those radio serials that were my first introduction to adult literature. A winter evening, the windows covered with black-out curtains, a coal fire, and my brother and I listening intently to the exciting stories coming from what was then called the wireless. *The Count of Monte Christo, The Lost World, A Tale of Two Cities* opened up a whole new world in the mind of a small boy.

I cannot remember when I first read *The Riddle of the Sands* – I spent my teenage years reading anything and everything that came my way – Childers was no doubt part of that exploration. I was certainly very familiar with the story, but not with the story of its author. When, a great deal later, I discovered the nature of his death, I was astonished. How could it be? What was the author of such a patriotic book doing in the IRA?

The question lurked at the back of my mind for many years as I occupied my time away from the sea and from writing books. It was only when I retired and had time to indulge myself in other things that I looked at last for an answer to that question. Finding it proved more difficult than expected. There were certainly biographies of Erskine Childers available, but they didn't answer the question; often they didn't even ask it.

The basic problem was that they were compartmental, just as Childers's life was compartmental. Each author had his own particular interest and concentrated upon that. The Pophams are excellent on his seafaring activities as is Boyle on his Irish involvement; Erskine Childers's own account of the Boer War is fine. But they seemed to be writing about different people. And there were gaps in the story which, because they did not fit into any obvious compartment, no one had seriously studied. It is this rounded view of Erskine Childers the man that I have tried to provide. I do not pretend to have entirely solved the mystery of Erskine Childers, but I do believe that, even more than usual, the child was father to the man.

1

Young Erskine

Robert Erskine Childers was born in the prestigious Mayfair district of London on 25 June 1870. The house, 60 Mount Street, lay close to the junction with Park Lane, offering easy access to the healthy, open spaces of Hyde Park. His brother, Henry, was then aged two. Over the next few years the boys were to be joined by three sisters, Constance, Sybil and Dulcibella. As to his Christian names, he was probably named Robert after his father, although the name was as common in his mother's family of Barton as amongst the Childers family. The name Erskine is much easier to pin down. Thomas Erskine was one of his mother's ancestors. A colourful lawyer in the late eighteenth century, he was a friend of Fox and Sheridan, making a name for himself by defending Tom Paine, George Gordon and the leaders of the Corresponding Society of London. Eventually, with the rise to power of the Prince Regent, he became Lord Chancellor. However, he soon grew bored with the post and retired, having found respectability far too dull for his tastes.

At the time of Erskine's birth, his parents, Robert Caesar Childers and Anna Henrietta Childers, had good reason to be optimistic about the future. Their marriage was a happy one; they now had two healthy sons and Robert was rapidly earning for himself a European wide reputation for his academic work. His field of study was important, even if somewhat obscure. Several years spent working as a civil servant in Ceylon had left him with a passionate interest in the Pali language. Pali had been in use in much of southern Asia as early as the seventh century BC. It continued to be the literary language of the area for a thousand years. All the greatest Buddhist writings were in Pali. Yet within Europe the language remained virtually unknown, even to the greatest scholars. None of the important Buddhist scriptures had been published in any European language, nor was there any Pali dictionary available anywhere in Europe. Robert determined to fill that academic vacuum.

His studies first bore fruit in 1869, when he published, in the *Journal of the Royal Asiatic Society*, an English translation of the *Khuddaka Patha*, one of the most important of Buddhist sacred texts. When his work was received with immediate and widespread acclaim, Robert began an even more exacting task, that of creating an English-Pali dictionary. In 1872, when the first volume appeared, academic honours poured down upon him. University College, London created especially for him the first Chair of Pali and Buddhist Studies. His old employers showed their appreciation in a more modest way by providing him with a nominally paid position as a sub-librarian at the India Office.

But Robert was not the only member of the family to venture into print in 1872. Anna also produced a book that year, although on a less ambitious scale and with less academic acclaim. Published in Plymouth, it was a translation of a work by a Swiss theologian, Ernest Naville, under the title of *Evil in the Universe*.

Academic fame, an improved financial position and the regular arrival of additional children all encouraged the Childers family to move to a larger house. They did not go very far, just a short distance up the Bayswater Road to 38 Clanricarde Gardens. Their new home was one of those tall, narrow, late Victorian houses; ornate enough to impress passers by, while taking up as little land as possible. The house was also guaranteed to exhaust housemaids; forcing them to spend their young lives in forever carrying bedding, hot water and coal-scuttles up and down numerous flights of steep, narrow stairs.

But the house did have very real advantages; especially for a family with young children. The road itself was a quiet cul-de-sac, with only the occasional tradesman or visiting hansom cab to disturb the peaceful scene. At the same time, only a short walk away, just the other side of the Bayswater Road, dangerous with horse-buses and heavy carts, lay Kensington Gardens. Once there, small children could play happily on the carefully tended grass, amongst the prams, parasols, nursemaids and sailor suits of late Victorian England.

Those early years of Erskine's life provided everything that a child could need. His parents were prosperous as well as intelligent. They loved one another and their children. He had brothers and sisters to play with; he had security and went short of nothing. But, although he was unaware of it, there existed a threat to the family's happiness, a dark cloud that marred the otherwise clear blue sky of their lives. Sometimes it grew in intensity, black and menacing, only to recede again, to become no more than a dark patch on the far horizon. But always it was there, never allowing his parents, and his mother in particular, to relax completely. Shortly after he celebrated his sixth birthday, the cloud spread, blotted out the sun and Erskine's happy little world was never the same again.

The Childers family came from the Doncaster area of Yorkshire, where they had lived certainly since Tudor times; Hugh Childers, a banker, being Mayor of Doncaster in 1604, with his home at Carr House. Socially they progressed by the slow but effective method of prudent marriages. Early in the eighteenth century Mildred Childers married William Walbanke of Cantley Hall, not far from Doncaster. By this means Cantley Hall soon became the Childers family home. A few years later the family acquired fame, of a sort, when in 1721 Leonard Childers bred a racehorse, called 'Flying Childers', which romped home in the 500 Guineas.

In 1797, Colonel John Childers married the youngest daughter and co-heir of Lord Eardley, bringing further distinction and prosperity to the Childers name. The colonel's five children, all boys, behaved according to established custom. Two of them entered the church, one the army, and one the diplomatic service. The eldest, who inherited the Eardley title, married the daughter of a local squire to extend further the boundaries of the family estates. Canon Charles Childers, Erskine's grandfather, had the good fortune to inherit from an elder brother the position of chaplain to the English colony in Nice, a post to which he clung, limpet-like, for the next forty years; turning down all offers of advancement. He was destined to be a major influence upon Erskine's life, an influence that was not always appreciated. He was, politically and in every other way, conservative to an extreme degree.

In 1860, his son, Robert Caesar Childers, whose second name came from an ancestor of his mother's, went out to Ceylon as a writer for the Civil Service. His new employers were quick to recognise his useful qualities. Promotion came rapidly, leading to his appointment as private secretary to the Governor, Sir Charles McCarthy. Later he was further promoted, this time to an important position in Kandy. Soon after arriving in Ceylon Robert Childers developed an unusually keen

interest in the country, its history, religion and languages. Blessed with
intellectual curiosity and a good ear, within a remarkably short time
he had mastered the complexities of the Sinhalese language to an extent
far beyond that demanded by the Indian Civil Service. His interest grew
rapidly into a passion, then into an obsession. Every moment spared
from official duties was thrown into his linguistic studies. Opportunities
for home leave were discarded in favour of yet more study. Leading
Sinhalese scholars, delighted to find an Englishman genuinely interested
in their subject, became eager to teach him all they knew.

It could not possibly last. Nineteenth-century Ceylon was not a healthy
place for an Englishman, not even one prepared to behave sensibly: to
take home leave whenever he could; to avoid over-exertion in the stifling
heat; to be careful what he ate. And Robert was not careful; he consistently overworked and never took home leave. In March 1864 his health
broke down and he was returned home an invalid. Gradually recovering
at his parents' home in Nice, he suffered a new upset when his mother,
who had been nursing him devotedly, developed a fever and died. His
father's behaviour towards his slow recovery wavered between anxiety
and impatience. Relations between the two men were not improved
when, with what Robert considered to be indecent haste, his father
turned his attention towards the courtship of a clergyman's widow,
whom he shortly married.

The arrival of his father's new wife, into what he still thought of as
his mother's home, led Robert to return to England as soon as he felt
well enough. Once more he turned his mind to his linguistic studies.
His luck however had changed, because it was at this time that he first
met Anna Henrietta Barton. Beautiful and intelligent, Anna was a
member of an old Irish Protestant family from County Wicklow. The
Barton's family home was Glendalough House, near the tiny village
of Annamoe. The first Barton to live in Ireland had gone over with
the Earl of Essex in the days of Elizabeth Tudor. The house and its
surrounding land came as rewards for services rendered in dangerous
times. But by now they had lived there three hundred years and had
put down deep roots. Ireland was their home and they loved it
dearly. They thought of themselves as being without question Irish
and resented interference in Irish affairs from English politicians such
as Gladstone.

Despite all this, they kept one foot firmly planted in England. Socially they mixed only amongst their own kind. Invariably their children were educated in England; frequently finding marriage partners there. They also provided a steady stream of recruits for the British Army and Imperial Civil Service. They were proud to be part of the British Empire and any suggestion of Irish nationalism was anathema to them.

Anna's own father had been Captain Robert Barton, of the Coldstream Guards. During the Zulu War of 1879 he commanded the Frontier Light Horse, a force of 156 officers and men. In the aftermath of the disaster at Isandlwana the British commander, Lord Chelmsford, badly in need of some sort of victory to save his military reputation, decided to attack a Zulu stronghold at Hlobane Mountain. It all went terribly wrong. A plan to climb the mountain in total darkness only succeeded in alerting the Zulu warriors of the British presence. During the course of the shambles that followed, Barton was ordered to take thirty men and establish contact with troops detached earlier. In attempting to carry out the order Barton ran straight into a force of 20,000 Zulus. He himself might well have escaped, had he not gallantly stopped to pick up a young lieutenant whose own horse had been killed. The resulting gallop for safety ended after seven miles when Barton's own horse, forced to carry two men instead of one, finally collapsed under the strain. The two men were cut to pieces.

After their marriage Robert Childers and Anna Barton set up home together at the house in Mount Street. To attend to their personal needs they employed a housekeeper, a cook and a parlourmaid. With the arrival of children the household staff was increased by the recruitment of a nursemaid. From time to time, as a welcome change from the unhealthy, smoke-filled air of nineteenth-century London, they took their growing family to the Bartons' home in Ireland. Anna then had the pleasure of showing her children the fields, woods and lakes that had been the favourite haunts of her own childhood.

Glendalough House was large, parts of it dating back to the seventeenth century. From time to time over the years, as the family prospered, the house had been added to, the latest addition being a stone façade, complete with mullioned windows and battlements. This no doubt had been intended to emphasise the age of the house, but had succeeded only in making it appear Victorian. Glen, as it was fondly called, was set in extensive grounds offering fine views stretching to distant mountains.

The Bartons themselves had once been part of the Protestant Ascendancy, the sector of Irish society that both guaranteed the continuity of British rule and gained most from it. Those days were largely gone, swept away by voting reforms that necessitated politicians looking towards a much wider Irish electorate. But as yet those changes had made little practical impact upon the Bartons themselves. They still retained considerable local importance, frequently serving in offices such as that of Justice of the Peace.

Their political opinions are made clear enough from their reactions to Parnell's rise to prominence in the early 1880s. There had been a time when the Bartons and their near neighbours, the Parnells, had been close friends. They had dined frequently at one another's houses and an annual cricket match had been played between the two families. But Charles Parnell's involvement in Home Rule politics ended that and, for a while, all contact between the two families ceased. Later, when Charles Barton became head of the household, the link was re-established, but never with the same closeness. There were to be no more cricket matches.

As landlords, the Bartons were considerate but paternalistic. It was their custom that every Barton child should adopt a local family, visiting them from time to time and giving presents at Christmas. Presumably the families concerned were then expected to express their pleasure and gratitude. Whether these adoptions were really appreciated is doubtful. The Bartons were, in any case, separated from their tenants, not only by money and social position but by the vast, almost unbridgeable gulf of religious belief.

Before very long, the formal link between the Childers and Barton families became strengthened further by a growing friendship between Robert's youngest sister, Agnes, and his wife's brother, Charles. Their fondness for one another gradually deepened and it surprised no one when, in 1875, they announced their intention to marry.

Meanwhile, back at their London home, the young Erskine was becoming acquainted with another man who was to have a great influence upon his life. This was his father's cousin, Hugh Childers. As a young man, straight from Trinity College, Cambridge, Hugh had departed for

Australia, where he flourished in the free and easy atmosphere. Settling in Victoria, he went into politics, becoming a member of that state's first cabinet. At the age of thirty he was sent to London as Agent-General. When his period of office ended he decided to remain in England to try his luck in the wider world of British politics.

Given his Australian background it is perhaps not surprising that Hugh chose to join the Liberal Party, rather than the Conservatives. In 1860 there was a by-election in Pontefract. Hugh stood as the Liberal candidate and won. Down in Nice the news was not well received. The Canon's political views were such that Gladstone, who had been for many years a personal friend, he now regarded as a dangerous extremist. The prospect of having a Liberal MP actually in the family he could only view with horror. Nevertheless, Hugh was even more successful in British politics than he had been in Australia. When the Liberals formed an administration in 1868 he was given the Admiralty. In 1880 he became Secretary of State for War; in 1882 Chancellor of the Exchequer; and, in 1886, Home Secretary. As a government minister he showed all the usual Childers characteristics: great concentration, remarkable attention to detail, and the tendency to damage his health by working himself into the ground.

Following his physical breakdown in Ceylon and his return first to Nice and then to London, Robert's health recovered only slowly and never completely. Throughout their marriage Anna had frequent cause to worry about her husband. Bouts of illness were common; bad weather invariably gave him severe colds that, going straight to his chest, he found difficult to shake off. Always there seemed to be something affecting a constitution weakened by the years spent in Asia. And he would insist upon working too hard, taxing his strength. Time after time Anna pleaded with him to take care, to rest, to think of his family. But it did little good; his obsession with linguistic studies drove him on and allowed him no rest.

Finally Anna's worst fears were realised. In the early months of 1876 Robert acquired a cold, one even worse than usual, one that took him weeks to shake off, weakening his resistance to worse threats. With the arrival of the first signs of spring came the realisation that he had contracted consumption. With a mixture of love for her husband

and the dread of losing him, Anna became a devoted nurse. She rarely left his bedside, seeing to his every need, night and day, but without success. He became steadily worse. Shortly after Erskine's sixth birthday party, Robert, knowing that he had only a short time to live and anxious for the health of his young family, departed for an hotel in Weybridge. He died there on the 25 July 1876, at the early age of thirty-eight. Only a few weeks before his death news came that French academics had awarded him the highly prestigious Volney Prize for scholastic excellence.[1]

Even worse was to come for the Childers family. Within a few months of Robert's death, it became apparent that Anna also had the disease. One terrible morning in late autumn, Erskine, puzzled and frightened, stood at an upstairs window with his brothers and sisters, watching as his mother was hustled into a cab by anxious relatives. She waved to the children and they waved back, but she departed without any of the accustomed hugs and kisses. He never saw her again. Taken to a sanatorium near Windsor, Anna lived for another seven years; seven long, lonely, painful years spent slowly dying. The last paragraph of the book by Anna published in 1872 read:

> To him who is unwilling to doubt the authority of reason and the value of conscience, and who preserves an invincible faith in the goodness of the principle of the universe, good shines forth even in the study of evil, and the murmurs of discouragement resolve themselves at last into a song of love.

Anna's faith in the goodness of the universe was put to a terrible test.

With the five children now effectively orphaned, the only recently married Charles and Agnes Barton offered to give them a home at Glendalough. The other adult members of the Childers family accepted the offer with gratitude and relief. Acquiring a large instant family immediately after their honeymoon was an unusual way to begin a marriage, but the house was large and well provided with servants, to whom a governess was soon added. Within a few years five small Barton children arrived one by one to keep their cousins company, making necessary an extra wing to the house.

For little Erskine the events in the few months following his birthday must have been both frightening and bewildering; especially the sudden disappearance of his mother. His brother, Henry, no doubt also felt the loss, but he was a little older and much less sensitive. The girls were all younger and much less aware. It would have been better for all concerned if Anna had died quickly. Especially for Erskine. Then, by mourning his loss, he could have come to terms with her absence in the normal, natural way. But instead she lived on. They wrote letters to one another, stilted letters, letters in which neither of them could express the emotions they really felt. Letters which, rather than healing the wounds, served only to keep them open.

Erskine also lived in a society in which men were not supposed to show their emotions and where little boys were expected to behave like men. Having no outlet for the depth of unhappiness that he felt, Erskine reacted the way children do in such circumstances – he turned in on himself. He developed the habit of taking long walks in the surrounding countryside, always alone. The walks enabled him to mourn the loss of his mother without being seen; and the physical exertion helped to ease his despair. He also developed a secret plan, a great dream for him to cling to, that helped him move his life onwards. He pledged to himself, that when he was older, like Saint George, he would ride forth, kill the dragon that held his mother captive, and bring her home to Glendalough in triumph.

Glendalough was his mother's home. This was where she had been born and where he had grown up. She had known the room he slept in, the tree he walked beneath, the stream he sat beside. In Erskine's young mind Ireland and his mother became inseparably linked, a link that was to remain for the rest of his life. There is also the likelihood that Erskine reacted to the disappearance of his mother in another, much more damaging way. With a feeling of guilt. Such a reaction is common enough from a small child faced with devastating and inexplicable events. The feeling that it is, in some way, his fault. His fault that his father has died; and that his mother has deserted him. From that springs the belief that he deserves to be punished. He then spends the rest of his life subconsciously punishing himself for his supposed wickedness.

A deep guilt complex of that type would account for aspects of Erskine's character and behaviour that were to be present throughout his life and which otherwise remain unexplained. Aspects which gradually strengthened with the passing of time until they became dominant features of his personality. There was, for instance, an asceticism that compelled him to self-denial of both alcohol and tobacco. He also constantly subjected himself to entirely unnecessary discomfort. And it could also explain his excessive courage, a courage that often appears foolhardy. So foolhardy that one acquaintance called him a crackpot.

When Erskine had first arrived in Ireland the Bartons had worried about him, not only because of his obvious unhappiness but also because he had a persistent cough. A cough which, given the fate of his parents, made them fear the worst. But his long walks in the clear air of the Wicklow Hills seemed to have solved both problems.

As the months passed the Childers family settled down in their new home. The Bartons were kind and did everything they could to help. Glendalough offered wonderful opportunities for children, especially for boys. They learned all the usual country pastimes; how to fish and ride and shoot. Around the house were 1500 acres of farmland, woodlands, and lakes to row a boat upon. Not far away were beautiful beaches with fine, clean sand for games and picnics. And, if the weather was bad, there was always the big house, ideal for games of hide and seek.

The two brothers were already beginning to show their own individual characters. In the schoolroom Erskine soaked up mathematics and English grammar like a sponge. Henry, on the other hand, treated academic subjects as terrible punishments which kept him from the more manly pursuits that he so much preferred. Mentally, the Bartons, with a long military tradition of their own, marked him down for the army. In 1878, aged ten, he went off to a preparatory school in England. Three years later they moved him to Harrow.

Erskine was different; the possibilities for him were much wider. The Bartons consulted both the Canon and Hugh Childers, well aware of the difficulties in getting the two strong-willed men to agree on anything. Somehow they produced a plan of campaign that satisfied them both. In 1880 Erskine, now aged ten, returned to England, destined for a preparatory school at Bengeo, near Hertford. Before long gratifying reports began to arrive at Glendalough. Erskine, they said, showed a natural aptitude for learning. They praised his studies of English literature, his writing composition and his rapid progress with in Latin and French.

By now Erskine's character was set. Much of it he had clearly inherited from his father, the good and the bad. His particular type of intelligence for instance: his easy acquisition of languages, his great attention to detail, and his amazing powers of concentration. Everyone who came to know him throughout his life was struck by the same thing, his ability to concentrate on what he was doing to such an extent that he became totally oblivious to everyone and everything around him.

But he had also inherited the other, dangerous, Childers characteristic, the tendency towards obsession. Erskine could not just be interested in a subject, he had to be overwhelmed by it. The same pattern occurred throughout his life. Someone, either a friend or relative, introduced him to some subject or activity, which he himself found interesting. Erskine took it up and before long it dominated his life. Whilst another man would add it to his interests or become tired of it and replace it with something else, Erskine surrendered himself to it totally.

As for other aspects of his character, they arose primarily from his childhood experiences, especially from that terrible year when he was six. The habit, first acquired at Glendalough, of going on long walks he was to retain for the rest of his life. Also retained was the tendency to hold something back, the unwillingness or perhaps the inability to reveal the depth of his feelings, even to the closest of his friends. And somewhere, far beneath the surface, guilt; a terrible guilt that gnawed at his very soul, crippling his personality and leading him to a violent death.

From Bengeo, Erskine progressed to Haileybury, also in Hertfordshire. Once the school had been the training-ground for recruits to the old East India Company. The end of John Company had also meant the death of the school. But in 1862 it had been recreated along more orthodox lines. Now, with an old friend of the Canon's as headmaster, the school seemed ideal for the academically minded Erskine.

Early in 1884, just as he was beginning to settle down in his new school, feeling less confused, making new friends, Erskine was called to the headmaster's study. He was told that his mother had died. Once more grief swept over him; the news meant the end of a dream, the great dream that had sustained him for so long. The belief that one day he would be reunited with his mother. Now it could never be. In the school, surrounded by other boys, most of whom he hardly knew, Erskine was once more forced to hide his feelings, to control his despair; to strengthen the walls that separated his emotions from his demeanour. Again he withdrew, took long walks through the Hertfordshire countryside, and sat alone on the grassy banks of the River Lea and grieved.

He later wrote, in a letter to his aunt, that the news of his mother's death ended his belief in religion. But too much significance should not be attached to that. People react to the events of their lives not in accordance with the nature of those events but in accordance with their own natures. Erskine's nature was such that religion was unlikely to play much part in his life. As he was later to show, he found it difficult to understand the power that religion could have over people. His mother was of course very different. The disasters that overwhelmed her life in all probability served only to strengthen her religious convictions.

For a while this new emotional shock delayed his academic progress. He did not do badly, usually ranking about the middle of his class, but he was capable of much more. Before long, as he recovered, he really began to show his mettle. Then the prizes came rolling in. Awards for Shakespearean criticism; for Greek and Latin translation; for essays and for art. Despite the fact that he normally wore glasses, he also became proficient in those non-academic activities to which English public schools attached so much importance. He was a member of the rugby fifteen, the rowing eight, the football eleven and was captain of paper-chases. And, as a change from all those physical endeavours, he was also secretary of the Senior Literary Society. Amongst the other boys he was invariably known as 'Perk'.

Erskine's rapid progress was watched with pleasure by Hugh Childers, who occasionally took time off from his duties at the House of Commons to visit his young and promising relative, visits that did nothing to damage Erskine's prestige in the school. Towards the end of each school term Erskine was able to look forward to returning to Glendalough, to his sisters and cousins, to the big, old house and the peaceful Irish countryside. Then there would be walks, games, rowing on the lake with Henry – the simple, quiet pleasures of being at home.

In June 1889, at the school speech day, he heard with great pride and delight that he had won a place at Cambridge. He was to go to Trinity College, the old college of Hugh Childers, who was, if possible, even more pleased than the young Erskine. Everything was going to plan; even the Canon was impressed. Returning to Ireland Erskine was met with more congratulations from his sisters and the Bartons. Henry, already away at Sandhurst, wrote expressing his own pleasure, although commenting upon the unfairness of so much intelligence going to one brother and so little to the other.

During the long summer days prior to taking up his place at Cambridge, Erskine resumed his old wandering habit. He ranged far and wide over the Wicklow Hills. With a pack on his back, map and compass in hand, he covered thirty miles a day, spending the night in a village inn before returning by a different route the next day. One morning he set out on just such an expedition. He had, however, only covered the first few miles of his planned walk when there came a sudden torrential rainstorm. With no cover available, in a matter of minutes he was soaked to the skin. The sensible thing would have been for him to retrace his steps and to return home in search of dry clothing.

But he was a young man and young men are not always sensible. He was also Erskine Childers, who once embarked upon anything was not easily deflected from his chosen course, and whose every instinct was to press on regardless and to stop for nothing. So he continued precisely as planned, oblivious of discomfort. When, several hours later, he reached the inn that was his intended destination, instead of immediately going to his room to remove his wet clothes, he stayed in the bar talking.

Was this just thoughtlessness? Or was it an early example of Erskine deliberately subjecting himself to discomfort? Either way, he paid a high price for his foolishness. By the time he reached home the next day he had a severe chill. Much worse, it soon became apparent that he had also contracted sciatica in his left foot. His doctors did everything they could, but the nerve was irreparably damaged. For the rest of his life he walked with a limp, a limp that brought to an end his involvement in most sports, although not his taste for long walks.

Early in that autumn of 1889 Erskine Childers became a student at Trinity College, Cambridge. Passing through the imposing Tudor gateway into the Great Court for the first time, looking around at the beautiful and historic buildings that surround it, must surely have given him a thrill of pride and excitement. So many great and famous men had been there before him. Now it was his turn; perhaps his turn to make a mark upon the long history of England.

He was not given accommodation within the college itself but found rooms with a Mrs Juler at No. 5 Bridge Street, only a short walk away, through All Saints Passage. There were clear advantages of living outside college, in the form of much less supervision. For Erskine there would be no necessity to clamber up ivy-clad walls after midnight; although given his character, it is unlikely that Erskine would have given the authorities much trouble in that respect.

During the next few weeks he gradually settled down in his new surroundings, finding his way about, making friends, establishing a fresh routine. Amongst the first things he did was to join the Cambridge Union. He regularly attended debates but intervened only rarely, being rather overawed by the seriousness of the discussions. He also doubted his ability to meet the high standard of oratory expected from those who took part.

Much more to his tastes were the proceedings of Trinity's own debating society, the Magpie and Stump. The society's meetings were held on alternate Fridays. They were presided over by a president wearing a dinner-jacket and a bright red tie who sat, a trifle precariously upon a table. Immediately opposite him stood a glass case containing two stuffed magpies sitting on a stump. All speeches were addressed to His Majesty the Bird, any other form of address being instantly ruled out of order. Every member attending was expected to speak for at least four minutes; failure to do so resulted in a fine of half a crown.

The evening's proceedings always began in a conventional manner with the formal reading of the minutes of the last meeting. At which point orthodoxy usually disappeared. Invariably a long and heated discussion took place, often resulting in the minutes being totally re-jected. If, at the end of this prolonged argument, there was any time left, they then held a debate upon some suitable topic. The subjects for debate varied enormously, sometimes dealing with serious questions of the day, such as the Parnell scandal, or the desirability of the rail-ways being brought under state control, on other occasions with more frivolous topics such as, 'The early bird catches the worm'.

Erskine was elected to membership on 15 November 1889. At the very next meeting he spoke in favour of a motion calling for the construction of a Channel Tunnel. The proposal was defeated by a narrow margin. At a later meeting he himself proposed 'that in the event of a Franco-German war the sympathies of this house would be on the side of the French'. Again he was outvoted. On a later occasion he spoke against Home Rule for Ireland. That time his side won.

He was far from being a great orator, finding it difficult to express his views concisely. Often he would speak at, or so it would seem to his listeners, interminable length, only to have the next speaker demolish his entire argument in two minutes flat. It was also noticeable that, in building up his case, he always preferred to rely upon an accumulation of facts, seeming reluctant to indulge in emotional appeals or oratorical flourishes.

As for his formal academic studies, these presented him with little difficulty. Study was second nature to him, just as it had been with his father. Latin and Greek absorbed him and he absorbed them, the inherent logic of classical subjects appealing to his particular type of mind. Intricacies of grammar that bored or baffled others he found both fascinating and simple to comprehend.

But his basic seriousness did not prevent him from making friends; friends who greatly influenced him and, in some cases, remained with him for the rest of his life. Walter Runciman, for instance, the son of a northern shipowner, and Eddie Marsh, the future secretary to Winston Churchill. There was also Ivor Lloyd Jones and Charles Trevelyan. These were his closest friends. Together they talked and argued, cycled about the flat Cambridgeshire countryside, and spent weekends sailing on the Norfolk Broads.

Longer holidays were spent back with his family at Glendalough. By now his Uncle Charles had died, leaving the widowed Aunt Agnes in charge of the house. She looked to Erskine for advice, preferring him to the older but less serious-minded Henry. It was a task that often required from him a fair amount of tact. Much of her temperament she had clearly inherited from her father, the Canon, which resulted in her having a rigid outlook on the world. Her religious views, for instance, were such that she would not allow the postman to come up to the house, because he was a Catholic.

In 1891 Erskine was elected secretary and treasurer of the Magpie and Stump Debating Society. By established custom he should, in the spring of 1892, have been promoted to president in an uncontested election. That, however, was not to be. An alternative candidate put himself forward, in the form of an eccentric and wealthy Scotsman, George Hamilton-Gordon, a son of Lord Stanmore. He was, in every respect, the complete opposite to Erskine, whom he clearly saw as hopelessly dull and scholarly. But Erskine had to work – he needed the degree, still having to make his way in the world. Hamilton-Gordon, on the other hand, aristocratic and rich, could afford to be more relaxed about his education. For him, the principal purpose of going to university was to enjoy himself. Not that he confined himself entirely to sport and japes. At the time he was campaigning for the presidency of the Magpie and Stump he was also teaching himself Russian, for the sole reason that he had been told the language was difficult to learn.

With the election contested, posters soon appeared in profusion in windows and on walls all over college and beyond, promoting their respective candidates. 'Which do you prefer? Mr Gordon's common sense or the intolerable gas of Mr Childers?' was answered by, 'Vote for Mr Childers – The Constitutional Candidate'.

The full flavour of the campaign is best described in the words of the *Cambridge Review*:

> The Magpie and Stump election produced the most singular entertainment which has been seen in Cambridge for a very long while. Throughout the college and in some of the street windows and other coigns of vantage were decorated with large posters; little sandwich-boys paraded the streets beseeching the passers-by in their most winning tones to vote for this or that candidate; many notices written in chalk on walls survive even now, and a considerable amount of ephemeral literature was freely circulated, of which the most amusing was Mr Childers' manifesto. The election itself was the largest and most delightful 'rag' which has taken place within our memory; almost everyone preserved the most perfect good humour, though some people who had squibs caused alarm by their fine indifference to danger, the danger to others that is.
>
> The battle was long doubtful, until Mr Gordon entered the field with a curious and antiquated piece of artillery known as a slogan, the sound of which so terrified the enemy that they broke and retired defeated. When the result had been made known, the fun still went on in the court with unabated vigour, and for some time the efforts which dons and porters made to obtain quiet were unavailing.[2]

The result of all this effort and excitement was that Hamilton-Gordon was elected president by 127 votes to 103. He then demonstrated his belief in old-fashioned sportsmanship by appointing Erskine vice-president, a post created especially for him. The following term Erskine was elected president unopposed.

On the face of it Erskine had taken all this in good part. But is that the whole story? Certainly he would have been less than human had he not been at least slightly irritated at Hamilton-Gordon's intervention. Erskine was an unusually serious-minded young man with whom tolerance was not a strong point. And within only a few years he was to show nothing but contempt for the British establishment and all it stood for, attacking it at every opportunity. Was it cause and effect? When he criticised cavalry officers for their conservatism and stupidity was it in part an unconscious blow against Hamilton-Gordon?

By this time Erskine was also editor of the *Cambridge Review*, for which he had often written articles. Suitable material for the paper was almost always in short supply, which meant that the editor frequently had to write more than half the paper himself. One article, anonymous but clearly showing the Childers style, was a skit on the Sherlock Holmes stories then fascinating the reading public for the first time:

> Had I known him less well I should have thought him either asleep or drunk, and to the prejudiced mind this conclusion would have been rendered probable from the fact that he had spent the morning making experiments on the effects produced upon the palate by forty-three different brands of Scotch whisky. He says he's writing a monograph upon the subject.

Having successfully obtained his degree, Erskine chose to stay on in Cambridge for another year to read law. His reasons are unknown; possibly he was advised to do so by Hugh Childers, who continued to be an important influence upon him.

Thanks to his friendship with Eddie Marsh, Erskine's social world during his final year at Cambridge widened considerably, bringing within it many of the most brilliant young men of his day. In July 1893 a small group of friends from Trinity spent a week together in Wales. The days were passed in strolling about the countryside, admiring the landscape, the evenings in reading to one another and in intellectual conversation. The group, in addition to Erskine, included Bertrand Russell,

Lytton Strachey, the Trevelyan brothers, Maurice Baring and Eddie Marsh. During the course of the holiday, Erskine had the distinction of teaching his intellectual friends the art of fishing. Although he enjoyed meeting them, such high-powered minds seem to have had little influence upon Erskine; he was never to be an intellectual himself. Throughout his life his tastes in reading rarely ranged outside his boyhood favourites of Dumas, Fennimore Cooper and Thackeray.

By the end of 1893, Erskine had succeeded in adding a law degree to his B.A. The following January he moved to London, where he enrolled with a Mr Scoones who ran a cramming establishment for the Civil Service examinations. Mr Scoones was small and elegant, with white hair and a little white beard. He was also a strict disciplinarian, inclined to violent fits of temper when any of his charges failed to learn the lists of French words with which he constantly supplied them.

In Erskine's case he is unlikely to have had much trouble. Study always attracted him and learning languages was something he found easy. Certainly, when the examinations finally arrived, Erskine came third, enabling him not only to enter the Civil Service but also to choose which department he wished to join. No doubt once more under the influence of Hugh Childers, Erskine chose to become a Committee Clerk in the House of Commons.

2

Sea Fever

Erskine celebrated his new employed status by acquiring the first home of his own. With his salary of £100 per year, plus the small income that he had from investments, he was able to rent a flat at 2 Mitre Court Buildings. Situated at the bottom of a small street running from Fleet Street to the Temple, his new home was both quiet and convenient.

The position of Committee Clerk in the House of Commons was not an occupation likely to set a young man's pulse racing. But for Erskine it did have its attractions. The duties involved drafting and continually redrafting proposed legislation; inserting and deleting clauses; and carefully selecting words and phrases to comply with the compromises reached by the politicians in the House. These were tasks perfectly suited to the Childers mind; the qualities required were precisely those his father had employed in translating the Pali language: concentration, attention to detail and clarity of language. Erskine slipped easily into the routine.

There were also other advantages of the work. There was, for instance, the continual interest of being close to the centre of government; of regularly seeing the most powerful men in the land; and of being amongst the most well-informed people in the country. Even the place of work was calculated to impress: an office in the Houses of Parliament, with all its grandeur. Large desks, plush seats, the walls lined with bookcases full of leather-bound legal volumes; ornate ceilings; and an air of calm, unhurried power. The very centre of the Empire.

Despite all of these points in its favour, it is true to say that of all Erskine's varied activities during his life, his long period of employment as a Committee Clerk is the only one that failed to inspire him, the only one that never became a passion. It remained just a job. But there was one other advantage in working at the House of Commons; one that Erskine made full use of, the long parliamentary recesses, much longer than today. With no politicians sitting there were no Bills, no amendments, nothing to do. A clerk was free to turn his mind to other interests, sport perhaps, or travel.

To his new colleagues in the office, Erskine seemed quiet, studious, rather dull. When work was slack he could be observed scribbling in a notebook; apparently he hoped one day to write a novel. As for what he did at weekends, away from the office, his colleagues had no idea; they assumed much of the same. Dull.

Then, somehow, word went round the office that he had a boat; that he went sailing. Perhaps there was more to him than they thought. Questions began to be asked as to where he kept it. Maidenhead, perhaps, or Henley. Greenhithe? Where's that? Down river? Gravesend? And where did he go on it? Thinking, perhaps Sheerness or Leigh on Sea. Where? Boulogne?

The 1890s was a time when the English, of all classes, of all backgrounds, suddenly discovered the sea. They had, of course, always seen themselves as a maritime nation, but most of them never went near it, certainly no nearer than the beach. Now all that changed. The lower classes, whenever they could afford it, went on paddle-steamers to Margate, down the Bristol Channel or along the South Coast. Their social betters, on the other hand, bought boats, seeing themselves as following in the traditions of Drake and Raleigh.

These new boats fell into several categories. There were, for instance, those owned by the rich and best described as gin palaces. They moved around the coast, from Cowes to Torbay or Weymouth and across the Channel to Dieppe or Honfleur. But they were little more than floating hotels. The second category were racing yachts which, over the years, became bigger and bigger, faster and faster, more and more expensive. They were usually owned by the same people who owned the gin palaces. You could not, after all, expect to be taken seriously at Cowes if you did not own a yacht. They were invariably manned by professional crews. As for their owners, they would no more dream of sailing their own yachts as would consider riding their own horses in the Derby.

But there was a third category of boat, the cruiser, ideal for men of modest means but with an urge for adventure. Unlike the other categories of boat, these were sailed by their proud owners, everywhere and in all weathers. The worse the weather, the more likely they were to be at sea. Often professional seamen, having with difficulty brought their vessels into port during a storm, would be amazed to see tiny yachts setting out for Heligoland or Cherbourg. Such yachtsmen had little interest in racing, being more often collaborators than competitors. They saw themselves as explorers, the natural inheritors of Cook and Frobisher. The Cruising Club, founded in 1880 and receiving a royal warrant in 1902, published small charts for its members and an annual magazine full of accounts of their voyages. It was this happy band of brothers that Erskine now joined. Within only a few years he was first a committee member, then its secretary. He also used its annual journal as a way of stretching his literary muscles.

That final year at university, 1894, was an exciting one for Erskine. The world suddenly opened out for him, offering unlimited promise. It had seen him meeting new, interesting people. There was the knowledge that he would soon be working for a living and would have financial independence. And, like so many others at that time, he discovered the sea. Erskine's first introduction to sailing was on the Norfolk Broads with his university friends. In Walter Runciman's care, he also discovered the type of yachts and yachting that Carruthers refers to in *The Riddle of the Sands*: 'My faultless attire, the trim gig and obsequious sailors, the accommodation ladder flashing with varnish and brass in the August sun, the orderly snowy decks and basket chairs under the awning aft.'

But it was his brother, Henry, who first demonstrated to him the pleasures of going to sea in a small boat, of pitting his wits against the elements. Throughout his life Henry was to prove adventurous. First, the army, seeing action in the Boer War; then to the Yukon for the gold rush; after that it was back to Strathcona's Horse for the First World War. Even when he did finally settle down it was on a farm in Nova Scotia. However, in the case of sailing, while it was Henry who first raised the interest, it was Erskine who became fanatical about it.

Shortly before Easter 1893, Erskine and Henry bought a boat. Knowing nothing whatever about boats, they naturally bought one that was totally unsuited to their needs. They planned to explore the Irish and Scottish coasts, and to visit all the little bays, estuaries and ports that came their way. The boat they bought was a former racing-yacht, named *Shulah*, with a huge keel requiring eight and a half feet of water. This meant that most small ports, the very places they most wanted to visit, were inaccessible to them. *Shulah* also had a mainsail and boom of monstrous proportions, designed for the large crews normally carried during races.

Being frankly ignorant of the sea, they thought it best to hire a professional skipper. He, quickly noting the inexperience of the owners and the size of the mainsail, promptly demanded a mate. At last setting sail, the skipper, even before they were out of Kingstown harbour, warned them that 'there would be a sea outside' and suggested they dress accordingly. They therefore donned their new, thick, unwieldy oilskins, mentally preparing themselves for huge, crashing waves, only to discover that there was only the lightest of breezes and the calmest of seas.

Having begun by making them look foolish, the skipper spent the rest of the voyage treating them like delicate passengers, and refusing to allow them to do or touch anything. Eventually, from some motive of his own, the skipper persuaded them, by means of much nautical jargon, that they needed to put into Belfast for repairs. In attempting to do so he only succeeded in running the boat onto a sandbank on a falling tide. Before long *Shulah* sat perched on her huge keel, propped up precariously by pieces of wood. When the tide rose again the crew resigned, refusing to work anymore for such unappreciative owners.

Relieved to be rid of one charlatan, the two brothers promptly hired another, who, it turned out, only wanted a free passage to Oban. The result is best given in Erskine's own words:

> He brought discredit on us in port, purposely ran us aground in leaving the bay, alleged damage to the keel and the need for docking, and when, in a flame of rage, we gave him instant notice to quit, demanded a sum so large as to suggest blackmail, insinuating our guilty intent to 'pile up' our damaged boat with an eye for the insurance.[1]

Happily it was a case of third time lucky. They found a young Scots fisherman who was content to allow them to do anything they liked, providing that it was understood that he was in charge. In his nominal care they reached Fort William without further incident. By then they had convinced themselves that they now knew all they needed to know about sailing; that 'professional help' was no longer necessary. When the time came to return to Ireland, they sailed *Shulah* alone. To once more quote Erskine: 'Memorable was the first morning, when we set the sails, weighed the anchor, and glided down the loch, uncriticised, unaided, masters of our fate.'[2] That first day, as they sailed down the often wild coast of the West Highlands, bound for the Clyde, the elements were kind to them, wind and currents working in their favour. They rapidly gained in confidence, even declining the convenient short-cut of the Crinan Canal in favour of the much longer and more adventurous route around the Mull of Kintyre. By the time they entered the Clyde they were beginning to feel that they knew it all, that their sailing apprenticeship was already over. But there is more to sailing than running before the wind in deep water with the sea all to yourself. Sooner or later you have to enter port; to navigate narrow channels; to find your way through a crowded anchorage. Then different arts are required, arts that can look easy when practised by others, but are difficult for the first-timer to achieve. This is especially so if the novices choose to arrive after dark, as Henry and Erskine did at Gourock:

> It was not until we actually entered Gourock Bay late on a dark, blowy evening, that we became thoroughly alive to some of the difficulties of short-handed sailing. Too long accustomed to solitude and sea-room, we came storming with magnificent nonchalance into an anchorage thickly dotted with anchor-lights swaying above hulls invisible in the darkness.
> We blundered miserably about, shaving a bow-spit here and a jigger there, until more by accident than design we brought up in an apparently free space, sullenly deaf to the cries of a dim figure on board a neighbouring yacht.[3]

Despite these occasional problems, the Childers brothers greatly enjoyed their new freedom. The following day saw them once more setting out, this time heading for the coast of Ireland. The arrival of another sunset finding them well away from land, they were able to savour to the full the pleasures of sailing at night. The swish of water under the bow, the wave-tops glistening, the mast-head drawing circles against a sky smothered in stars, the flash of a distant lighthouse, and the darker shape of a passing steamer. An experience never to be forgotten. Early the next morning they approached their home port, tired but content:

> In the longest and hardest passages, however, there comes a moment when

you begin to feel definitely that all is well, when humour banishes care and
fatigue, and the thought of arrival in port inspires a splendid exaltation.
Rockabill light was far astern, Howth light, as we approached, succumbed to
the strengthening dawn, and at last, blear-eyed, worn out, but unspeakably
proud and happy, we swung round the pierhead of Kingstown Harbour,
picked our way smoothly and warily – although alas with no one to applaud
– among the still sleeping yachts, dropped our anchor, stowed our sails and
slept.[4]

That first voyage had taught the Childers brothers a great deal; and
not only about boats. But it was obvious that *Shulah* didn't meet their
needs, that something smaller and more manageable was required.
Advised that the best place to sell her would be Plymouth, they decided
to sail her there. Leaving Kingstown on 22 September with a nice
north-westerly breeze, they started off in fine style, only to have the
wind turn southerly on them. They beat to and fro all night, but made
little ground. The next day they reached Waterford where, the wind
continuing from the south, they wisely lay up for two days. Then they
set off again, the wind now light but westerly. Eventually they rounded
Land's End and crept into Penzance. The following day, despite alternate
rain and fog, they moved on to Plymouth. That was their final voyage
in *Shulah*, which they successfully sold the following spring.[5]

Despite the fact that *Shulah* had been, in some ways, a disappointment,
Henry and Erskine had both enjoyed and profited from the experience.
But while Henry had acquired a taste for sailing, just as he had a taste
for riding or climbing, Erskine had become addicted. For years to come
every moment that he could spare from work was spent on and around
boats. Naturally, being Erskine, he set out to do it properly, to study
the subject in depth, to know all there was to know about ships and
the sea.

In the Easter of 1895, with *Shulah* sold, Erskine bought a replacement,
officially called *Marguerite*, but usually known as *Mad Agnes*. The new
boat, which according to Erskine was dirt cheap, was only eighteen feet
long and half-decked. She was clinker built with a draught, when the
centre-board was up, of only two feet six inches. *Marguerite*'s cheap
price was probably her principal attraction, because Erskine was, in other
respects, less than enthusiastic about her. In an article written for the
Cruising Club Journal, he commented: 'The drawbacks and difficulties

of cruising in such a boat do not need enumeration, and I should not have tried it had my choice been free.'⁶ One obvious drawback was her lack of a proper cabin:

> As for sleeping accommodation, I have a specially designed bell-tent of oiled canvas, laced round the combing, when in use. Our couches consist of two reindeer-hair mattresses, which make most efficient life-preserving gear.⁷

But despite her disadvantages, it was *Mad Agnes* that Erskine established at Greenhithe, convenient for his London home. Every weekend he spent aboard her, employing a Kent seaman, Bob Earles, to teach him the finer points of sailing. He also set himself to learn navigation, a subject which, given his usual dedication, he quickly mastered. The same year he joined the Cruising Club, whose annual magazine soon began publishing regular articles by him.

Within only a few weeks of buying *Mad Agnes* Erskine set out on a ten-day cruise. From Greenhithe he sailed single-handed to Folkestone. There he was joined by two of his old university friends, one of whom was Ivor Lloyd-Jones. A few days later they crossed the Channel, 'spent an evening of wild dissipation in Boulogne', stayed the night in an hotel and sailed back the next day. The return journey, 'what with calms, heavy showers and changeable airs took fifteen hours'. They arrived back at Folkestone tired but triumphant at four in the morning.

Much of that summer Erskine spent with Lloyd-Jones exploring the muddy rivers and creeks of the Essex coast. Then, on 6 July, he set out alone on his most ambitious cruise so far. Leaving Greenhithe at about midday, he sailed *Mad Agnes* down the Thames and then up the Medway to Rochester, where he stocked up with provisions. Two days later he set off once more:

> I sailed on till 9 p.m., when I anchored about two miles off Herne Bay to take some sleep. Set tent, dined and turned in at 10 p.m. At 3 a.m. on the 9th, I got under way on the ebb with light south-west breeze and ran to Margate, where I let go outside the harbour and completed my night's sleep.⁸

This is Erskine the yachtsman at his most typical. Not content with beginning his night's sleep anchored two miles off Herne Bay (a far from comfortable spot in an eighteen foot boat), he then completed it outside Margate harbour, exposed to every wind and current, rather than take shelter inside. As he later explained in the *Cruising Club Journal*:

> I may say that I always made a point of keeping in open anchorage at night in preference to the inside of a tidal harbour, whenever and wherever this was possible. I have the strongest antipathy to the dirt, odours, publicity and general discomfort of a quayside berth in a crowded basin.[9]

He reached Folkestone on the 11th, where he remained until the 14th, staying with friends. The voyage was then resumed as far as Hastings, where a local fisherman clearly misread the character of this slightly-built, rather diffident young man:

> Had myself put ashore for shopping and newspapers. Aboard again at 4.30. Unpleasant contre-temps with the men whose boat I had used to shore and back. One came aboard and asked an exorbitant sum, blustered and refused to leave my boat till paid. I offered more than a fair sum and said he might stay as long as he liked, but that I was going to sail with the tide. Then made tea and sat down to read. After an interval of silence, heard much altered voice consenting to a somewhat less sum. Took no notice till the demand descended to my original level, when I promptly paid him and he decamped in low spirits.[10]

Late on 18 July he reached Bembridge, on the Isle of Wight, where he kept to his usual perverse rule by anchoring outside the protection of the harbour, despite worsening weather:

> A test night for my tent. It blew hard all night, first from the west, then from the south, with a deluge of rain, but managed to spend a very comfortable night, and woke up to a fine blowy day.[11]

The next day he returned home by train. Two weeks later he was back again, still alone, to spend a week exploring the Solent, with a base close to Brownsea Island. But not always alone:

> Spent the next few days sailing about the sheltered waters, generally three-reefed in very stormy weather, with limited cargoes of small South London boys, a camp of whom had been organised by some friends of mine. It is interesting work (even with shifting boy-ballast) exploring that labyrinth of creeks and islands.[12]

A few weeks later, once more alone, he continued further west to

Poole, in Dorset. On 20 September he was joined by Henry. On the 25th, despite bad weather, they sailed across the Channel to Cherbourg, which they found not entirely to their liking.

> Generally speaking we were disappointed with French soil. Cherbourg itself was very commercial and banal, and Cherbourg cuisine was, let us hope, not representative of French culinary genius. We spent a pleasant evening though, with coffee and billiards, and a concert.[13]

As was usual throughout their visit to France, Erskine slept on board the yacht, anchored in the most exposed position he could find, while Henry adjourned to the comforts of an hotel. Despite all Erskine's protestations about the 'discomforts' of harbours, it is difficult to see his behaviour as anything but masochistic.

Some days later *Mad Agnes* approached Le Havre in darkness, with freshening winds and a rising sea. They hove to for a while, waiting for daylight. Then, in the early morning light, not being sure of the port entrance, which was greatly obscured by mist, Erskine chose to follow a local fishing-boat. At first everything went fine. Until, that is, they approached the harbour entrance, with the fishing-boat in the lead. Suddenly, the wind veered violently. For a moment, the local boat, already battling against a strong current, appeared motionless, hovering between safety and disaster. Then the natural forces overpowered her, lifting her like a toy boat in the bath, and threw her bodily at the massive stone pier of the harbour entrance. She instantly capsized, her keel clearly visible amongst the breaking waves and flying spray.

On board *Mad Agnes* there was a moment of shocked horror. Then Erskine swung the tiller hard over. Helped by the same strong current that had assisted in the destruction of the fishing-boat, the yacht swept narrowly but safely past the stone pier. Fighting against both wind and sea, *Mad Agnes* moved slowly away from the dangers of the shore, eventually returning to Cherbourg. The next morning they were relieved to read in a local newspaper that the seven man crew of the fishing-boat had all been rescued. By now autumn gales were arriving in rapid succession. Apparently even Erskine could be cautious sometimes, or perhaps Henry was insistent. Either way, instead of being sailed back to England, *Mad Agnes* was lifted onto a Channel steamer and brought back as deck cargo. Upon his return Erskine was awarded the Admiral de Horsey Silver Cup by the Cruising Club for the best cruise of 1895.

For Erskine, the following year, 1896, was dominated by the deaths first of Hugh Childers and then, only a few months later, of the Canon. Each had, in his own way, played an important part in Erskine's youth. Hugh, ever since the premature death of his cousin, had done everything he could to help the orphaned children. They, and Erskine in particular, had good reason to feel gratitude towards him. *The Times*, in its obituary for him, commented: 'Although Mr Childers can hardly be ranked as a great statesman, he undoubtedly had the merit, not always possessed by greater men than himself of being an honest politician and an excellent official.' As for the Canon, he had never recovered from the fearsome reputation acquired when the children were small. Later they had largely blamed him for the exile of their mother. He had remained chaplain in Nice until 1884, at which time he was aged seventy-eight. But leaving Nice after all those years did not represent retirement. Instead he became rector of Armthorpe, in Yorkshire, a post that he retained until his mid eighties. Death finally came to him in Florence at the age of ninety.

Apart from those two family bereavements, the year passed quietly enough, with Erskine exploring the South Coast of England on *Mad Agnes*. In the office his nautical activities had raised his prestige considerably. But questions about his seafaring experiences invariably produced anecdotes designed more to show his incompetence than his skill. So far as his colleagues could discover, he spent most of his time at sea only narrowly avoiding one disaster after another.

The year 1897 began modestly enough, with Erskine and Ivor Lloyd-Jones in Essex exploring the Blackwater and Colne estuaries, frequently running aground, always a hazard in those misleading waters. Crossing the Blackwater, making for West Mersea, Erskine was 'bewildered by a forest of masts'. They ran straight onto a hidden sandbank on an ebb tide. It meant a long wait for the tide to return; embarrassing but not dangerous. In April, becoming more ambitious, wanting to explore further afield, and to do so in greater comfort, he sold *Mad Agnes*.

Early in August Erskine bought his third boat, *Vixen*, a former lifeboat and destined to be famous as the model for *Dulcibella* in *The Riddle of the Sands*. She was a thirty foot cutter. According to Erskine, 'No one could call the *Vixen* beautiful. We grew to love her in the end, but never to admire her'. As for *Vixen*'s cabin while under Erskine's care, thanks to his novel we have a full description:

> Two long cushioned covered seats flanked the cabin, bounded at the after end by cupboards, one of which was cut low to form a sort of miniature sideboard, with glasses hung in a rack above it. The deck overhead was very low at each side but rose shoulder high for a space in the middle, where a coach-head roof with a skylight gave additional cabin space. Just outside the door was a fold-up washing stand. On either wall were long net-racks holding a medley of flags, charts, caps, cigar boxes, hanks of yarn, and such like.
>
> Across the forward bulkhead was a bookshelf crammed to overflowing with volumes of all sizes, many upside down and some coverless. Below this were a pipe-rack, an aneroid, and a clock with a hearty tick. All the woodwork was painted white, and to a less jaundiced eye than mine the interior might have had an enticing air of snugness. Some Kodak prints were nailed roughly on the after bulkhead, and just over the doorway was the photograph of a young girl, 'That's my sister', said Davis.[14]

The middle of August 1897 found *Vixen*, with only Erskine on board, moored at Boulogne. His original plan had been to pick up Henry and Lloyd-Jones, sail down Channel, work his way either across or round the Bay of Biscay to Bordeaux, and then through the Languedoc Canal to the Mediterranean, where he would spend the winter. He described the project as 'the dream in my heart'. But the fates were planning otherwise. That summer saw strong south-westerly winds rolling in from the Atlantic day after day; making it impossible for a small yacht to make much headway down Channel. On the 20th he was joined by Henry, straight from climbing in the Austrian Tyrol. On the 23rd Ivor Lloyd-Jones arrived from London. The next day, with a gusty south-west wind driving low dark-grey clouds before it, they gave up hope of making the Mediterranean that year. Instead they came up with an alternative plan. Running before the wind, they sailed northwards, up the French and Belgian coasts until, turning up the estuary of the Scheldt, they reached Dordrecht on the 29th. As the fictional Davies explained it:

> We had a splendid sail to the East Scheldt, but then, like fools, decided to go through Holland by canal and river. It was good fun enough navigating

the estuary – the tides and banks there are appalling – but further inland it was a wretched business, nothing but paying lock-dues, bumping against schuyts and towing down stinking canals, never a peaceful night like this – always moored by some quay or tow-path, with people passing and boys – heavens! Shall I ever forget those boys! A perfect murrain of them infests Holland: they seem to have nothing in the world to do but throw stones and mud at foreign yachts.[15]

Continuing through the Dutch canal system, they went via Rotterdam, Utrecht, Loenen and Muiden, eventually reaching Amsterdam on 11 September, where Lloyd-Jones was forced to leave them and return home. A few days later, *Vixen* sailed down the North Sea Canal, through the great sea-locks at Ijmuiden, and out, back into the North Sea. While moored at Amsterdam, the Childers brothers discussed what to do next. The plan, devised at Boulogne, of exploring the Dutch canal system, they had completed successfully. But they still had some time to spare. Should they now push on further to the north, or return to England? Typically they decided to place their future into the hands of fate. If, when they once more reached open sea, the wind blew from the east, they would cross the North Sea and make a leisurely journey home. If, on the other hand, a west wind blew, then they would go with it, to the Frisian Islands.

If, on the 16 September 1897, an east wind had blown across the bleak Dutch polders, *The Riddle of the Sands* would never have been written, at any rate not in the form that we know it. But, as it happened, on that fateful day, when *Vixen* left the shelter of Ijmuiden and lifted her bow to meet the swell of the open sea, she once more met a brisk south-westerly wind. Erskine, the decision made for him, swung over the helm, took the boat about, and set a course for the north. The routes taken by *Vixen* and *Dulcibella* continue to coincide. As Davies explains in the novel:

'The weather had been still and steamy, but it broke up finely now, and we had a rattling three-reef sail to the Zuider Zee. Well, I followed the Dutch islands, Amelund, Schiermonnikoog, Rottum (outlandish names aren't they), sometimes outside them, sometimes inside. It was a bit lonely, but grand sport and very interesting. The charts were shocking, but I worried out most of the channels.'

'All sand', said Davies enthusiastically. 'You can't think what a splendid sailing-ground it is. You can explore for days without seeing a soul. These are the channels you see; they're very badly charted. This chart was almost useless, but it made it all the more fun. No towns or harbours, just a village or two on the islands, if you want stores.'

'They look rather desolate', I said.

'Desolate's no word for it; they're really only gigantic sand-banks themselves.'

'I made a passage of it to the Eider River, took the river and canal through to Kiel on the Baltic and from there made another fine passage up to Flensburg.' [16]

Vixen passed through the Kiel Canal lashed to the side of a trading ketch, *Johannes*, with a skipper called Bartels, 'a little man in oil-skins and sou-wester was stooping towards us in the cabin door, smiling affectionately at Davies out of a round grizzled beard'. Upon their arrival at Kiel on 12 October, Henry was forced to leave for England. Erskine continued on his own to Flensburg, which he used as a base for exploring the nearby coast:

> The fjord here was about a mile broad. From the shore we had left the hills rose steeply, but with no rugged grandeur; the outlines were soft; there were green spaces and rich woods on the lower slopes; a little white town was opening up in one place, and scattered farms dotted the prospect.[17]

About three weeks later, on 3 November, Henry having rejoined him, they began the return journey, meeting Bartels and the *Johannes* for a second time at Kappeln. 'I took my apples to Kappeln', he said sedately, 'and now I sail to Kiel and so to Hamburg, where my wife and children are.' They passed back through the Kiel Canal in his company. Then, on their way back to Holland, they explored other islands and small ports that Erskine was later to make use of in his narrative.

> A low line of sand-hills, pink and fawn in the setting sun, at one end of them a little white village huddled round the base of a massive four-square light-house – such was Wangeroog.
>
> Benserseil. A paltry bleak little place.
>
> Nordeney. A lighthouse appeared among the sand-dunes on the island shore, and before darkness fell we dimly saw the spires and roofs of a town, and two long black piers stretching out southwards.
>
> Rottum. This queer little one – it has only one house on it.[18]

Reaching the Dutch port of Terschelling on 14 December, they lay the boat up there for the winter, returning to England by steamer from the Hook of Holland to Harwich. Christmas, as usual, was spent with the family at Glendalough.

The following spring, that of 1898, Erskine, with a paid hand, Alfred Rice, an Essex man from Burnham, crossed to Holland. Together they brought *Vixen* back to England. A few months later, in June, Erskine, accompanied part of the way by a friend, William Le Fanu, sailed *Vixen* round to Burlesdon, in Hampshire. That was to be his new base. The rest of the summer was spent roaming freely along the South Coast from Sussex to Cornwall.

That autumn he moved house, to a much larger flat at 16 Cheyne Gardens, Chelsea. Not far from the river, the flat was modern, convenient and in a fashionable area. He was to share it with his three sisters; the first time the four of them had lived together in London since those dreadful events more than twenty years earlier. The young women had just arrived from Ireland. All three were now in their twenties and still unmarried. Doubtless it was felt that the wider social world of London was more likely to bring them into contact with suitable bachelors than the rural seclusion of County Wicklow. If that really was the motive for the move, it was but partially successful as only one of them was destined to marry.

In October Erskine set off on a new and very different seafaring adventure. He sailed from Liverpool on a tramp steamer, the *West Indian*, bound for Port of Spain, Trinidad. The ship was old and slow, with a top speed of only 9½ knots. The voyage took eighteen days, but Erskine found much to interest him:

> There were only three other passengers, a couple by the name of McCarthy and their daughter; golden haired, eighteen – and a very good sort with no rot about her. The third officer was an old dour, silent, grizzled man of SIXTY-TWO, looking like some gnarled tree trunk on a blasted heath. He never speaks or unbends except to the cabin-kitten when he thinks he is unobserved; and then he expands in an elephantine tenderness. A strange, silent riddle of a man.[19]

From Barbados he wished to travel to Grenada, where he had an invitation to stay at Government House, but getting there proved un-expectedly difficult. Eventually, despite cries of horror and dire warnings from the local Europeans, he booked a passage upon a 'sloop', one of the small sailing ships that plied the islands. She was called *Faith* and seems to have been appropriately named.

> [I] was pulled out towards the *Faith*. She looked a shapely little craft of about twenty tons, so crowded was she with men, women, things, other passengers and six sailors, all Negroes, and stacks of casks, baskets and miscellaneous deck cargo, down to pigs and hens.
>
> The rigging was in a shocking condition of age and dilapidation. I expected the peak halyard to go at every puff. Things soon began carrying away: beginning with the topping lift, hastily mended with a pathetically elementary knot. The sails were dotted with holes, and I don't believe there was a single spare rope on board. There was an ancient compass in a cage, but I scarcely think anyone knew its properties; certainly there was no chart. Grenada was 'somewhere over there', expressed with a wave of the hand covering a third of the horizon.[20]

Being the only European on board Erskine was given a sort of cubby-hole to sleep in; known to the crew, with remarkable accuracy as 'the doghouse'.

> A long low kennel standing on the starboard side – just room for a man to lie down. Sound as my sleep that night was, it succumbed at last to a persistent banging and flapping of spars and sails, while the sluggish wallowing of the hull suggested that we were not underway. Peering out I saw the helmsman fast asleep at the tiller.[21]

He spent a week in Grenada, exploring the island on horseback, before catching the mail steamer to St Vincent. A further voyage by 'sloop' from St Vincent to St Lucia was, compared with his first such voyage, 'less amusing and a good deal more hazardous'. During much of the voyage he was forced to take over and sail the ship single-handed, all of the official crew being sea-sick.

By the time Erskine returned to England, in the early months of 1899, the possibility of a new, different kind of adventure, loomed on the horizon. The likelihood was that, before very long, Britain would be at war. For young men at the turn of the century war still had a romantic

ring to it, a chance for brave men to show their courage in the name
of patriotism. Pictures came into their minds of brave crusaders; comrades fighting selflessly side by side; dashing deeds against impossible
odds; and the eventual return to enraptured and beautiful women. Only
the brutal realities of the Somme were to end such romantic dreaming
forever. Erskine was an imperialist. Given his class and time, it would
have been remarkable had he not been. The Barton and Childers families
alike were heavily involved in the Empire, politically, administratively
and militarily; they had been for hundreds of years. That the British
Empire was a 'good thing', not just for the rulers but also for the ruled,
was to Erskine self-evident. On those occasions when he sang, 'wider
still and wider', he really meant it. To him, the Jameson Raid of 1895,
when Cecil Rhodes and his friends had attempted to seize Johannesburg
for the British, had been humiliating only because the courageous doctor
had not been given the support that he deserved. He had in fact been
betrayed by short-sighted and timorous politicians. Erskine accepted,
without question, that in all arguments about Johannesburg and the
goldfields the British were entirely in the right. He believed that
the Boers were tyrants, bullying British men, women and children. He
also believed that something should be done about it; in the name of
justice and freedom.

In common with most wars, the roots of the South African War were
deep and complicated; the conflict being caused as much by the mutual
incomprehension of the two sides as by the policies they followed.
Neither side really wanted war, but equally neither side understood the
consequences of having one. To the British, the Boers were a handful
of farmers who would be unable to put up much resistance when faced
by professional troops. A clear demonstration of power was all that was
necessary. The Boers, on the other hand, thought that, when it came to
the crunch, the British wouldn't fight or, at any rate would put up only
a token resistance. Given that situation, war was almost bound to break
out sooner or later.

In 1897, following the Jameson Raid, the British government sent Lord
Milner to South Africa as High Commissioner. Unfortunately, the
cabinet was divided as to precisely why they had sent him. The Prime
Minister believed that he had gone to bring about a 'just peace'; to end
those dangerous misunderstandings that bedevilled relations between

the two sides. Others however, led by Joseph Chamberlain, saw no reason for showing weakness, believing that a strong policy would enable them to obtain everything they wanted without the need for war. As for Milner himself, upon arrival in South Africa, he promptly set out to provoke the war, with all the foresight of a small boy poking a lion with a stick.

Shortly before Christmas 1898 came one of those trivial incidents that so often act as a trigger for war, when a drunken boiler-maker from Bootle was shot dead by a Boer policeman. The news spread quickly through Johannesburg, losing nothing in the telling. Anger grew rapidly with both sides adopting hard-line positions. Someone suggested a petition to the Queen, begging for her protection. In an attempt to calm matters, the local British agent refused to pass it on to London. But his attempt at peacemaking was brought to nothing when the Boers reacted to the petition by arresting the better-known signatories, thereby further inflaming the situation. On 14 January a protest meeting held just outside the city was broken up by a Boer mob armed with chair legs, while the police stood by doing nothing. When the policeman finally appeared in court he was acquitted; the judge commending him for doing his duty. A new petition was raised, now with 21,000 signatures. Placed in a cardboard box it was taken by train direct to Lord Milner in Cape Town, who accepted it with open arms; as manna from heaven.

Erskine meanwhile, back at his desk in the Houses of Parliament, was perfectly placed to observe history in the making. Believing that war might break out at any time, and anxious not to miss it, he restricted his sailing to the South Coast. Easter was spent tacking to and fro off the Isle of Wight. Summer weekends passed much the same way.

While *Vixen* sailed peacefully about the Solent, the drift to war continued. The two sides negotiated, sometimes seeming close to success, but always failing to break through the wall of distrust and misunderstanding that separated them. Warned of their military weakness in South Africa, on 8 September the cabinet, pushed by the belligerent Chamberlain, authorised the dispatch of ten thousand men as reinforcements. The Boers, hearing of British troop movements, moved their own army up to the border with Natal. On 2 October the Orange Free State, allies of Kruger, began their own mobilisation. Seen from Pretoria the position was now clear: the British were set upon war.

Only one question remained. Should the Boer republics sit and wait to be attacked, or get their own attack in first, before the British were ready? The answer was obvious.

The Boer War was, in many ways, a typically British war. To most people in Britain war seemed inevitable sooner or later; it had done for years. Yet, when war came, it took the government entirely by surprise. For decades successive governments had followed a policy of cheese-paring the armed forces; cutting a bit off here, a bit off there. Now, having got themselves involved in a war, they discovered, to their total astonishment, that they had neither the men nor the material to fight it with. The Secretary of State for War, Lord Lansdowne, warned of the threat posed by the Boer army, which outnumbered British forces in South Africa by five to one, came up with a contingency plan to deal with the danger. He told his generals that, in the event of war breaking out, they were not to mount an attack for three months. By that time, he assured them, large reinforcements would have arrived from England. That the Boers might not be so obliging as to wait that long before themselves attacking seems not to have occurred to him. But then, they wouldn't dare, would they? A bunch of farmers?

On 9 October, while Erskine, having finally given up waiting for the war to begin, was cycling in the Dordogne with Le Fanu, the Boers presented Britain with an ultimatum, the kind of ultimatum known to be unacceptable. Just three days later they invaded Natal. The British public, despite all the efforts of the press to stir up their patriotism, refused to take the war seriously. When news of the Boer ultimatum came through, the *Times* commented that 'by tea-time we shall be at war'. The public, taking up the phrase, began referring to the 'tea-time war'. That other phrase so beloved by the British at the beginning of every long war, 'all over by Christmas', was felt to be hopelessly pessimistic.

Opinions soon had to change. By the middle of November the British Army, outnumbered and scattered in penny-packets all round the frontier, had suffered a series of humiliating defeats. Boer forces were now deep into Natal, with the towns of Ladysmith, Kimberley and Mafeking all under siege. Worse was to come. On 15 December, Sir Redvers Buller, much against his better judgement, was compelled to attempt the relief of Ladysmith by mounting a frontal assault against a superior, well dug-in army. The British forces were driven back, suffering 1200 casualties. Having given Buller an impossible job to do, when he failed to achieve it the politicians naturally piled all the blame on him.

Countries throughout Europe now began to discuss Britain's defeat, regarding it as inevitable if not already an established fact. But in Britain it was seen differently. Queen Victoria, now in her eighties declared, 'We are not interested in the possibilities of defeat'. The British public heartily agreed with her. Government and people alike began to take the war seriously: new generals were appointed; new armies began to be formed; and guns and ammunition were purchased in great quantities regardless of cost. And not only in Britain itself. Australia, New Zealand and Canada offered men. The whole Empire prepared for war. And so did Erskine Childers.

One of his colleagues in the office, Basil Williams, was a member of the Honourable Artillery Company, training with them regularly. Shortly after Christmas it was announced that the company was to form part of the City Imperial Volunteers, a force being raised by the City of London for service in South Africa. Basil Williams volunteered. Knowing that Erskine, spending his holiday at Glendalough, was also keen to be involved, Basil sent him a telegram:

> YOU SHOULD COME OVER AT ONCE AND VOLUNTEER.
> I'VE ALREADY TAKEN STEPS TO DO SO.

Erskine's response was immediate. Sending a telegram to say that he was on his way, he begged his friend to have him enrolled. It might be imagined that an artillery unit that already had all the volunteers it needed would not be wildly enthusiastic at acquiring a slightly-built man, with no military training, wearing glasses and walking with a limp. Nevertheless, Erskine was determined to join them.

3

Soldier

Only a few days after Christmas 1898 Erskine travelled to London in great haste. For anyone wanting danger and excitement, war offered the perfect opportunity. But for Englishmen major wars were rare events. There had not been one for more than forty years. If he missed this chance he could be too old when the next opportunity came around. It was true that he might be able to join another regiment, but there was the very real danger that the war might be over before he got there. Anxious not to waste any time, the moment his train reached London he went straight to the barracks of the Honourable Artillery Company, where he applied for service as a driver. He faced the usual form-filling, interviews and a medical examination. The medical presented him with no real problem. Despite his gammy leg, thanks to his constant sailing and fondness for long walks, he was far fitter than most young men in England. One of the great scandals of the time was that 30 per cent of the volunteers for the army had to be rejected on medical grounds. Many did not even have enough strength to carry a rifle.

There followed a long and frustrating week of waiting. A week spent scanning the press for news of the war. Of watching for the postman, sometimes hopeful, sometimes pessimistic. Then at last it came. Acceptance. He was off to war. A few days later formal enlistment took place at the barracks, in the presence of the Lord Mayor dressed in full regalia, while a band played martial airs. The short ceremony over, Erskine returned to his flat. Back to waiting.

On 9 January the enlisted men were ordered to report to barracks. The next three weeks were exhausting. Constant heavy manual labour humping guns and shells about, cleaning stables, grooming horses, and always drill, gun-drill, riding-drill, rifle-drill – endless drill. Given his social background, many of the activities were already familiar to him. Riding for instance, although not on horses such as these, and shooting.

As for sleeping in barracks, that was like being back at school. As the date of embarkation neared, the pace of activity quickened. Uniforms were issued, kit received, instructions given. Guns were dismantled, packed and sent to the docks. Horses were groomed and inspected by vets. At last everything was ready. It remained only for the men and their horses to report to the ship, *SS Montfort*, which lay waiting for them in the Royal Albert Dock.

At two o'clock on the morning of 2 February a long line of silent horsemen wound their way out through the barracks' dimly-lit gateway into the empty streets of St John's Wood. The weather was atrocious, an English winter at its worst. A strong, ice-cold wind from the east drove large wet snow-flakes into the faces of the men, while, beneath the feet of the horses, three inches of slush covered the road, making riding difficult. For hours they trudged slowly through the back streets of north London, the men huddled miserably beneath their capes against the foulness of the weather; the horses frequently slipping on the ice-covered road. At least, they thought, South Africa would be better than this.[1]

When they finally reached the ship, just after seven, there was no rest or refreshment for the men. Priority was given to getting the horses on board, not an easy operation with quay, gangways and ship's deck all thick with slush. The animals were then groomed, fed and watered. Only when the horses had been made comfortable were the men able to attend to their own welfare. Erskine, in his first letter home, described the soldier's accommodation on board, such as it was:

> Thence we crowded still further down to the troop-deck – one large low-roofed room, edged with rows of mess-tables. My entire personal accommodation was a single iron hook in a beam This was my wardrobe, chest of drawers and an integral part of my bed; for from it swung the hammock.[2]

Because of the delay in getting men and horses on board, the ship missed the tide, not getting under way until two the following morning. Next day the *Montford* sailed down Channel, giving anyone on deck the chance of a last glimpse of the English coast. But Erskine had little opportunity for such sentimental farewells. He was much too busy. For the first week of the voyage he was detailed to attend to the horses; a full-time job, feeding and watering, grooming, haying-up three times a day, and keeping the whole stable deck clean.

In bad weather attending the horses was both difficult and dangerous. Climbing into a stall holding two large nervous animals, with the ship pitching and rolling beneath him, while trying to avoid being kicked, stood upon or crushed, required both courage and dexterity. And bad weather soon arrived. As Erskine wrote to his sisters:

> Soon after leaving the Bay, we had some rough weather. 'Stables' used to be a comical function. My diary for the first rough day reads:

> About six of us were there out of about thirty in my sub-division: our sergeant, usually an awesome personage to me, helpless as a babe, and white as a corpse, standing rigid. The lieutenant feebly told me to report when all horses were watered and feeds made up. It was a long job and at the end I found him leaning limply against a stall. 'Horses all watered and feeds ready, Sir.' He turned on me a glazed eye, which saw nothing: then a glimmer of recollection flickered, and the lips framed the word 'feed' no doubt through habit; but to pronounce that word at all under the circumstances was an effort of heroism for which I respected him. Rather a lonely day.[3]

On 9 February the ship reached the Canary Islands and anchored off Las Palmas. The day was warm and still, the sky a deep clear blue. The men crowded the decks, grateful for the calm sea; relishing the sunshine and unable to go ashore, but pleased to see land again. With the bad weather behind them, the next fortnight had at least some elements of a pleasure cruise, the men competing for deck space and enjoying impromptu concerts until, on 26 February, the ship entered Table Bay and anchored.

Two days later came the hard work of, first, unloading horses and equipment, and then unpacking and assembling the guns. These were brand new 12½ lbs Vickers-Maxim field guns, the most modern in the army. The unit had the good fortune to be financed by the City of London rather than by the Treasury. This meant that their equipment was the best that money could buy. While the men were all reservists or volunteers, their officers and NCOs had been seconded from the regular army, many of whom only now joined them. The next two weeks were spent getting everything in order and in training. Their camp site was far from pleasant, having been used by many units before them.

The grass was almost entirely worn away, there was rubbish everywhere, and always there was the pervasive smell of old latrines. But, at last, on 20 March, they were on the move again, by train to Stellenbosch.

One week later they moved on again, to Piquetberg, where they were to guard a railway bridge, though from whom was far from clear. There they remained, guarding a railway bridge that no one seemed inclined to attack, while the days ticked by, becoming weeks. Men, all keyed up for action, became bored and irritable.

Companies of Yeomanry used to arrive, and leave for destinations with enticing names that smelt of war, and night after night rollicking snatches of 'Soldiers of the Queen' would float across the valley from the troop trains as they climbed the pass northward.[4]

By now the whole military situation had been turned around, although not by military skill. New commanders had been appointed, Roberts and Kitchener, who pushed forward aggressively. But the real reason for their success was simply numbers. Men, guns and equipment were arriving in ever-increasing quantity. From being outnumbered by the Boers at the beginning of the campaign, the British soon greatly out-numbered them. By the end of the war the British army in South Africa amounted to almost 450,000 men, plus hundreds of artillery pieces and mountains of ammunition.

On 15 February Kimberley was relieved, on the 28th Ladysmith. On 13 March British troops entered Bloemfontein, the capital of the Orange Free State. Seen through Erskine's eyes and those of the men with him, the war was rapidly being won – but without them. They had not come all this way just to watch trains go by. April 15 brought great news. Their captain received a telegram which, knowing their concern, he read out to them. They were to proceed to Bloemfontein, as soon as the railway could take them. They were delighted and could hardly wait. Bloem-fontein, they knew, was close to the front line. At last there was a chance of action. But alas, there was that proviso. When the railway could take them. It seemed the railway couldn't take them. They had low priority. Troops were still pouring in through Cape Town, all destined for the front. The HAC would have to wait. Another month passed. On the 12 May Mafeking was relieved, provoking great jubilation in England. And still Erskine and his comrades gloomily watched the trains go by.

Only much later did they learn the reason why their force had been put carefully to one side and kept out of the war for so long. It was the ultra-modern guns they had. The General Staff didn't trust them, as new-fangled things that could not be relied upon.

On 19 May, almost three months after their arrival in South Africa, a train was at last found for them. With great relief the men clambered up into open goods wagons. Trundling slowly northwards, with frequent unexplained stops in the middle of nowhere, for the first time they saw signs of fighting:

> At a stop at a shanty (can't call it a station) a man described a fight for a kopje just by the railway. Coleskop was in view, a tall, flat-topped mountain and later we steamed into the oft-taken and retaken Colesberg Junction and were shown the hill where the Suffolks were cut up. All was barren veldt again, and the strangeness of the whole thing struck me curiously. Why should we be fighting here? There seemed to be nothing to fight for, and nothing to get to when you had fought.[5]

A few hours afterwards they crossed the Orange River, entering enemy territory for the first time. Just outside Bloemfontein the train ground to a halt. They were ordered off. Scrambling down from the trucks the mood of the men was not good. By now they knew the signs and they feared they were going to be held in reserve again. Their fears were entirely justified. They remained there nearly a month, doing nothing and hearing of more victories won by others.

On the 26 May, Hamilton's army invaded the Transvaal. Two days later the Orange Free State was formally annexed to the British Crown. Erskine watched the ceremony:

> One out of four was allowed to go to town and see the Proclamation of Annexation read. I was lucky enough to be picked, tumbled into proper dress, and hurried down just in time. The usual sight as I passed the cemetery, thirteen still forms on stretchers in front of the gate, wrapped in the rough service blanket, waiting to be buried.
>
> I found the Market Square full of troops drawn up and a flag-staff in the middle, with a rolled-up flag on it. Soon a band heralded the arrival of the Governor and staff-officers. Then a distant voice began the proclamation, of which I couldn't hear a word except 'colony' at the end. Then the flag was unrolled, and hung dead for a minute, till a breeze came and blew out the

Royal Standard. Bands struck up 'God Save the Queen', a battery on a hill above the town thundered out a rough salute, everybody cheered, and I was standing on British soil. I saw not a single native Dutchman about, only crowds of the khakied of all ranks and sorts. After this little bit of history-making I hurried back to the commonplace task of clipping my mare's heels, an operation requiring great agility on the part of the clipper.[6]

18 June saw them entrained once more, moving slowly forward, this time as far as Kroonstadt.

A curiosity of the Boer War was that, until Roberts entered Pretoria on 5 June, very few men on either side had any clear understanding of the type of war in which they were involved. Politicians and generals on both sides had from the start thought in terms of capturing towns, hence the Boer sieges of Mafeking, Kimberley and Ladysmith and the British eagerness to relieve them. But the Boers were predominately farmers who, even more than most farmers, regarded towns as dens of vice populated by parasites. Roberts believed that once he had occupied Pretoria and Bloemfontein the war would be effectively over. When he entered the capital of the Transvaal on 5 June he sat down and waited for a formal surrender. He did nothing to stop Boer soldiers in their thousands from departing northwards, rifles in hand.

The Boers, and their best generals in particular, saw things differently. At last free of the dictates of meddling politicians, they would fight the war as they had wanted to fight it from the beginning, as a guerilla war on the veldt. The veldt seen through British eyes was an endless, almost featureless plain, relieved only by the isolated hills called kopjes and the occasional, usually dried-up, river bed. An arid and alien world. A land of extremes, sometimes freezing cold, more often burning hot; where stifling clouds of dust turned overnight into glutinous mud.

From now on the conflict took on many of the characteristics of a naval war, in which there were no strategic positions to capture. A war entirely of manoeuvre, the object being to corner your opponent, to catch him at a disadvantage and to avoid being caught at a disadvantage yourself.

Ironically, the only man on the British side who had understood this from the beginning was the much maligned Buller. He had seen it all before, in the Zulu War. But his attempts to persuade his political masters that Ladysmith was not worth fighting for and should be abandoned only resulted in him being branded as a defeatist. They preferred to waste hundreds of lives in their determination first to hold it and then to relieve it.

Even as the overconfident Roberts was approaching Pretoria the new style of warfare was already beginning. On 31 May the Irish Yeomanry, a force comprising the cream of the Irish Protestant aristocracy, discovered as they approached Lindley that it was in enemy hands. Rather than withdrawing while they still had time, they chose to sit and wait for reinforcements. By the time those reinforcements arrived it was too late, the Irish Yeomanry no longer existed, except as prisoners of war. They left eighty dead behind them.

On 4 June a convoy of fifty-six food wagons, with an escort of 160 men, was ambushed and captured. The very next day, De Wet, a name that was to become very familiar to Erskine and his friends, fell upon the railway station at Roodewal, between Kroonstadt and the Vaal River. A battalion of the Derbyshire Regiment, just arrived from England and still green, was effectively destroyed. Stocks of food and ammunition worth half a million pounds were stolen or burnt. These were hardly the actions of a defeated army.

An early result of this change in the nature of the war was that Erskine and the HAC, who had spent months trying to get to the front line, now found that the front line had come to them. Kroonstadt, their new base, had been occupied for more than a month and had been designated as 'cleared of enemy' long since. But soon the country surrounding it became De Wet's favourite hunting ground, as Eskine was soon to discover. But first there came a scare:

> 22 June. At 7 a.m. coffee and porridge and at 7.30 orders came to harness-up sharp. There followed a whole series of contrary orders, but we ultimately harnessed up and hooked in; and soon after marched away. About three miles off, after climbing a long hill. we unlimbered the guns in a commanding position, and remained there till dark, in the close and fragrant neighbourhood of about twenty dead horses. I believe we had something to do with some possible or probable fight, but what, I don't know. A very dull battle. We marched back at dark and bivouacked near the town. I slept by my horses, very cold.[7]

But that 'dull battle' marked the end of the unit's prolonged inactivity. The very next day saw them entering fully into the war. On 23 June part of the HAC, with Erskine among them, were given the task of escorting a convoy going to Lindley, fifty miles to the east. The convoy comprised a long line of ox-wagons, together with a few traction engines pulling trucks and a train of mules; an interesting mixture of technologies. A company of the 'Buffs' made up the bulk of the escort.

Since the disaster that had befallen the Irish Yeomanry, the town of Lindley had acquired an evil reputation as the centre of frequent ambushes. As a town it had never amounted to much, with no apparent reason for existence. No visible roads led to it, no fields surrounded it. By the time Erskine headed that way what rudimentary signs of civilisation there had once been were gone, having been destroyed as the town continually changed hands. Even the church was a complete ruin.

For the first few days of the journey the long line of creaking wagons ambled peacefully along, filling the air with clouds of dust that were visible for miles across the open plain. For the HAC the only problems came from the heat, the flies, the constant thirst and the abysmally slow progress. Then, early on the morning on the 26th, they came under attack for the first time:

> 8 a.m. We are in action, my waggon at present halted in the rear. We harnessed up at 3.45 this morning and marched some miles to the top of another hill, overlooking another plain, a crescent of steep kopjes on the left, occupied by the Boers. The convoy halted just as a spattering of rifle-fire ahead struck on the still morning air, and the clatter of a maxim on the left flank. We trotted down the hill, plunged down a villainous spruit and came up on to the level, under pretty heavy fire from the kopje on our left.[8]

For the next three days Erskine's unit behaved like a destroyer defending a naval convoy. The Boers were all around them, probing for a weak spot, hoping to get at the wagons as they lumbered slowly forward. The HAC dashed to whichever part of the convoy came under attack, fired off a couple of dozen shells, then dashed somewhere else. Whether they ever hit anything they never knew, but the convoy crept forward unharmed. Erskine's function in all this was to keep the guns supplied with ammunition. He loaded his two horse waggon with shells, charged across open ground to the guns, unloaded and rushed back for more. All this under constant fire from the enemy. While the guns could make use of whatever cover they could find, he had to rely on speed, luck, and the inaccuracy of the Boers' fire for survival. He was in his element, never happier than when in danger, his only complaint being the incompetence of the enemy.

On 29 June the convoy finally reached Lindley intact. Not that it made much difference to Erskine's unit, as the Boers promptly besieged Lindley itself, or more correctly, the place where Lindley had once been. Now, instead of defending a moving convoy, the HAC defended a static one. In practice it made little difference. The Boers circled the town like Red Indians and the HAC moved with them, firing sometimes at one hill, sometimes at another. Whether they hit anything they had no way of knowing. But luckily nothing hit them.

In the early hours of 2 July they harnessed up and marched out of Lindley, towards the east. They were now part of one of the biggest and most complex operations of the war. According to intelligence reports, the last major force under De Wet's leadership, comprising eight thousand men, was sheltering in the mountains close to the border with Basutoland. It was now intended to catch and destroy them. Towards this end a force equivalent to three divisions, divided into five columns, was to converge on the mountains to trap the Boer army within them. They would then break through one or more of the surrounding passes, which would place the Boers completely at their mercy. Erskine and the HAC formed part of a brigade under General Paget detailed to advance on the central pass, known as Slabbert's Nek. Fighting began almost immediately.

3 July. 8.30 p.m. The Boers seem to have some special dislike to our waggon. They have just placed two shells, one fifty yards in front of it, and the other fifty yards behind. The progress of a shell sounds far off like the hum of a mosquito, rising as it nears to a hoarse screech and then plump. We mind them very little now. There is a great competition for the fragments as curios.

The Boers had a gun on a ridge, which we dislodged, and the infantry took the position. About 2.30 it began to rain again and poured all the afternoon in cold, sloshing torrents. We finally went up the kopje ourselves over a shocking piece of rocky ground near the top, fired on the retreating Boers from there, and then came down the other side.

> Soon afterwards came an old story. It was about five and had cleared up. A staff officer had said that there were no Boers anywhere near now and that we were to march on and bivouac. We and the Munsters were marching down a valley, whose flanks were supposed to have been scouted, the infantry in column of companies, that is, in close formation and all in apparent security.
>
> Suddenly a storm of rifle-fire broke out from a ridge on our right front and showed us we were ambushed. The Munsters were nearest to the ridge, about 600 yards, I should say. We were a bit further off. I heard a sort of hoarse murmur go up from the close mass of infantry and saw it spread out. Our section checked for a moment, in a sort of bewilderment, but the next and almost without orders, guns were unlimbered and whisked round, a waggon unhooked, teams trotted away and shrapnel bursting over the top of the ridge in quick succession. All this time the air was full of a sound like the moaning of wind from the bullets flying across the valley, but strange to say, not a man of us was hit.[9]

This short, unexpected, skirmish at last established the military usefulness of the HAC and their modern guns. Reports to General Paget, presumably from grateful officers of the Munsters, were full of praise, both for the unit's quickness of response and for the accuracy of their fire. From now on they were to play their full part in the mounting campaign. And the respect between unit and general was mutual:

> Paget is already very popular with us. We trust his generalship and we like the man, for he seems to be one of us, a frank, simple soldier, who thinks of every man in his brigade as his comrade.[10]

Not that Erskine had much idea what was going on; he had to rely entirely upon rumours:

> It is said that the mythical Clements is now one march behind us, our scouts having met up today. Other mythical generals are in the air. I am getting used to the state of blank ignorance in which we live.[11]

After two more days on the march, with only occasional contact with the enemy, the column reached within three miles of the small town of Bethlehem. They then encamped to await further orders. It was now 5 July. Three days later a second column, of two thousand men, under General Hunter, joined them and occupied the otherwise deserted town.

The net was slowly being drawn around the Boer army. To the east, piled high above the horizon, stood a range of mountains, wild and majestic, their red peaks scattered with snow, sparkling prettily in the African sunlight. Beyond the mountains, and encircled by them, lay the Brandwater Basin, an area of rich grazing-land, the last remaining Boer stronghold. Within it, around the small town of Fouriesburg, sheltered De Wet and seven thousand men. That range of mountains offered protection to the men behind them. Access to the valley was restricted to only a handful of narrow and winding passes, easy for a small force to defend. But if an attacking army blocked those passes and then succeeded in forcing its way through one of them, there could be no escape for the men inside. From being a safe haven, it would become a trap. It was the intention of General Hunter to do precisely that.

By now, for the British troops, De Wet had acquired the kind of respect that a later generation of soldiers was to confer upon Rommel. He seemed to have an almost magical ability to strike when least expected; only to vanish again whenever superior forces were brought against him. If he and his army could be caught and destroyed, Boer morale would most certainly slump. The end of the war might then at last be within sight.

But the aptly named General Hunter had difficulties of his own to overcome. The coordination of five separate armies, moving across rough and largely unmapped territory, presented him with every kind of logistical problem. Communication between units was constantly threatened by guerrilla activities. Supplies of food and ammunition were dependant entirely upon the movements of the almost medieval ox-cart. Although Paget arrived at the rendezvous on the 5th, Hunter on the 8th, and other units within the next few days, they were compelled to delay further advance until the arrival of their supply wagons. These eventually lumbered in on the 20th, their animals almost exhausted. Erskine meanwhile had gone sightseeing:

> 12 July. Williams and I got leave to spend the morning out, and walked into Bethlehem over the veldt. A rather nice little town, but all the stores shut, and looking like a dead place. It was full of troops. Some stores had sentries over them, for there had been a great deal of looting.[12]

Beyond the mountains the slow advance of superior forces had not gone unnoticed by their opponents. On the 15th, while Hunter waited, cursing with impatience, at Bethlehem, De Wet, together with 1800 men, slipped quietly through Slabbert's Nek out into the open veldt and away. Before leaving, he recommended the other commanders to follow his example. They, however, without his inspiring presence, dithered, argued, and chose to do nothing. Two days later their chance was gone. Paget's force, including the HAC, moved forward to close the Slabbert's Nek bolt hole. They dug in and waited. Erskine, sitting around, waiting for the battle to begin, wishing they would get on with it, was in a pensive mood:

> I suppose it arises from the nature of my work, but, speaking for myself, I feel no animosity to anyone. Infantry, no doubt, get the lust of battle, but I don't for my part experience anything like it, though the gunners tell me they do, which is natural. One feels one is taking part in a game of skill at a dignified distance, and any feeling of hostility is very impersonal and detached.[13]

In common with many soldiers 'fighting on a foreign field' there were times when Erskine wondered what he was doing there. Often of an evening, sitting by the guns, watching the sunset, he discussed it with Basil Williams. Back in England, the war had seemed straightforward. But this was no longer so. The Boers, whom the newspapers back home had pictured as cruel brutes, he now found to be brave and honest farmers. He saw Boer women, their meagre belongings piled on a cart, watching impassively as their homes were deliberately burned in front of them. That the British cause was just, he never doubted. But did it have to be like this? He could not help but wonder. As Basil Williams wrote much later:

> Both of us, who came out as hide-bound Tories, began to tend towards more liberal ideas, partly from the jolly democratic company we were in, but chiefly, I think, from our discussions on politics and life generally.[14]

Over the next few days the other escape routes through the mountains were blocked, one by one. On 22 July an officer explained to Erskine's unit what was intended to happen next. As Erskine commented: 'It is most novel and unusual to know anything about what one is doing. It makes a marvellous difference to one's interest in everything, and I have often wondered why we are not told more.'

Shortly after dawn on the 23rd, simultaneous attacks were mounted against two of the passes: Hunter upon Ratief's Nek and Paget against Slabbert's. Close to the peak of Slabbert's Nek the waggon road ran close to an African kraal, which the Boers had strongly fortified by extensive and well-hidden trenches.

3.30 p.m. We and the 38th have been raining shell on the Boer positions and on their guns. It looks like an impregnable position. The Royal Irish, I hear, are attacking the right hand bastion; the Munsters, I think the left and there is a continuous rattle of rifle fire from both. Our teams, waggons and limbers, have been shell-dodging under the brow of the hill. They have fallen all around us, but never on us. One which I saw fall, killed five horses straight off, and wounded the Yeomanry chap who was holding them.[15]

At dawn the attack was resumed, beginning with an artillery bombardment of the Boer positions. But the lack of response from the Boer guns soon made it obvious that most of the enemy had withdrawn during the night. An extremely strong defensive position had been given up with hardly a fight.

We got away, and marched up through the nek, up and down steep grassy slopes, and through the site of the Boer laager. We halted close to the emplacement where one of the Boer guns had been yesterday. There was a rush to see some horrible human debris found in it. I was contented with the word pictures of enthusiastic gunners, and didn't go myself.[16]

At Retief's Nek the defence was much more determined. Hunter's troops, almost all Scots, faced riflemen skilfully hidden in the rock-strewn hillside. They suffered casualties. In taking one hollow, high up the mountain, the Black Watch and Seaforth Highlanders had eighty-six men killed or wounded. But, as at Slabbert's Nek, the British superiority in artillery told in the end, the opposing army slipping away into the mist. Once through the pass the two invading columns joined up and advanced rapidly.

There was a strong, cold wind, and we kept our cloaks on all day; a bright sun though, in which I thought the brigade made a very pretty spectacle in its advance, with long streams of mounted troops and extended infantry on either flank.[17]

Pausing only to wait for General Rundle's force, which had entered the valley through yet another pass, the British pushed on, the Boers still retreating before them. Two questions remained: had the easternmost pass been successfully sealed, and how many men were still within the net? The first question was soon answered by the sound of heavy guns to the east. That pass too was safely blocked. The HAC meanwhile tagged along behind:

> 27 July. Hooked in and waited for the whole convoy to file by, as we are to be rearguard. It took several hours, and must have been five or six miles long.
>
> Suddenly the whole valley opened out to another wide circle bounded by mountains on all sides, some wearing a sprinkling of snow still. Here we came to the pretty little town of Fouriesburg, and joined the general camp, which stretched as far as you could see, thousands of beasts grazing between the various lines, and interminable rows of wagons. At night camp fires twinkled far into the distance and signals flashing from high peaks all around.[18]

The Boers, finding themselves hemmed in, and without effective leadership in the absence of De Wet, requested negotiations. Over the next few days talks took place between Hunter and the Boer generals. The outcome was never in doubt. The Boers had no possibility of escape, any further resistance would be pointless, just a waste of lives. It was now simply a question of pride. Hunter, as a concession that he could afford to make, and anxious to get after the elusive De Wet, agreed to allow the Boers to keep their waggons. It was enough to satisfy the demoralised Boers, who surrendered without further argument.

Erskine, meanwhile had discovered that the telegraph office in Fouriesburg was operating normally, apart that is from the usual army red tape. Getting round it gave him a new social experience, one that edged his political opinions another notch to the left.

> He said that to pass the censor it must be signed by an officer, so I had to look for one. After some dusty tramping I found a Captain of the Staffords, saluted, and made my request. We were, I suppose, about equal in social station, but I suddenly – I don't know why – felt what a gulf the service put between us. He was sleek and clean, and talking about the hour of his dinner to another one, just as if he were at a club. I was dirty, unshaven, out at knees, and was carrying half a sack of fuel and felt like an abject rag-and-bone

picking ruffian. He took the paper, signed it, and went on about his confounded dinner.[19]

With the fighting over, for the moment at any rate, the HAC were
able to turn their minds to more pleasant matters. To food for instance.
Although a great deal of looting had taken place, some of the local farms
were still able to provide the soldiers with almost forgotten luxuries,
such as eggs, butter and freshly baked bread. But the period of relaxation
was inevitably short. De Wet was still at large and there were prisoners
to deal with:

> 31 July. The first batch of 250 prisoners have come in, and are herded near.
> They are of all ages from sixty to fifteen, dressed in all varieties of rough
> plain clothes, with some exceptions in the shape of khaki tunic, a service
> greatcoat, etc. Some seem depressed, some jocular, the boys quite careless.
> All were lusty and well fed.[20]

Final figures for the operation showed almost 4500 prisoners taken,
including three generals; at a cost to the British of thirty-three dead and
242 wounded. A remarkable victory by any standards. On the 2 August
Erskine's unit left Fouriesburg performing a new task, as escort to long
lines of prisoners. For the next week they wended their way slowly across
the veldt, now uncannily devoid of enemy. The land was not, however,
unpopulated:

> 7 August. Marched for several hours before camping about 12.30 After dinner
> I walked over to a Kaffir kraal and bought fuel, and two infant's copper
> bangles. I was done over the bangles, so made it up over the fuel (hard round
> cakes of prepared cow dung), filling a sack brim full, in spite of the loud
> expostulations of the black lady. They were a most amusing crowd, and the
> children quite pretty.[21]

On 9 August, despite the unpleasantness of being caught for several
hours in a dust-storm, they reached Winberg, where they handed over
their prisoners. The next day they set off to rejoin the rest of Paget's
Brigade, then chasing De Wet somewhere to the north of Pretoria. They
began with an eleven mile march to Smalldeel, which they reached the
following afternoon. The place was aptly named: 'a dreary little tin
village round a station, built on dust, and surrounded by bare, dusty
veldt'. But they were not there long, just long enough to receive a large

stack of letters accumulated during their recent travels. Joining a train of open railway waggons heading for Pretoria, they also had leisure to enjoy them. The train was slow, the nights in the trucks cold.

14 August. Sleepy heads rose from the sea of blankets and blinked out to see the crossing of the Vaal River, and a thin, sleepy cheer hailed this event; then we relapsed and waited for the sun.[22]

Later that day they reached Pretoria, where they were reviewed by General Roberts. But to men cut off from civilisation for many months it was the following evening that provided the real pleasure:

We came to the Central Square, where we made for the Grand Hotel, and soon found ourselves dining like gentlemen at tables with tablecloths and glasses and forks, and clean plates for every course. The complexity of civilized paraphernalia, after the simplicity of a pocket-knife and mess-tin, was quite bewildering.

We ordered a bottle of claret, the cheapest being seven shillings. The waiter when he brought it paused mysteriously, and then, in a discreet whisper to Williams, said he supposed we were sergeant-majors, as none under that rank could be served with wine. Williams smilingly reassured him, and Driver Childers did his best to look like a sergeant-major, with I fear, indifferent success.

We walked home about 8.30 the streets all silent as death, till we were challenged by a sentry near the outskirts of the town, and asked for the counter-sign, which we didn't know. There were muttered objections, into which a bottle of whisky mysteriously entered, and we bluffed it out. I have never found ignorance of a counter-sign a serious obstacle.[23]

On 16 August they left Pretoria with their old friends of Paget's brigade to scour the area either side of the railway between Pretoria and Petersburg, once again in pursuit of De Wet. The fighting took on the familiar pattern of sudden attacks of rifle or shell fire from an unseen enemy, answered by shell fire of their own. As warfare it could be very frustrating, especially for those kept in the dark about what was really happening:

19 August. Some days are very irritating to the soldier, and this was a typical one. We harnessed up and stood about waiting for orders for five hours. At last we moved off, only to return immediately; again moved off, and after a few minutes halted; finally got more or less started, and marched five or six

miles, with incessant short halts, at each of which the order is to unbuckle wither-straps and let horses graze.[24]

Other aspects of army organisation also continued in the old familiar way:

> He brought a waggon full of clothing and tobacco which was distributed after we had come in. There were thick cordoroy uniforms. If they had reached us in the cold weather they would have been more useful. It is hot weather now.[25]

The intermittent fighting was inconclusive; with De Wet evading yet another carefully planned operation to entrap him. What successes there were proved modest:

> 23 August. There was a stir and general move just now. I got up and looked where all eyes were looking, and saw a solitary Boer horseman issuing from the bush, holding a white flag. An orderly galloped up to him, and the two went into the hut where the general is. The rumour is that a thousand Boers want to surrender. Rumour reduces number to one Boer.[26]

On 24 August Erskine, who had for some days been suffering from a sore place on the sole of his foot, a familiar complaint known to the soldiers as Veldt Foot, was helped into an RAMC ambulance. He shared the covered waggon with six other soldiers, some from the Wiltshire Regiment and some from the Munsters. His comments about the Munsters illustrate clearly his incomprehension at that time of the Nationalist movement in Ireland, then just beginning to stir uneasily after a period of quiescence:

> It was pleasant to hear the rich Cork brogue in the air. It seems impossible to believe that these are the men who Irish patriots incite to mutiny. They are loyal, keen, and simple soldiers, as proud of the flag as any Britisher.[27]

And yet, within only a few years, he himself would be one of the most extreme of those same Irish patriots. But if he was not yet ready to become an Irish Nationalist, the war was nevertheless proving to be an education for Erskine. It was bringing him into contact with all manner of men, men that he would never ordinarily have met in class-ridden Britain. Men such as the Wiltshires, to whom he took an instant liking: farming lads for the most part, ill-educated, but honest, good-natured and cheerful, despite their wounds. Increasingly, he found himself more in sympathy with these ordinary soldiers than with their officers, whom he often found both arrogant and incompetent.

After some days spent trundling uncomfortably in the waggon at the rear of the army, the decision was made to use the now reopened railway to move the sick and wounded to hospital in Pretoria. To Erskine the transformation was miraculous:

> August 30. I write lying luxuriously on a real spring-mattress bed, between real sheets, having just had my fill of real bread and real butter, besides every comfort, in a large marquee tent, with a wooden floor.[28]

Lying in bed all day, with not much to do, other than wait for the next meal to come round, Erskine turned his mind towards the question of leadership and the relationship between officers and men:

> The popularity of officers depends far more on the interest they show in the daily welfare of the men, in personal fellowship, in consideration for them in times of privation and exhaustion, when a physical strain which tells heavily on the men may tell lightly on the officers ... I have got the impression that more might be done in the army to lower the rigid caste-barrier which separates the ranks.[29]

The period as a patient at the Yeomanry Hospital in Pretoria, enabled Erskine's foot to respond rapidly to the combination of rest, good food and careful nursing. On the 4 September he was astonished to receive a letter addressed to his brother, Henry, whom he had assumed was still with his regiment in the Transvaal, where he was part of Buller's army. The letter was addressed to Henry Childers, Hospital, Pretoria. Erskine asked an orderly to discover whether Henry was in one of the numerous other hospitals that all but surrounded Pretoria. But the orderly was unable to find any trace of Erskine's brother. Three days later Erskine, waking from an afternoon sleep, heard someone asking, 'Is Childers here?' He now learned that Henry, wounded in the foot, was in a convalescent camp about a mile away. Having received letters addressed to Erskine, he had asked a friend to discover where Erskine was. The next day, when Henry turned up in a carriage and pair, they spent a wonderful afternoon together. There was much to talk about. A couple of days later Henry returned, this time as a patient, his CO having overthrown all manner of army regulations to have him transferred.

A week later, both men were moved to the convalescent camp that Henry had so recently left. The following day they were moved once more, this time to a rest camp about four miles away. Once settled in, Erskine was appointed office orderly to a Captain Davies. At first he found his new job, sweeping, dusting and tidying the office, something of a novelty, 'parlour-maid's work' being new to him. When not being a parlour-maid he functioned as a messenger. But neither occupation offered him much in the way of inspiration and he soon tired of them.

The increasingly bored Erskine made frequent applications to return to his unit. All his efforts failed, he was never told why. His frustration was not even eased much when Captain Davies promoted him to ordnance clerk; the Byzantine complexities of army accountancy amazed him. But eventually relief came in an unexpected way. On 27 September he heard that all members of the City Imperial Volunteers were to leave for home the following Monday. That same afternoon he had the pleasure of rejoining his old unit, which lay encamped just outside Pretoria.

The following five days were passed trundling slowly southward in open railway trucks amidst much joking about De Wet blowing up the line in front of them. When Erskine awoke on the morning of 7 October it was to find the train standing in the docks at Cape Town, with their ship moored nearby. They returned to England on the *Aurania*, the horses being left behind for other units to use. Basil Williams also stayed behind, intending to catch a later ship. The voyage was uneventful, apart from frequent bouts of bad weather. To the men, eager to be home, it seemed interminable. But even the longest voyage comes to an end. On the afternoon of Saturday 27 September the *Aurania*, about ten hours late, entered Southampton Water. Eagerly the men lining her decks watched the shore: the green fields, the oaks and the elms, the church spires, people waving from small yachts. They were home. But not just yet. The ship slowed and stopped. The anchor-chain rattled. A tug approached but was turned away. There was a long and puzzling delay before they were told the news. No one was to come aboard; and no one was to go ashore. They must all remain where they were – until Monday.

On the morning of that same day, people poured in their tens of thousands into central London to watch the arrival back in England

of the City Imperial Volunteers. The main railway termini saw a continuous stream of packed trains arriving full of excited passengers, many
of them wearing the national colours or carrying flags. Soon the planned
route of the march from Paddington Station to the Guildhall was lined
by eager, patriotic faces. But all were destined for disappointment.
Because of bad weather the ship carrying the men was still fighting its
way up the English Channel. Eventually an announcement was made,
which spread slowly through the disbelieving crowd. The parade was
postponed for two days.

Slowly everyone drifted away, quietly returning to their homes. They
seem to have taken the news calmly, certainly there are no reports of
any trouble. The aborted event did, however, inspire a cartoon in the
Illustrated London News. It shows a disappointed young lady saying to
her gentleman friend, 'Well. I dunno. Something rotten always seem to
'appen when I go out with you'.

Down in Southampton Water, the liner lay at anchor for the rest of
Saturday and all day Sunday, her passengers gazing forlornly at an
inaccessible shore. At last, shortly after eight on Monday morning, to
the sound of ship's sirens and the whistles of dockyard cranes, the ship
moored against the quay. There were the inevitable crowds, cheering
lustily as the first men in khaki came down the gangway. They were the
men of the HAC, Erskine among them, and clearly excited at the
reception they were given.

The special train bearing the troops to London was decorated with
laurel leaves, the arms of the City of London and the CIV emblem.
Throughout the journey people waved and cheered from station platforms, roads and fields. In the late morning the train, diverted to
Paddington because it was considered to be more convenient for the
parade, finally arrived in London.

Before a large cheering crowd, the troops formed up and set off on
the welcoming parade. The people of London, as if determined to make
up for their earlier disappointment, had turned up in even greater
numbers than on Saturday. Although police and soldiers lined the route,
the numbers were so great that the enthusiastic populace constantly
spilled across the road, often bringing the procession to a halt. The
mounted infantry went first, followed by the field artillery, then the
Cyclist's Corps, and finally the massed ranks of infantry, the mile long

procession taking twenty minutes to pass any one point. Outside the National Gallery the crowd was so huge that the troops were forced to thread their way through in single file. On they marched, along the Strand and down Fleet Street. When they reached Temple Bar, they paused to fix bayonets, a rare privilege to which they were entitled. Shortly afterwards there came an unfortunate incident when an over-eager spectator fell sixty feet from a roof, landing on a woman, who was killed instantly. The man then stood up and calmly limped away.

The soldiers, finally reaching St Pauls, attended a thanksgiving service. That completed, they proceeded to Guildhall to be formally welcomed back and congratulated upon their military valour by the Lord Mayor. The speeches at last over, the march resumed; on through Moorgate to their barracks in Finsbury Circus, where a sumptuous banquet was laid on for them. Erskine was home.

4

Author

When Erskine arrived back in England at the end of October 1900, it was to receive a pleasant surprise. Throughout his period in South Africa he kept a diary, written up whenever he could find a spare moment. He also wrote regular letters to his sisters on whatever scraps of paper came to hand. These he asked to be circulated amongst his family and friends, then kept safely for his return. He hoped that he might later be able to make use of them in some literary form.

His sisters did as they were told, passing the letters round, then carefully storing them, in his old room at Glendalough, pending his return. Amongst the numerous friends who thus had the opportunity to read them was a Mrs Thompson, who had known Erskine since his days at university. She was greatly impressed by the letters; so impressed that she in turn showed them to Reginald Smith, a partner in a publishing company, Smith, Elders. He too liked what he read. Thus it came about that, when Erskine returned to London that autumn, he found Reginald Smith eagerly awaiting him, with an offer to publish.

That a publisher was interested in the letters is not at all surprising, their commercial potential was obvious enough. For one thing, they had topicality. Wars always provoke amongst the general reading public a demand for books about them, the Boer War being no exception. But the letters had much more to offer a publisher than a routine account of the war. Erskine was always at his best, both as a man and as an author, when he was not being too serious. Once he climbed onto one of his pet hobby-horses his best qualities tended to disappear; his normal good nature and sense of humour vanishing, to be replaced by intolerant dogmatism. But in his letters from South Africa Erskine was not trying to convert anyone to anything. Instead he was simply relating his experiences and observations of the war to his own family. This meant that the letters were written in a direct, entertaining style, one that greatly appealed to the ordinary reader. What was more, he wrote not as a senior army officer or professional war correspondent but as a driver in the horse artillery. His experiences were those of an ordinary soldier with whom the man in the street could readily identify. This greatly increased the attraction of the letters to the reading public.

For such a literary task Erskine was well equipped, his talent for both description and narrative being difficult to fault. Take for instance his letter written during a train journey, rolling across a war-stricken veldt in an open railway-truck:

> I have received about thirty letters. It is an orgie, and I feel drunk with pleasure. All the time the train rolls through the wilderness, with its myriad ant-hills, its ribbons of empty biscuit tins and dead horses; its broken bridges, its tiny outpost camps, like frail islands in the ocean, its lonely stations of three tin houses, and nothing else beyond, no trees, fields, houses, cattle, signs of human life.

The circumstances under which they were written give the letters an especial immediacy, a quality they still have a hundred years later. At the same time there is also a timeless quality about them. He is writing about the Boer War. But the pictures of a soldier's life that he gives could equally apply to every war from Troy to the Falklands. He tells of long periods of boredom; of sitting about for days or weeks on end, his unit apparently forgotten by everyone. Of sleeping beneath the guns on starlit nights, waiting for a battle to begin. Of outbreaks of violence that end as suddenly as they begin. And of the ageless problems of the soldier's life, the struggles of living in the open, the weather, the dust, the thirst, the hunger and the flies. Above all, he tells of the comradeship that men have always discovered amongst the dirt, discomfort and dangers of war.

There are also examples of Erskine's gentle sense of humour over incidents that would be familiar to anyone with experience of service life:

> As I anticipated, there has been a crisis over my lack of a saddle at the last moment, various officers and NCOs laying the blame, first on me, and then on each other, but chiefly on me, because it was safest.

He even gives advice on the correct way to perform 'fatigues':

I and a dozen others slouched off under a corporal, who showed us to a sergeant, who gave us to a sergeant-major, who pointed to a line of tents, and bade us clean up, but to the trained eye there were some minute fragments of paper and cigarette-ends. Now the great thing in a fatigue of this kind is:

1. To make it last. No good hurrying, as fresh futilities will be found for you.

2. To appear to be doing something at all costs.

3. To escape unobtrusively at the first opportunity.

It is of the greatest importance in a fatigue to have an implement; it is the outward symbol of labour; if observation falls on you, you can wipe your brow and lean on it; you can even use it for a few minutes if necessary. Without some stage property of this sort only a consummate actor can be seen to be busy.

When, later in 1900, the book appeared in the shops, under the title of *In the Ranks of the CIV*, it was well received, one critic expressing surprise that an 'ordinary soldier' could write so well. The reading public 1also approved; within the year the book had gone through three editions.

But Erskine, at that time, was feeling discontented with life. Like many another soldier returning from war, he found settling down to the dull routines of civilian existence difficult. For him, more than most, the contrast between the excitement and companionship of Slabbert's Nek and the daily drudgery of 'the lethargic institution', as he called the Commons Committee Room, was just too great.

In an article in *The Times*, published much later, Erskine wrote about his return voyage from Scotland on *Shulah*, with only Henry as company. Commenting upon the difference in character between himself and his brother shown during that early seafaring adventure, he wrote: 'In my brother a childlike optimism, in myself a temper tinged with philosophical doubt, but ready enough to follow a decisive lead.' Again and again throughout his life Erskine responded readily 'to a decisive lead'. Sometimes he was led in a good direction, sometimes in a bad one, but always he followed it, and always he went to extremes. Henry introduced him to the sea; he became a yachting fanatic. Basil Williams led him to the HAC – and thence to war.

Now, back in England, Erskine continued his association with the unit, training with them every week. But, being Erskine, that was nowhere near enough; he had to be the finest and best trained man in the force, ready for action whenever called upon. While the other members went through the training sessions, content to do as much as necessary but no more, Erskine worked ferociously at everything, behaving as if they really were at war. At the end of those training periods his fellow soldiers invariably adjourned to the nearest pub for a few pints. But not Erskine. Instead, he chose to give up alcohol altogether and dramatically cut down on his smoking. Ostensibly this was done in the interests of physical fitness, of becoming the finest possible HAC driver, but the real motive was probably more psychological than physical.

These weekly training sessions at St John's Wood were not enough for Erskine. He considered joining another regiment, one that would take him back to the war in South Africa. For the war still continued, despite the optimism of General Roberts. Although disgusted by the way the newspapers continued to portray the Boers, as well as critical of some of the methods being used against them, Erskine still supported the British cause. He also had an underlying need for danger and discomfort, for a regular dose of adrenalin to keep at bay the childhood ghosts. As an alternative to returning to the war, he once more considered his old dream of becoming a novelist. He thought of writing a book based upon the voyage that he and Henry had taken to the Frisian Islands on *Vixen*. He gave the project a great deal of thought, but couldn't work out the best way of doing it. That was the trouble really; although unsettled, he could not make up his mind what to do next. What he badly needed was a decisive lead.

The lead, as is often the case in life, came when he least expected it and from an unexpected source. Amongst those favourably impressed by Erskine's book of war experiences was the Colonel of the HAC, Lord Denbigh. He wrote to Erskine, congratulating him on the work, and invited him to spend a weekend at his country house, Newnham Paddox, near Rugby. Erskine, taking up the offer, was soon writing to his sisters: 'He is a young man with a young and charming wife and a bevy of little children. They have a lovely red house full of Van Dykes, Rubenses and Reynoldses.'[1] Over the weekend that Erskine spent as a guest of the Colonel, the two men were in one another's company a great deal, indulging in the traditional country house activities. They rode, fished and shot together. But most of all they talked; their conversations ranging widely over a variety of military and political topics. For the first time Erskine learned why the City Imperial Volunteers had been returned to England so suddenly and so soon. It seems that the then Lord Mayor of London, keen to share their glory, was anxious that they should arrive back in the City during his term of office. He therefore wrote to Roberts, who was an old friend, asking if the unit could be released early. Roberts, who was in one of his 'the war's almost over' moods at the time, saw no reason for refusing. Hence their early discharge.

Lord Denbigh (who cannot have been that young, despite Erskine's description; he had fought at the Battle of Tel el Kebir in 1882), with the experience that goes with such a rank, had no great difficulty in getting his visitor to open his heart to him and to admit to his current discontent. The Colonel persuaded Erskine not to return to South Africa, assuring him that there was no shortage of young men willing to be soldiers. He suggested instead that his talents would be better employed in further writing. By way of encouragement, he asked Erskine to write an official account of the HAC's part in the war.

This, gentle, kindly nudge from Lord Denbigh was sufficient to set Erskine off on a new course, a course that he was to maintain for some years. The simple suggestion of a book on the war led Erskine to write a series of books; to turn himself into a military analyst and to attack head on a large part of the military establishment. In short, direct to another obsession.

With a decisive lead provided for him, Erskine's discontent was overcome. Every moment not employed in the office was now committed to the fresh challenge, to the new book. Although in some respects this second book dealt with actions already described in his original account, the new one covered a much wider field. The HAC was an artillery company, and as such did not usually operate on the battlefield as a single unit. In addition, at an early stage of its period in South Africa the company was split into two, each part fighting on a different front. Erskine now had to describe the experiences of both units and knit the two together.

There was also a major difference between the two books in that the first was published in the same way that it had been originally written, in the form of letters. Turning the letters into a book was really just a question of selection; of deciding which to include and which to leave out. The second book, on the other hand, was written entirely afresh. It was based partly upon Erskine's own experiences, where his diary was obviously useful, and partly upon the memories and records of other members of the company.

But despite this difference in content, the same pleasant, straightforward style was employed, with occasional touches of soldierly humour. The descriptions of fighting are, if anything, even more vivid than in the first book:

> The cordon of Boers, in closing in, fired the veldt, and the flames, driven by a favourable wind, licked their way up to our very guns and horses, while the whole atmosphere became murky with smoke, through which the sun appeared as a dull crimson ball, as in a November fog in London. Some of us can see now that pandemonium of yelling Kaffirs, plunging cattle, blaspheming transport officers, and panting traction-engines, through which we forced our road, and so climbed out of that accursed spruit, under its pall of lurid smoke.[2]

The HAC in South Africa was published in 1903.

With the second book completed, Erskine turned his attention back to sailing, both as an activity and as a source of literary inspiration. It is not clear precisely when he sold *Vixen*, probably before leaving for South Africa. Yachts need regular attention and he had no idea how long he would be away. Now, in partnership with Le Fanu and A. H. Dennis, he bought a replacement, a fifteen ton, thirty-three-year-old yawl, named *Sunbeam*. In the early summer of 1903 he and his two friends spent a fortnight sailing along the south coast as far as Weymouth. He also bought a motorcycle. Speed, with its strong element of danger, appealed to him throughout his life. But although *Vixen* had departed, the yacht continued to exert a continuing influence on Erskine's life, soon bringing him, through its fictional form, a popularity which lasts to this day.

The *Riddle of the Sands* begins with Carruthers, a young, rather fastidious Foreign Office official, being invited by someone he had known at

Oxford to join his yacht, then lying at Flensberg. The yacht is quite clearly *Vixen*, renamed *Dulcibella* in honour of Erskine's favourite sister. The description of the fictional yacht is almost word for word identical with a description of *Vixen* given by Erskine in an article he had published in the *Cruising Club Journal*. Together the two young men, while exploring the Frisian Islands and the adjacent coast, discover and foil a German plan to invade England. They also unmask a British traitor.

The plot is built around Erskine's own Frisian voyage, which gives the story a strong feeling of authenticity, an authenticity that is further strengthened by the fact that almost all the characters in the book are based upon real people. The owner of *Dulcibella*, Davies, is almost certainly a portrait of Erskine himself, or more correctly a portrait of Erskine as he saw himself, not always the same thing. But in Erskine's case the portrait is really quite remarkably accurate, especially in those elements of his personality that were to become increasingly, and dangerously, dominant as he grew older. The portrait is therefore of considerable interest:

> He wore an old Norfolk jacket, muddy brown shoes, grey flannel trousers (or had they been white?) and an ordinary tweed cap. The hand he gave me was horny, and appeared to be stained with paint; the other one, which carried a parcel, had a bandage on it which would have borne renewal. I thought he gave me a shy, hurried scrutiny.[3]

The character of Davies also shows other features of Erskine's personality commented upon by people who knew him well. The reticence, the periods of introspection, the intense concentration upon what he is doing to the exclusion of everything else, the untidiness. And there is also another aspect of Erskine's character that comes out through the author's pen, his strong belief in a personal destiny:

> I glanced round at Davies. He had dropped the chart and was sitting, or rather half-lying, on the deck with one bronzed arm over the tiller, gazing fixedly ahead with just an occasional glance around and aloft. He still seemed absorbed in himself, and for a moment or two I studied his face ... I had always thought it commonplace, so far as I had thought about it at all. It had always rather irritated me by an excess of candour and boyishness. These qualities it had kept ... but I saw others. I saw strength to obstinacy, and

courage to recklessness in the firm lines of the chin; an older and deeper look in the eyes. Those odd transitions from bright mobility to detached earnestness ... seemed now to be lost in a sensitive reserve, not cold or egotistical, but strangely winning from its paradoxical frankness. Sincerity was stamped on every lineament.[4]

Now, if Davies is Erskine, who then is Carruthers? It has been suggested that he too is Erskine; a sort of alter ego. But the truth may be much simpler than that. If almost all the characters in the book are based directly upon real people, why should Carruthers be any different? How does the book describe him? As 'a young man of condition and fashion, who knows the right people, belongs to the right clubs, has a safe, possibly brilliant future in the Foreign Office'. So who did Erskine know who fits that description? Certainly not Henry. How about Walter Runciman? He was a friend of Erskine's at Cambridge and introduced him to sailing. He did indeed know all the right people and belong to all the right clubs. At the time in question he worked at the Foreign Office. As for being destined for a brilliant future, he finished up a cabinet minister. He also owned a yacht, the *Waterwitch*, with facilities that Erskine was constantly teasing him about:

> a brand new line of battleship. I will go and smell round your boat at Lymington at Easter perhaps and it will be interesting. A bathroom, ye Gods what debauched luxury! A ladies cabin! Shades of our Viking forebears![5]

Portraying Runciman, only thinly disguised, as Carruthers, would be a rather amusing joke, easily understood by their friends.

The various German characters were portraits of men that Erskine had met during his exploration of the islands: Captain Bartels of the *Johannes*; Commander Von Brunning of the torpedo-boat, *Blitz*; and a whole host of minor unnamed characters whom Dickens would have been proud of, including a river-pilot:

> Installed before a roaring stove, in the company of a buxom bustling daughter-in-law and some rosy grandchildren, we found a rotund and rubicund person who greeted us with a hoarse roar of welcome in German, which instantly changed, when he saw us, to the funniest broken English, spoken with intense relish and pride.[6]

The only people in the book who seem to have been pure inventions on Erskine's part are the British traitor, Dollman, and his daughter, Clara. Erskine certainly had a great deal of trouble with Clara and what he called 'the love interest'. That is hardly surprising; it was not something he knew much about. Although he was now in his mid twenties, he seems to have had remarkably little to do with women.

Partly that is the result of his class and time. It is difficult for us to appreciate just how segregated the sexes could be at the turn of the century. At the age of ten Erskine was sent to preparatory school, then to Haileybury, both of course single sex schools. After that it was Trinity College, Cambridge; no women there either. Then it was off to the House of Commons, equally devoid of women. As for his other interests, he was unlikely to meet many girls in his style of yachting and there were no women in the HAC.

But there must have been more to it than that. Other men managed. There were girls to be met, his sisters must have had friends; his friends must have had sisters. Possibly he never tried very hard, preferring not to take the risk. For there still remained the emotional legacy of the death of his mother. He had been deeply hurt and had built up defences to protect the scars. Such defences are not easily removed, even when the desire to remove them exists. The capacity to love means the willingness to risk getting hurt; it was not easy for Erskine to take that risk.

In the circumstances it is not perhaps surprising that the fictional Clara probably owes much more to romantic novels than to any girl he is likely to have met:

> I can see her now stooping in at the doorway, treading delicately, like a kitten, past the obstructive centre-board to a place on the sofa table, then taking in her surroundings with a timid rapture that broke into delight at all the primitive arrangements and dingy amenities of our den.[7]

As for the traitor Dollman, the dangers implicit in modelling him upon a real person are obvious enough. Erskine also seems to have had difficulty in deciding whether he is really wicked, or a figure of tragedy. As a result he never really come alive, remaining a dim figure lurking in the shadows. At about the same time, the German ambassador in London was explaining to his masters in Berlin, 'The English always find it difficult to believe that anyone has genuinely evil intentions'. Erskine was nothing if not English.[8]

But where are the origins of *The Riddle of the Sands* to be found? In looking for the inspiration for Erskine's writing we need to look no further than his favourite reading. We know that, despite his highly cultured university friends, he never showed much inclination for intellectual interests himself. We also know that in his period as editor of the *Cambridge Review* he wrote humorous articles for the magazine in the style of the Sherlock Holmes stories. It is those early writings and their origins that provided the seed from which *The Riddle of the Sands* grew.

There had been spy stories before Erskine Childers wrote his. Ever since the Franco-Prussian War, the public mind had been teased by thoughts of unscrupulous foreigners plotting against the straightforward, cricket-playing British Empire, and against the Royal Navy in particular. There were indeed several such stories involving Sherlock Holmes himself.

The Sherlock Holmes stories, with which Erskine was so familiar, were originally serialised in the *Strand* magazine, which also regularly published spy stories. Just as Conan Doyle produced detective stories that raised the level of that genre to new and more respectable heights, so Erskine Childers did the same for the spy story. In the way that only a handful of specialists are familiar with the fictional detectives before Sherlock Holmes, so only a handful are familiar with the early stories of espionage.

The Sherlock Holmes stories also had an even more direct influence upon *The Riddle of the Sands*. The Conan Doyle influence is obvious from the opening pages when the conventional Carruthers has his dull existence suddenly enlivened by a call for assistance from the skilled, enthusiastic, very unconventional Davies in the solving of a puzzle. And the ability of Davies to make sense of the tidal flows and currents swirling round the sand-banks of the Frisian Islands is not unlike the ability of Holmes to understand the flows and currents of criminal activity in fog-bound London.

If the espionage predecessors of *The Riddle of the Sands* have been long forgotten, many of its successors are regarded as classics. The calm, quietly patriotic Englishman strolls through twentieth-century literature from Richard Hannay to George Smiley, overcoming dastardly foreigners and being curiously diffident with beautiful women. Their activities are not confined to literature. Many of the stories have appeared as films and television dramas. Perhaps the most original and characteristically English film legacy of Carruthers and Davies is *The Lady Vanishes*, in which Naughton Wayne and Basil Radford portray Charters and Caldicott, two upper-class Englishmen travelling across Germany by train shortly before the outbreak of the Second World War. Obviously intended to be only minor characters in the drama, they brilliantly steal the limelight by calmly, almost absentmindedly, dealing with bullets, knives, dead bodies, wicked foreigners and beautiful mysterious women with many a cry of, 'I say, look hear, old man' and 'Would you mind awfully, old chap'. Their only continual source of concern is the dreadful possibility of missing the start of the Test Match at Lords.

How are we to account for the continuing popularity of *The Riddle of the Sands* into the very different world of the early twenty-first century? There is no mystery to this. It is well written, has a good story with a mystery at its heart, and what it has lost in topicality it has gained in nostalgia. And it is above all, in the old phrase, a rattling good yarn.

Erskine had great difficulty in writing *The Riddle of the Sands*, much more than any of his later books. He thought about it for several years before he began working on it and spent two more years writing it. There were times when he became thoroughly sick of the whole project, wishing that he had never started. But, of course, once started, it was impossible for him to stop, to admit himself defeated.

In January 1901, he wrote to his aunt, 'I have not begun that book yet. I forgot before coming away to get the diary of that cruise from the flat.' Four months later, he wrote again, 'I have not begun the Baltic book yet. I fear it would be no good without pictures. I also fear the story is beyond me.'[9] In the spring of 1902, in a letter to Basil Williams, he wrote, 'I'm finding it terribly difficult as being in the nature of a detective story. There is no sensation, only what is meant to be a convincing fact. I was weak enough to "spatchcock" a girl into it and now find her a horrible nuisance. I have not approached Reginald yet.'[10]

When the book was finally finished, shortly after Christmas 1902, he sent it, with considerable relief but not much optimism, to Smith, Elder. At that point, the only aspect of the book he was really satisfied with was the title. Reginald Smith, at Smith Elder, immediately returned the manuscript to him, asking, according to Erskine, for 'large chunks to be cut out of it'. But at least he hadn't turned it down. With the help of his sisters, who willingly submitted themselves to the boring and seemingly endless chore of checking and rechecking the manuscript, Erskine did as he was told, although not without argument.

At the core of his disagreement with his publisher was the key question of the precise nature of the book. When several years earlier he had first begun planning it, he had been following his old dream of becoming a novelist. But now, thanks to Lord Denbigh, he saw his future in terms of a military analyst. For him, the whole point of the book was the serious message it contained: the German threat and British ill-preparedness to deal with it. The entertainment value of the story was only incidental. He no longer saw the book as a novel and objected strongly at the publisher's insistence upon describing it as such, although it is difficult to see what else it could possibly have been called.

The difficulty really was that, at that time, most novels in England were written for women. The great improvement in the education provided for girls, combined with the lack of employment opportunities for them, created an enormous market for suitable books for them to read. Novelists such as Arnold Bennett and John Galsworthy eagerly met that requirement. Male readers, on the other hand, were almost totally neglected, at any rate by English novelists. The very word, 'novel', came almost to mean a book for women. *The Riddle of the Sands*, on the other hand, was a male-orientated book, offering little of interest to the feminine reader. Its spectacular success encouraged other authors to write books for men, leading the way through Buchan to Fleming, Le Carré and the other masculine novels of every type that fill station bookstalls today.

In May 1903 the book was published, despite Reginald Smith's grave misgivings. He need not have worried; he soon had a best-seller on his hands. The response to the book's arrival in the shops was immediate acclaim, from all quarters. Sales promptly took off and stayed high. By the end of the year *The Riddle of the Sands* had gone through three editions, plus a special cheap edition that sold several hundred thousand copies. It was without question the book of the year; Erskine Childers was the new sensation. Rather to his embarrassment, he became the target of society hostesses, who vied with one another for his presence at their exclusive soirées.

That the book achieved instant success on such a scale was pure luck; the kind of luck that inspires the dreams of authors and publishers alike. Had the book been published two or three years earlier, when Erskine first began working on it, its reception would have been much more muted. Certainly there would not have been quite the chorus of approval that it did receive. As it was, the timing could not have been better.

The reason lay in a change in perception amongst the British of their position in the world. The Boer War had shown Britain to be completely isolated; devoid both of friends and allies. At the same time German nationalism was becoming increasingly bellicose and the German press violently anti-British. With the death of Queen Victoria in 1901 and her replacement by the Francophile Edward VII, British foreign policy took a new turn. But such a complete change of direction could only be conducted gradually, if the government were to take the public with them. Anything that would assist the government in making that change was to be welcomed.

Meanwhile Germany, under the leadership of the dangerously unstable Kaiser Wilhelm II, was jealous of British naval strength, and resentful of its power. The Kaiser, encouraged by the clever and unscrupulous Tirpitz, set out to challenge British naval power by developing a strong navy of his own. It was a challenge that Britain could ill afford to ignore. For the Kaiser a large navy was necessary only to serve his vanity and ambition; for Britain it was a question of national survival.[11]

In the spring of 1902, the British Admiralty was advised by their naval attaché in Berlin that the rapidly growing German High Seas Fleet was of such a design that it could only be intended for war against Britain. Their latest and largest battleships were incapable of carrying sufficient fuel for operations much beyond the confines of the North Sea.[12] The Admiralty secretly began to plan a naval base at Rosyth as part of their reply to that German threat. At the same time work began upon designing a new and revolutionary type of battleship.

Meanwhile, British newspapers were discovering the growing fanaticism of German nationalists. They reacted by beating the nationalist drum themselves. Articles in German magazines expressing demands not only for colonies in Africa and Asia, but also for their right to seize large areas of Europe, including Holland, were eagerly pounced upon and widely publicised. Germany was increasingly being portrayed, with some justification, as a bogeyman.

In February 1903, while Erskine was busy on his final rewrite of *The Riddle of the Sands*, an editorial in the *Morning Post* stridently declared, 'There is a menace growing up in the east which cannot be ignored'. Demands for the government to 'do something' became widespread. Not that the government minded such demands in the least; they served its ends very well. Plans were already well advanced for new naval bases and a rapid expansion of the fleet. Public pressure helped remove opposition from treasury and pacifist critics alike.

Towards the end of his book Erskine wrote:

> We have a great and, in many respects, a magnificent navy, but not great enough for the interests it insures, not built or manned methodically, having an utterly inadequate reserve of men. We have no North Sea naval base, no North Sea fleet, and no North Sea policy.[13]

He also called for the formation of a Royal Navy Volunteer Force to be established, one that made use of the untapped skills and enthusiasm of the yachting fraternity:

> 'I know what you mean', said Davies, 'There must be hundreds of chaps like me – I know a good many myself – who know our coasts like a book – shoals, tides, rocks, there's nothing in it, it's only practice. They ought to make use of us as a naval reserve'.[14]

In March, just before the publication of the book, a Bill was placed before Parliament to do precisely that. Fact was rapidly catching up with fiction. Erskine added a postscript to the book acknowledging the measures being taken by the government, hinting that they came in response to the activities of Davies and Carruthers. But he demanded more. He also advocated that all Britons should have some military training; a suggestion that caused some elements of the German press to be even more paranoid than usual.

To a government planning a very expensive programme of naval armament, Erskine's book could not have come at a better time. It is not in the least surprising that amongst those expressing admiration for the book was the Prime Minister, Lord Rosebery. But, if government ministers were delighted with the book, some of their senior civil servants were not. The First Lord of the Admiralty, Lord Selborne, soon found himself facing a phalanx of backbench members. All were demanding reassurance that their East Coast constituencies were not about to be invaded by rapacious Huns.

Swiftly ordering his staff to investigate the threat, the minister was not satisfied until they provided him with a lengthy report declaring that the scenario described by Erskine was absolutely impossible. However, it may not be entirely a coincidence that the annual naval manoevres, held later that year, concentrated upon the problem of repelling an attempted landing upon the East Coast of England by an unspecified foreign power. As for the Germans, it is now known from documents held in their archives that their General Staff produced contingency plans for a surprise invasion of England as early as the spring of 1896. Their intended landing area was the Suffolk coast between Aldeburgh and Yarmouth.

There is also another curious coincidence. Towards the end of the book Carruthers rescues some charred papers from the stove of a villa on Nordeney, which the traitor, Dollman, had been using. The papers are found to be the German plans for an invasion of England. As it happens, there was a large villa on Nordeney, the summer home of the German Foreign Minister, von Bülow.

Inevitably, not everyone was so enthusiastic about the book. The anonymous critic in the *Times Literary Supplement*, looking down from his lofty throne, found it all too tiresome. In common with Erskine, he was far from happy with the 'love interest', but he thought there should be more of it; and much less sailing:

> But the book can only be read by the aid of large maps, railway guides and special information about things nautical. The traitor has a pretty daughter, otherwise there would be no 'love interest'.
>
> 'There was a flutter of lace and cambric, and she was in his arms, sobbing like a tired child, her little white feet between his great, clumsy sea-boots, her rose-brown cheeks on his rough jersey.'

The wearied critic of fiction 'could lie down like a tired child' before he reaches this conclusion, so outworn is he with shoals, sands, channels and glances at the chart. The heroine, in the maze of the mystery, 'complained that her head was going round'. The heroine is to be sympathised with, a plain tale with no colouring would be more readable than this bewildering romance.[15]

He was, however, very much in the minority. Praise came from all directions. The Prime Minister, Lord Rosebery, meeting Erskine in the House of Commons, stopped to express his appreciation of the book. 'He wanted to know how much was fact and talked delightfully on the various subjects suggested by the book, urged me to write again.' The *Westminster Gazette*, commenting upon the appearance of the third edition of the book in January 1904, described it as 'a literary accomplishment of much force and originality'. The newspaper then went on:

> It was manifestly, however, intended to be something more than that ... This is a book with a purpose, clearly stated and strongly enforced. It is meant to secure our national safety. Mr Childers is no panic monger; he does not install suspicion or hatred of Germany, but simply accepts statements repeatedly and deliberately made by German authorities, and indicates how the danger might be met.

There is, however, within the book one strand that is curiously out of line with popular opinion of the time. On several occasions Davies expresses admiration of the German Kaiser: 'He's a fine fellow, that Emperor'; 'He really is a splendid chap'. That is not at all how most people in England saw Wilhelm II in 1903. Quite apart from his scarcely concealed envy of British power, the Kaiser had precisely that strutting officiousness that always grated against the British character. To them his attempts to emphasise his Prussianness by upturned moustaches and over-rigid bearing simply appeared ridiculous. The British public reacted as they invariably did to such men; they made him a figure of fun. The press were quick to see the possibilities; cartoons mocking him becoming more and more common. His increasingly frequent diplomatic indiscretions were pounced upon with undisguised glee. 'Witless Willie', they called him. That Erskine should be so far out of line with prevailing opinion in Britain is interesting. It suggests that he did have a certain sympathy with more dictatorial methods of government than the usual Westminster-style muddling through that he was so familiar with. Certainly, the older he got the more dogmatic and intolerant he became.

Through his friendship with Eddie Marsh, who seemed to know everyone, Erskine was now introduced to many people in positions of power and influence. He met, for instance, Winston Churchill. It has even been suggested that *The Riddle of the Sands* was written at Churchill's instigation as part of an anti-German crusade. But, at that time, Churchill, strongly influenced by his association with Lloyd George, was a Radical Liberal. His primary interest being social reform, he was opposed to increased arms spending, wanting the money spent on pensions and social security. As for the German threat, Churchill simply refused to believe that it existed; a position he was to continue to maintain until the Agadir Crisis of 1910 at last changed his mind.

That Erskine would continue to write was not in doubt. He had in fact already committed himself to yet another book on the Boer War. But this was an undertaking that he had given rather unwillingly. It came about when Eddie Marsh introduced him to Leo Amery, a near neighbour of Erskine's in Chelsea. A long-established journalist on the *Times*, Amery was then heavily involved, as general editor, in producing *The Times History of the War in South Africa*.

Having already written the first two volumes himself, Amery was now working on the third. For the last two volumes he had engaged Basil Williams. Basil, however, although busy completing volume four, was about to return to South Africa to work with Lord Milner in implementing the new peace agreement. He would therefore be unable to write the final volume. Erskine was now asked to take on that task. He was far from enamoured with the idea. Although the financial terms offered were attractive, the amount of research involved would be prodigious. In the end he agreed, more to please Basil, who was feeling guilty at leaving a job half done, than to satisfy Leo Amery. Erskine did, however, insist that he must be allowed to finish the HAC book first. As we have seen, he also completed the long-planned *Riddle of the Sands*.

It might be expected that Erskine, who had long wanted to be a novelist, having at last not only produced a novel but a best-selling one, would now write more of them. His great aunt Flora shrewdly suggested that he travel. Perhaps, bearing in mind his classical studies, he could go to Greece. It would, she thought, help to broaden his mind, and possibly give him the background for a new book. It is greatly to be regretted that Erskine did not take up that suggestion. His talents were perfectly suited for either novels set in foreign locations, or for writing travel books. He had the ability vividly to describe a landscape or person. He could also do it with humour, having a good eye for the more amusing aspects of human nature.

But he rejected the suggestion out of hand. By now he was firmly set on becoming a military analyst and he would not be deflected from it. As for the success of *The Riddle of the Sands*, in his eyes that only confirmed the correctness of his chosen course. He did not see the book as a successful novel; indeed he didn't see it as a novel at all. He had set out to awaken the government and people of England to a foreign threat; the book's success had done precisely that. Everyone said so and constantly praised him for it.

That then was to be his future. He would write a series of books drawing attention to the weaknesses of the British armed forces. He would point out where the War Office and the generals were going wrong, and he would give advice on correct battlefield tactics. That there might be some reluctance on the part of the military establishment to take notice of the opinions of a part-time driver in the horse artillery seems never to have entered his head.

The result of that decision was that Erskine would, in the years to come, write only serious books, books designed to be influential. Books in which the best qualities of his writing, his descriptive talents and his sense of humour, were ruthlessly excluded. Books which hardly anyone read and which influenced almost nobody. But before he could embark upon his own literary projects he had first to write the volume on the Boer War promised to Leo Amery more than a year before. He had as yet done almost nothing about it, having pushed it to one side first for the HAC book, then for *The Riddle of the Sands*. When he did begin work on it, he found the task even more daunting than he had expected; the amount of research involved was colossal. The HAC book had involved only one unit of the enormous army that Britain had sent to the war. With the new volume, he needed to understand the involvement of every regiment in the entire army. And being Erskine there could be no short cuts, he had to do it thoroughly.

During the summer, Erskine and his friends embarked upon their most ambitious seafaring expedition so far. A. H. Dennis, with three friends, a paid hand and 'a small cabin boy who had never even seen the sea before' sailed *Sunbeam* along *Vixen*'s old route across the North Sea, through the Frisian Islands and the Kiel Canal and on to Flensburg. At Flensburg there was a reshuffle of crew as the old trio of Erskine, Ivor Lloyd-Jones and William Le Fanu replaced some of the others, including presumably the cabin boy. The new crew then had the pleasure of exploring the beautiful waters that surround Denmark, performing a rough figure of eight around the islands of Funen and Zealand. They visited a number of the small, picturesque towns that dot the Danish seaboard including Svendborg, Nyborg and Faborg, perhaps the most attractive of them all.[16]

That year, 1903, saw Erskine advancing strongly in all directions. At the House of Commons he received promotion to Clerk of Petitions. As he wrote to Basil, now busy in Cape Town, 'I know nothing about petitions. It's sixty pounds a year extra and I find it gives me more work than I ever expected.' There was also another project for Erskine to consider. In 1896 the Ancient and Honourable Artillery Company of Massachusetts paid a visit to London as the guests of their parent organisation, the Honourable Artillery Company. There now came an invitation for a return visit in September to Boston and other American cities. Erskine was, at first, very reluctant to take part. Being a teetotaller he found the prospect of 'a round of drinking and feasting' singularly unattractive.

Had he known the details of the programme being planned for them in America he would have had even graver doubts. In Boston alone they were budgetting for spending $251,000 on the visit; this sum including such interesting items as $30,000 on banquets, $15,000 on wine, $8000 on cigars and $50,000 on private entertainment.[17] None of this was likely to appeal to the ascetically-minded Erskine Childers.

Other members of the HAC also had doubts, but of a more fundamental nature. They wondered how a British military unit would be greeted in Boston, a city with such close Irish links. The Americans, however, seemed very keen to have them; and Lord Denbigh was eager for them to go. He was also anxious that the force should 'make a good show' and that as many members as possible should make the trip. Erskine, largely out of respect for the Colonel, eventually allowed himself to be talked into it, with consequences that were totally unexpected.

5

Marriage

Erskine and the other members of the Honourable Artillery Company sailed from Liverpool by a Dominion Line ship, appropriately named *Mayflower*, on 23 September 1903. The voyage lasted nine days. Lord Denbigh's request for a good turnout had been fully met. One hundred and sixty-five men took part in the trip, of whom more than seventy had fought with the unit in South Africa.

To them this new voyage, paid for by their American hosts, presented quite a contrast with their experiences of sailing on the *Montfort* three years earlier. Instead of closely-packed hammocks, they were now provided with comfortable cabins, offering every possible facility. No need now to queue for the privilege of washing at a cold tap, or having to search for a few square feet of deck space upon which to sit. The food too bore little resemblance to that served up to them during their earlier South African expedition.

But, although they had neither horses nor guns to attend to, they continued to behave like the military unit they were proud to be. Anxious to make a good impression upon their American hosts, they had a training session every morning, which varied in character day by day. Their uniforms were regularly cleaned and inspected, and an assortment of drill and sword exercises performed.

On their first evening at sea the company laid on a concert for the enjoyment of their fellow passengers. Amongst the entertainment thus provided, Private Lobb offered a humorous song, entitled, 'I'm a Jonah Man'. Private Fisher sang. 'Yo, Ho, Little Girls', whilst their commander Lieutenant Colonel the Earl of Denbigh provided, 'Love's Coronation', followed by 'Alouette' as an encore. All items were well received. On Sunday morning, divine service was held on deck by the Rev. Dr Leighton-Parks, who gave an address upon the topical theme of 'The Miracle of the Anglo-Saxon Race'. In accordance with maritime custom, the last night at sea saw a Fancy Dress Ball, with Lord Denbigh appearing as Father Neptune and Lady Denbigh as Britannia.[1]

In Boston, meanwhile, excitement was mounting. The local press had for weeks been stirring the interests of its readers with the thrilling and unique prospect of the coming event. Old battles were recalled, new friendships welcomed. Much was made of the fact that no British military unit had been to Boston since General Howe had sailed away in defeat a hundred and fifty years before.

The newspapers explained in some length, and with surprising accuracy, the precise nature and functions of the HAC as compared with its American equivalent. They gave potted histories of the company and its officers, including details of the unit's activities in the recent war. The press were particularly interested in the circumstances which led to Major Budworth, one of the officers taking part in the visit, being awarded the Victoria Cross. The ladies were not forgotten either. The fact that Lord and Lady Denbigh were leading the visitors offered a rich source of speculation and advice concerning dress fashions, social etiquette and similar niceties. It was said that Lord Denbigh was a close friend of the King and a possible future Ambassador to the United States.

At midnight fifty members of the Boston Ancients, as they liked to call themselves, left harbour in a specially chartered steamer to greet their English visitors while still at sea. Others had already gone to the tip of Cape Cod, hoping to provide a display of welcome from there, a project sadly foiled by fog.

Unlike their British guests, the Boston Ancients were not a functioning military unit and were not subject to military discipline. While their unit did have its own uniform, most of their members chose to exercise their right to wear the uniform of whichever branch of the armed forces they had previously served in, even when that unit no longer existed. They were also, for the most part, much older than their visitors, sixty of their members having fought in the Civil War forty years earlier. But none of this in any way dampened their enthusiasm either for their own unit or for the forthcoming visit.

By four in the morning the men of the HAC were up and about, giving their uniforms a final brush and their rifles a last inspection. Breakfast was taken at 6.30; it was barely completed before the American welcoming party, led by Colonel Walker, boarded the ship. That morning's edition of the *Boston Post* declared, in huge banner headlines: 'HONOURABLES ARE HERE'. The paper was in fact a little bit premature with the news. At the time the newspaper first appeared in the streets, the ship was still edging its way cautiously through a thick fog that completely blanketed the New England coastline.

Any lingering doubts as to the kind of reception the company would receive in the American city were dispelled when the ship entered Boston harbour. Every ship, large or small, was smothered in bunting. British and American flags fluttered gaily everywhere. Three warships, USS *Chicago*, HMS *Retribution* and a French vessel, the *Trude*, were dressed overall, their decks lined from end to end with waving sailors. The air was filled with the sound of sirens and whistles; church bells rang, bands played, crowds waved ecstatically. Fort Warren fired a twenty-one gun salute: an American welcome at its most exuberant. On *Mayflower*, meanwhile, the officers and men of the HAC stood watching and waving, almost overcome by the sheer enthusiasm of their reception. They had expected nothing like this.

Later that morning a grand parade took place when the English visitors, accompanied by a British style military band borrowed from Halifax, Nova Scotia, marched, in full-dress uniform, from the harbour and through the centre of the city.

> First the Corps of Cadets, the gallant Ninth, the Lancers, and the British Naval and Military Veterans, then the Boston Ancients. Then at the sight of the Earl of Denbigh, hats went up in the air and a host of shouts broke forth. The red-coated Honourables, in their tall bearskin hats and gold-laced coats, seemed highly elated with the ovation given them. Their typical English faces and general youthful appearance formed a great contrast to the Boston Ancients who preceded them. The Boston men looked older and the Putnam Guards especially seemed to deserve the name of Ancients.[2]

Throughout the whole length of the march, despite continuous and sometimes heavy rain, the Englishmen were welcomed by huge crowds who lined the streets in their thousands, cheering and waving. At every window of the eleven story buildings, women and children waved flags and shouted themselves hoarse. As the *Boston Post* expressed it, without exaggeration, 'Heroes returning from victorious wars could get no greater reception'.

One detachment wore the dark blue artillery uniform with its brilliant gold facings and the natty Eton jacket. The other detachment wore the old and time-honoured British scarlet topped with huge bearskins. This was the picturesque uniform, the one the crowd was longing to see and they cheered its wearers with a will.

And what a contrast was presented between the appearance of the English and American soldiers. The Englishmen, in their natty showy uniforms, gold lace showing everywhere, looked strange and foreign beside the quiet unembellished uniform of the Massachusetts Militia. The English walked as if on dress parade; the Americans as if on pleasure bent. The cocky, trippy, snappy, jerky step of the English tactics showed in striking contrast to the easy, long, graceful swing of the American soldiers.[3]

That evening there was a formal reception for the HAC officers at the State House. According to the local press, upon their arrival, 'Men jumped in the air and cheered, while women waved their handkerchiefs and their umbrellas'.

The next morning the visitors entertained the Bostonians by parading their regimental colours before a large and appreciative audience. In the early afternoon a special train carried them to Providence in nearby Rhode Island. Once more they were met by packed streets and large, enthusiastic, flag-waving crowds. In the evening, before returning to Boston, they were the honoured guests at a banquet for a thousand people, dining on the local specialities of clams, bluefish and ears of green corn.

The following day, being a Sunday, naturally began with a church parade, witnessed by 30,000 people. The wiser members of the company no doubt rested in their hotel rooms in the afternoon, especially if they had seen that day's *Boston Sunday Post*, with its headline referring to the banquet promised for that evening:

ANCIENT ROMANS OUTDONE

Neither the wonderful feasts of the Augustinian Caesars nor the dazzling sumptuousness that transformed the halls of Louis XIV's palace into epicurean bowers can rival the dinner which the Boston Ancients have striven and planned for as a welcome to their guests from across the sea.

With its customary love of statistics, the paper then went into considerable detail as to the planned expense of the forthcoming meal. It wrote of a total cost of $60,000, of the employment of 300 waiters, of seventy-five wine-waiters, and of the provision of 400 gallons of the oldest, finest, wines.

During the course of the banquet, held in Symphony Hall, the Governor of Massachusetts declared, to shouts of agreement, that 'America and Britain will never again be at war against one another, though they may be at war with each other'. Lord Denbigh, in reply, assured his hosts, 'Bunker Hill monument will ever stand before Britons as an example of how colonies ought not to be governed', a comment that was received by his hosts with applause and cries of approval. During the banquet each of the hundred or so tables was shared between members of the two companies, enabling them to get to know one another as individuals.

The visitors spent Monday morning on a steamer trip round the harbour, witnessed as always by huge crowds. As a typically reticent Englishman, Erskine found some aspects of American friendliness and hospitality rather difficult to deal with. As he wrote to Basil Williams:

> One is introduced to any passer-by, never remembers his name, and has a tiresome business of evading taking drinks with him. The drink question is a perfect curse and I believe I offend people right and left, but it can't be helped.[4]

The following day saw the start of a two thousand mile tour of north-eastern America and Canada, beginning with a train journey to New York, including a four hour stop-over at Fall River. In New York, staying at the Waldorf, they visited the officer cadets at West Point, where, for the first time, the American press found the drill of their own servicemen smarter than that of their English visitors. The same newspapers caused considerable offence in Boston by their mockery of the Ancients and their uniforms. Leaving New York, the HAC travelled on to Washington, where they paraded in front of the White House, being inspected by the President, before attending a four hour reception given by Mrs Roosevelt.

Later that same day they departed on the evening train bound for Buffalo and Niagara Falls. By this stage of the trip a number of the men were beginning to feel the strain of constant travel and of the frequent banquets provided for them. Not surprisingly, upset stomachs presented the main problem. These, however, were usually blamed not on the rich food or the overabundance of alcohol but on the curious American fondness for iced water. This, it was felt, was freezing delicate English stomachs which were not used to such a strange beverage.

By 11 October they were in Toronto, and on the 12th in Montreal. The Canadians, while welcoming their visitors in large numbers and in a friendly fashion, were not nearly so extravagant, either in expenditure or reception, as their American cousins. It did, however, provide a welcome interlude of calm before the men once more crossed the border to face more enthusiasm and yet more banquets.

Returning to Boston by rail through Vermont provoked fresh excitement. Not only did crowds pack the platforms of every station where the train stopped, but little groups of people stood by the trackside, eager to see them go by and to wave a friendly greeting. The arrival back at Boston on 14 October meant a final huge and expensive banquet, this time at the Somerset Hotel, attended by four hundred guests. The following day most of the company left for home, sailing from a harbour surrounded by 75,000 men, women, and children all come to say goodbye, maintaining their excitement to the end. It had been quite a trip. Towards the end of the tour Erskine wrote to Basil Williams:

> As to behaviour, I believe we have got through without open scandal – mercifully, for the primitive instincts of the HAC set towards debauchery, and when champagne is perpetually flowing like water the descent to Averno is abnormally easy, especially, as our escort, a hundred members of the Boston Company, aren't noted for their sobriety, celebrated as they are for many things.
>
> They are all elderly and stout. They all wear different uniforms, some dating from antiquity, and look strangely like participants in a fancy dress ball or pantomime. Indeed I believe the Ancients rather resent being reminded that we can fight and are visibly disappointed that we were not more their equals in age and girth.[5]

Seen from any viewpoint, but particularly from the British, the visit had been an immense success. The only slight embarrassment came from the twenty-eight men of HMS *Retribution* who went ashore to see the sights and chose not to return. The ship was forced to sail without them.

When the festivities were over and the rest of the company sailed off to England, Erskine chose to stay on in Boston for a while. He had heard so much about the beauties of the New England fall, it seemed a shame to come all this way without seeing it. He also felt the need for a period of calm after all the excitement and constant feasting of the previous two weeks. Renting a room at the University Club, he soon established a routine more in keeping with his usual way of life. Hiring a motorcycle, he set off each day to explore the surrounding countryside. Every evening he returned, tired, to have a bath, dine alone, and then retire to his room for a quiet read and an early night. One morning, setting off as usual up Boston's Beacon Hill, his machine suddenly coughed, gave a splutter or two and then stopped. Erskine had a quick look at the engine. The cause of the trouble he found easy enough to diagnose, but to repair it he required a spanner, something not supplied with the hired machine.

He looked about him. On either side of the road stood large, imposing houses. Choosing one entirely at random, he walked over and knocked on the door. It was opened by Dr Hamilton Osgood, a member of a long-established Boston family and a well-known physician. Noticing the stranger's English accent, Dr Osgood questioned him further. Learning that Erskine was a member of the English regiment that had recently caused such a stir in the city, the doctor invited him in to meet his wife and daughter, Mary. That evening Erskine returned to the house again, this time for dinner. He sat opposite Mary. Further evenings followed. Then whole days. Accompanied by Mary, Erskine explored the city, being introduced to more and more of the family's relatives and friends. Only three weeks later, Erskine proposed to Mary. Rather to his amazement, he was accepted.

Mary Alden Osgood, invariably known as Molly, was in her mid twenties, with auburn hair and a pleasant smile. She was also a young woman who had known more than her fair share of physical suffering. At the age of three she had suffered a skating accident that seriously injured both her hips. Tubercular abscesses developed, first in one hip, then in the other. Despite a succession of long and painful operations, up to the age of ten Molly was unable to walk at all. Further operations followed, enabling her, slowly and painfully, to learn to walk. By the time she was thirteen she could manage with crutches. Later, after yet more operations, she was able to replace the crutches with sticks. But, in spite of all this medical attention, she was effectively to remain a cripple for the rest of her life. Having undergone and overcome such terrible trials in her childhood, Molly had not surprisingly grown into a woman of great courage and strength of character. That Erskine, who had had to overcome childhood tragedies of his own, was attracted to such a woman is perhaps only to be expected. They were also qualities that had been present in his own mother.

The wedding took place on 6 January 1904 at Trinity Church, the city's largest Presbyterian establishment. The ceremony was performed during particularly severe winter weather, which frequently brought fierce blizzards sweeping across the city, bringing traffic to a complete standstill. Despite this, Boston society turned out in force. January was normally such a depressingly dull month for social occasions in the city. A fashionable wedding offered its inhabitants an opportunity for dressing up which they were determined not to miss. The *Boston Post*, while showing little interest in the bridegroom, naturally paid great attention to the ladies' dresses, which showed a curious fondness for black:

> A number of very beautiful gowns were worn at the Childers-Osgood nuptials, which showed to special advantage against the background of Mr Doyle's decorations of foliage in combination with myriads of Easter lilies. Mrs Hamilton Osgood was richly clad in black velvet, with a small toque and had with her the Misses Childers of London who were attired much alike in grey with large black hats.[6]

The wedding service was conducted by the Bishop of Massachusetts, a family friend of the Osgoods. Erskine's youngest, and favourite, sister, Dulcibella, was one of the bridesmaids. In the absence of Basil Williams, still busy in Cape Town, Erskine's cousin, Robert Barton, performed the service of best man. After the wedding, the couple departed for Europe, where they spent their honeymoon making an extended tour of Italy.

When they eventually returned to England, Erskine and Molly's first task was to go house-hunting. After some searching, they found just what they wanted, in the form of a flat at 13 Embankment Gardens, Chelsea. Conveniently, it was only a stone's throw from Erskine's old flat in Carlyle Mansions, where his sisters continued to live. In describing their new flat to his father-in-law, Erskine wrote:

Counting a room in the basement which goes with it, it has seven rooms, excluding the kitchen, etc, and servant's bedroom. We shall have a drawing-room, dining-room, study and two little rooms with a communicating door for you. Three of the rooms look out on the extensive gardens of Chelsea Hospital.[7]

The early months of 1904 saw Erskine settling down again in London, with a new wife and a new home. In this way began the happiest period of his life. Molly provided the love and companionship he badly needed. She also, for a while, put to rest the legacy of childhood tragedy. The desire for discomfort and danger died away under the influence of quiet domesticity. Other aspects of his life, however, continued much as before. While Parliament was sitting he went off to work every day to his office in the House of Commons, leaving Molly to run the household, plan their meals and supervise the servants.

Whenever his official work was slack, he turned his attention towards *The Times History of the War in South Africa*, slowly grinding his way through it. Most of his leisure time was also sacrificed to the same cause. With his customary thoroughness he studied countless documents, official and unofficial. In search of facts, he wrote to generals and politicians, and had discussions with army officers and ordinary soldiers. No loose ends went unpursued.

Quite often, when working at the House of Commons, and finding that he needed papers from home, he wrote a letter to his wife requesting them. This he would have delivered by messenger, who then returned with the items, together with a letter from Molly. These letters, however, were not always strictly necessary. As would only to be expected, given his character, when Erskine finally fell in love he did so totally. Molly became his new obsession and the dominant influence in his life; far too much so in the opinion of many of his friends, who felt that he was allowing his own personality to be submerged by hers. Whenever he was away from her, sometimes for only a matter of a few hours, he wrote letters to her, declaring his love for her; then waited anxiously for a reply from her. Having at last found a replacement for his mother, Erskine lived in dread of losing her; of her suddenly vanishing, the way Anna had done so many years before.

Back on Chelsea Embankment the couple lived a busy social life. The arrival of the sociable, attractive Molly, together with the literary fame obtained by Erskine himself, brought numerous new friends into their orbit. They did not live in high society, neither of them caring much for such pretensions. They much preferred interesting people to ancient titles or modern fashions. But they held the occasional dinner party and were invited to parties by others. They also made and received less formal visits:

> We are going out a good deal and there is very little time alas for reading and the quiet life. But we've had some interesting parties with the Sargents, among others (John Sargent and Henry James were there), and at the Trowers where Molly revelled in a marvellous collection of Japanese things, and we've met Sir George Clarke, the ex-Governor of Australia and present members of the triumvirate who are reorganising the national defence system and giving us a new army.[8]

Erskine, however, did not neglect his old friendships and activities, still training regularly once a week with the HAC. As for sailing, his father-in-law had promised the couple that, as a wedding present, he would have a yacht specially built for them, to their own design. Erskine, however, was cautious. Although Molly had apparently done some sailing in American waters, he thought it best, in view of her lameness, to carry out an experiment before committing his father-in-law to the not inconsiderable expense of a brand new yacht. He therefore made use of *Sunbeam*, which he owned in association with his old university friends Le Fanu, Dennis and Colomb. The newly-weds spent several weekends together sailing along the South Coast, reaching as far as the Cornish port of Fowey. Gradually Molly, from being the coddled passenger, heavily wrapped up in oilskins and countless woollens, became the mate, taking the helm, cooking and keeping watch 'with the eyes of a sea-eagle'.

Before the year was out Erskine was sufficiently satisfied with Molly's seafaring abilities to tell her father of the design of boat they both wanted. They chose to have one designed and built by Colin Archer at his yard in Larvik, at the mouth of Oslofjord. Archer was a Scottish-Norwegian who had previously designed Nansen's *Fram*, in addition to numerous lifeboats and fishing-vessels. When built, the new yacht, which was forty-four feet long overall and with a thirteen foot beam, had all the beauty of line to be expected from her Scandinavian origin.

Below, she had three cabins: a two-berth sleeping cabin, complete with WC; and a companionway, with another bunk in it, leading to a main saloon, where there were two more berths. There was also a fo'c'sle, which contained the galley.[9] Clearly the days when Erskine could safely mock the facilities of Runciman's *Waterwitch* were coming to an end.

During the August of 1905 the new boat was delivered to Bursledon by a Norwegian crew, led by a Captain Knudsen, with Lloyd Jones on board as a representative of the owner. Her name, *Asgard*, ostensibly came from the doomed home of the Gods in Norse mythology, but the similarity between the names Asgard and Osgood is probably of more significance. On 30 August Erskine and Molly, together with a friend, Laurie Rainsford, sailed the new boat for the first time, contenting themselves with cruising about the Solent, having occasional mock races against other yachts. They were delighted with every aspect of her. The following month the two of them, in spite of Molly being five months pregnant, set off on a month's voyage aboard her, getting as far west as the Helford River.

In December 1905 Molly gave birth to a fine healthy son, who they named Erskine Hamilton Childers. This brought to an end Molly's yachting activities for some time. Compensations did, however, come in the spring, when they made a voyage to Norway as passengers on a steamer. Their busy social life, both formal and informal, continued much as before. That Molly's literary tastes were rather different to those of her husband is shown by a letter from Sir Frederick Pollock, the writer on jurisprudence, to Oliver Wendell Holmes:

> Tomorrow I am going to see two charming Americans. Mrs Erskine Childers of your state, with whom I am reading Dante's *Purgatory* in such times as we can steal, and Elizabeth Robins of Kentucky. Mrs Erskine Childers is a modern marriage by capture – her husband went to Boston with the Hon. Artillery Co. and brought her home. They are devoted to sailing a small boat (she can steer of course) and their baby rising some six months is known as the Admiral.[10]

Erskine meanwhile had, to his considerable relief, at last finished the *Times* book on the Boer War promised to Leo Amery several years before. The volume, tightly written and six hundred pages long, dealt with the final, guerilla phase of the struggle. It related a complex story to which the author had given much time and thought. Unfortunately, there now arose a heated dispute between author and editor. Leo Amery was a disciple of Milner; Erskine one of Milner's most determined critics. Amery, believing that the criticisms of Milner in the book went too far, insisted upon rewriting sections of the final chapter. Erskine, angry and determined not to be silenced, insisted upon including a protest in his preface to the volume: 'Mr Amery, in his capacity as general editor, has largely remodelled my draft of this chapter and, as it now stands, he is solely responsible for it.'

Despite this disagreement, the two men continued to be on friendly terms until the contentious issue of the future of Ireland separated them at last in 1916. Amery, in his own memoirs, makes no mention of the quarrel, choosing instead to praise unstintingly the work of his fellow writer:

> The story of that protracted fight between the mobile and mechanical conceptions of warfare, between the heavy-footed pursuer with his widespread nets and the pursued with his elusive escapes and raids, between Boer stubbornness and Kitchener's unflagging energy, was told in full with consummate skill in the handling of his material and with sympathetic insight by my poor ill-fated friend, Erskine Childers.[11]

The book, which was published in 1907, is an immensely detailed, densely written scholarly work. Unlike Erskine's earlier books, however, it does not make easy reading, there being no place in it for the best aspects of his writing. There are none of his vivid sketches of army life, no word pictures of a country at war, and humour is completely absent.

To the military historian, wishing to know the activities in the war of a particular regiment or artillery unit, it is no doubt extremely valuable. But to the ordinary reader, forced to hack his way through dense thickets of military terminology, it is rather heavy fare. As Amery himself admitted, 'The minuteness of detail devoted to "battles" that in the world wars of our day would be dismissed as mere incidents may now seem exaggerated'. The book also has another fault that was to characterise much of Erskine's work from now on. As with his criticisms of Milner, Erskine all too often defeated his own ends by his harshness, by his refusal to take into account the feelings of others, and by his failure to temper criticism with diplomacy. Despite describing himself as a military analyst, when it came to mounting attacks himself he seemed incapable of anything but the direct frontal assault. He could have achieved so much more had he adopted a more subtle approach. Instead he chose words guaranteed to raise hackles, especially in the cavalry:

> The regular cavalry formed the permanent foundation; but the profound conservatism which, as in most regular armies, characterised this arm, debarred it from setting such an example of vigorous originality as was urgently needed for the conduct of the campaign.[12]

With the *Times* book now, at last, out of the way, Erskine turned his attention to another book on military strategy and tactics. Misled by the nature of the runaway success of *The Riddle of the Sands*, he saw himself becoming a major influence on military thought, genuinely believing that politicians and generals alike, eagerly seizing upon his ideas, would rush to adopt them. Molly has been criticised for encouraging him in this course, for supporting him in his belief that his future lay as a military analyst, and for failing to convince him that he would be better employed in writing another novel. But this is to misunderstand the influence that Molly had over Erskine. She had precisely the same power over him that most women have over their husbands. She had the power to encourage him upon the course that he had already set himself; she had no power to change that course. If ever a man was headstrong, that man was Erskine Childers. So far as we know, only once during their marriage did Molly seriously attempt to divert him from his chosen course; and on that occasion she failed completely.

In August 1906, Erskine and Molly, together with Ivor Lloyd Jones and a paid hand, called Amor, edged *Asgard* away from her Hampshire moorings, raised her mainsail and set off up-Channel, bound for the Baltic.[13] The weather which had, for some weeks, been fine, suddenly worsened. Although the strong south-west wind served their purpose well enough, the torrential rain was much less welcome. Nevertheless, with full sails they ran before the wind along the length of the South Coast, rounded the North Foreland and swept across the North Sea to Ijmuiden in fine style. Then it was along the old familiar route of Texel, Terschelling, Cuxhaven and the Kiel Canal. For a while the weather around Jutland was fine, giving them splendid sailing, as they worked

their way, in easy stages, up the east coast, first to Flensburg, then on
to Aarhus.

Some idea of the relationships between the various crew members
can be deduced from a crew list drawn up at that time by Molly:

Erskine	Slave driver	Very severe
Molly	Charwoman	Fractious
Ivor	Driven slave	Patient, but complaining
Amor	Paid hand	Would cook while sinking [14]

Molly also wrote, rather touchingly, in a letter to her family back in
Boston: 'Whenever Erskine says I have done well – as he sometimes
does – then I feel proud – But I have so much to learn still ... and of
course I am no good at the ropes, for they are so heavy.'

From Aarhus they turned eastwards again, making for the north coast
of Funen, eventually putting in at Nyborg. By now it was well into
September, the days growing short, the weather worsening. A cold wind,
sometimes up to gale force, and often with driving rain, swept in from
the east, a forewarning of the approach of winter. Molly again:

At 8 I went below – in answer to Erskine's comments, undressed, found
myself soaked through and through. I rubbed myself dry, put on dry things,
was seasick, and got into my bunk cold, hungry, exhausted, despairing. In
five minutes I was glowing and hot all over, rested, happy and deliciously
sleepy, too sleepy to want to eat, and seasickness forgotten. I was seasick only
because everything was on its head below, and I was so miserable. But I loved
it all the time on deck and had not one qualm. [15]

Concluding that it was now too late in the season for their original
plan of pushing on to Helsinki, they made instead for the small port of
Svendberg. There they lay the boat up for the winter, intending to
continue their explorations to the eastern Baltic the following year. But
that voyage was destined not to take place; and the reason is not difficult
to find. Even before they returned from the Baltic, Molly found she was
pregnant again. Unfortunately, unlike the first occasion, this new preg-
nancy proved to be very difficult. When their second son was finally
born and named Henry, in February 1907, he was sickly and malformed.
Although everything was done for him, he survived for only nine
months. At the same time Molly's own health gave Erskine serious cause
for concern.

Precisely what happened to *Asgard* during this period, and for some time to come, is something of a mystery. Obviously it was impossible for Molly to go to the Baltic in 1907. It is unlikely that, given the difficult situation at home, Erskine felt able to go without her. Probably some of their friends sailed her back from Denmark. But what is more curious is that there are no records at all of Erskine's seafaring activities from the moment when the yacht was left at Svenberg, in September 1906, until they once more departed for the Baltic in June 1913.

Although, over the years, Erskine wrote numerous articles about his voyages, for a wide variety of publications, they are completely silent about this period. What is more, there are no logbooks, no letters mentioning the yacht, nothing. This does not of course mean that they didn't sail in her, but it does suggest that they didn't venture very far. It is also true that, at this time of his life, Erskine was extremely busy; in all probability he simply wasn't able to find the time for lengthy voyages.

What he had done, meanwhile, was to write the first of a series of yachting articles for the *Times*. He had, for ten years or more, written regularly for the *Cruising Club Journal,* and occasionally for other yachting magazines. But the *Times* articles were a new venture, written very much for commercial purposes. Being tired of the Committee Clerk's dull grind, he was seriously considering realising a long-held dream of becoming a full-time writer.

Not that he had any money worries; his father-in-law was extremely generous. Bank drafts came from him regularly, sometimes for as much as a thousand pounds. But Erskine was too proud and independent a man to be satisfied with living off his wife's relatives, however generous they might be. Hence he produced the articles, which could be written much quicker than the book he was planning. It would be interesting to know precisely how they came to be written. Did Erskine approach the *Times*, or did someone with influence at the *Times* suggest the project to him? The second alternative could well be the truth, because his own inclination seems to have been for more books on military strategy.

Either way, the articles mark the last flowering of the old Erskine Childers style, the style that began with *In the Ranks of the CIV* and reached its peak with *The Riddle of the Sands.* The articles were varied in nature. Some of them gave advice about cruising in particular geo-graphical areas. There was one about the South Coast, another about the much lesser known estuaries and salt marshes of Essex:

> if you wish to put to a supreme test your capacity to love Essex as she deserves to be loved, you cannot do better than explore the Roach and its branches on a grey day when a searching wind from the east moans over the flats, when colours are toned down to the neutral and a sense of infinite desolation lays hold of the senses.

Other articles were about areas further afield that he knew well; the Frisian Islands, Denmark and Holland. He also wrote articles about cruises that he had done himself, such as that first voyage with Henry on *Shulah*, or the Frisian voyage on *Vixen*. All were published between June 1907 and August 1910, many of them, like the one about Essex, reflecting his fondness for bleak, lonely places, such as his beloved Frisian Islands. He had a rare ability to produce within the reader the wish to visit the most unlikely places; to make even monotony of scene sound enticing:

> One must learn to look for beauty, not in lucid blue seas and sunny wooded cliffs, but in vast almost featureless distances. For the mainland coast the eye must be content with a fine pencil-line of grey, dotted with a windmill or two, an occasional spire, and a rare clump of trees. Above all, one must love sand in all its manifestations; the delicate pink of island-dunes in the evening glow, and all the infinitely various and subtle hues – from umber to pale straw – of dry or drying flats. Monotony of scene must be a joy in itself, and inspiration must be found in a kind of solitude which, if the spirit is not tuned to it, seems more dreary than the dreariest moorlands and the most naked mountains.[16]

While Erskine was looking increasingly to writing as a profession, Molly, eager to see him make his mark in the world, was trying to push him into politics, without as yet much success. Over the years his political opinions had moved slowly but steadily leftwards. He went to South Africa a diehard Tory, but returned with views closer to what was then the centre of British politics. Since then he had continued the leftward drift until, by 1907, it would be correct to call him a Liberal but not really a Radical.

Politics did not as yet attract him. He had his opinions, but there was no one issue which he felt strongly enough about to campaign for or against. On the question of social reform, he was never to have much interest, despite the appalling social deprivation that was obvious enough in the London of his day. Votes for women he considered unnecessary. In the same way, on the question of Home Rule for Ireland, he simply saw no real reason for it. He was a Liberal of the old school, with little in common with the up and coming members of the party such as Lloyd George or Churchill. Unlike them, he believed only in gradual reform based upon the existing constitution. Anyone who campaigned for reform of the constitution itself he was liable to regard as a dangerous fanatic.

In the summer of 1908, Erskine and Molly left London for the clean air and tranquillity of Glendalough. It was a relief to escape from the hectic rush and dirt of London, not to mention the political turmoil as suffragette riots mingled with demonstrations of the unemployed. Later they set off with Erskine's cousin, Robert Barton, on a motor tour of central and western Ireland. They were particularly interested in visiting the rural cooperative societies then being organised by Sir Horace Plunkett and his friends. Upon his return to Glendalough, Erskine wrote to an astonished Basil Williams: 'I have come back finally and immutably a convert to Home Rule as is my cousin, though we both grew up steeped in the most irreconcilable sort of Unionism.' [17] He had in fact completely changed his whole opinion on the future of Ireland virtually overnight. In the process, he had also discovered a new obsession, the strongest of them all. So what had happened? Who had given him a decisive lead this time? It was certainly not Sir Horace Plunkett and his friends; they had no wish for Home Rule, viewing the whole idea as irrelevant and dangerous, something that, given the religious differences within Ireland, could tear the country apart. As for Molly, she had brought with her from Boston the strong beliefs and prejudices about Britain and Ireland that continue in New England to this day. But she had not converted Erskine to Home Rule before; there is no obvious reason why she could have done so now.

So who does that leave? It leaves Robert Barton, the man who had been responsible for organising the expedition in the first place. The man who was already interested in the subject. No one was better placed to influence Erskine than Robert Barton; the two cousins had grown up together. He had been best man at Erskine's wedding – Henry was the only man with closer ties. Once the decision was made, Molly would probably have encouraged the development, but it must almost certainly have been Robert Barton who initiated it. On the previous occasions when he had been given 'a decisive lead', Erskine had always quickly overtaken the provider of that lead. This time it was to be different, and there was to be no slowing of enthusiasm by either man. Both were to become more and more fanatical about the cause they had adopted. But always it would be Barton leading, with Erskine usually following some way behind. For Erskine, the consequences were to be disastrous.

6

New Interests

At about this time, in 1907 or 1908, Erskine discovered a new way of indulging his old fondness for long walks. He became a member of a remarkable rambling club. Known as the 'Sunday Tramps', it was precisely that kind of lightly organised, slightly eccentric society that could only exist in England. Elsewhere at that time it would have developed upon more rigid, quasi-military lines. Its founder had been Leslie Stephens, the author and editor of the *Dictionary of National Biography*. Holidaying in the Swiss Alps, Stephens acquired a taste for climbing and mountain walking, not activities easily practised in central London. His wish for some similar activity in congenial company eventually led him to the possibilities of a rambling club. In 1879 he wrote to a number of his literary friends, asking whether they would be interested in taking part in regular twenty mile Sunday walks. He received an encouraging response and the idea quickly blossomed. Every Sunday morning, rain or fine, the little group of friends set out together for a leisurely stroll through the variety of countryside that lay within easy reach of their London homes.

Each week they explored a different area; one week it would be the North Downs, the next Burnham Beeches and Windsor, the following one Epping Forest and the Essex flats. The list of men who were, at one time or another, members of the club, reads like a catalogue of the writers and thinkers of late nineteenth and early twentieth century England. Robert Bridges, Roger Fry, Leonard Woolf, John Buchan, George and Charles Trevelyan, John Simon, John Maynard Keynes, William Rothenstein, F. W. Maitland.

Together they tramped the fields and muddy lanes of south-east England, in sun, rain or snow. Obviously they talked, without doubt they argued, sometimes perhaps they even quarrelled. But any such disagreements soon succumbed to the necessity of putting one foot in front of the other as they faced yet another mile in one another's company. And at midday they found some old country inn where they paused to satisfy their need for food and drink.

At this, the most settled period of his life, no doubt influenced by Molly, Erskine was at his most sociable. Amongst his many new friends, in addition to fellow writers, there were also a number of men who came to share his passion for the sea. These included Robert Woodhead, who frequently cruised with him, Major Alfred Ollivant of the Royal Artillery and F. W. Maitland, the historian, both of whom Erskine taught to sail. And one young man who was to become particularly close to him, Gordon Shephard.

Shephard was a professional soldier, destined to become the youngest brigadier in the Royal Flying Corps. When he first met Erskine and Molly, in August 1909, he was trying his hand as a yachtsman. Inspired by *The Riddle of the Sands*, he sought advice from the older man. Erskine, like most yachtsmen, was only too pleased to give what help he could to keen beginners. Shephard was delighted to meet a man he so much admired. As he wrote to his mother:

> I dined yesterday with a great yachtsman, a clerk in the House of Commons, but nevertheless a good radical. He strongly recommended me to go to Texel and work south to Flushing or only to the Hook and then back. His name is Erskine Childers. I have hired a yacht, but cannot get it till 29 August, which is a nuisance.[1]

The two men quickly became firm friends. Intelligent and dedicated, Shephard learnt very quickly. Within a few years his voyages, in Baltic and Norwegian waters, would become more ambitious even than Erskine's. His explorations took him to areas previously unvisited by British yachtsmen, including St Petersburg and the northernmost reaches of the Gulf of Bothnia.

But all these new social acquaintances did not mean that Erskine neglected his old friends. Basil Williams, in particular, remained close to him. Now returned from his South African labours, Basil stayed solid and true for the rest of Eskine's life, never once wavering – no matter how much he disagreed with his old friend's political activities.

Despite the tragedy of little Henry, and Molly's own continued weakness, it was not long before she was pregnant again. Their third son,

Robert Alden, was born early in 1910. To everyone's profound relief the new arrival was strong and healthy, soon to become a perfect companion for young Erskine, then aged six.

In 1910 Erskine had a new book published, a work of military analysis, which carried the title, *War and the Arme Blanche*. The subject was one that he had pondered over for a number of years, ever since his period in South Africa. During the periods of enforced idleness that punctuate a soldier's life in the field he had thought a great deal about the nature of warfare and of leadership. Although only a driver in the Horse Artillery, he had observed with a critical interest the functions and relative effectiveness of the various military arms.

Following his return to England he retained his fascination with military matters. In his customary way he read extensively upon the subject, making himself something of an expert in all aspects of it, both tactical and strategic. He also developed strong views, views that he felt compelled to express to the world, confident that they would be listened to with the respect he felt they deserved.

The phrase *Arme Blanche* is best translated as 'Cold Steel' and, in this particular context refers to the cavalry sabre. It was Erskine's contention that the sabre, as an effective military weapon, was completely obsolete and should no longer be carried. He believed that the only suitable weapon for modern cavalry was the rifle. In his book, he presented his case logically and eloquently, basing his arguments upon the recent military campaigns in South Africa and Manchuria. He was able to show that during the course of the Boer War the cavalry had discovered for themselves the uselessness of a sabre when faced by an enemy armed with modern rifles. During the later phases of that war the British cavalry had discarded their sabres completely, taking up rifles instead. However, at the end of the war, conservative elements within the army, ignoring the lessons learned at such cost, had once more reinstated the sabre to its previous pre-eminent position. This, they claimed, was justified because the South African War was inherently different from other wars and could therefore not be used as a pretext for drastic and unnecessary change. This, Erskine now argued, was simply not true. He then presented his case at some length, with all the skill and method to be expected from a man holding a law degree. Each opposition claim was carefully demolished; and his own arguments being supported by evidence drawn directly from the battlefield.

The book was in fact something of a *tour de force* that might, despite his amateur status, have had considerable influence upon the less hide-bound officers in the army. Unfortunately, the book had one fault; and a serious one. While his arguments were well-reasoned and skilfully presented, the whole tone of the book was intolerant and unnecessarily provocative; it was almost guaranteed to annoy most cavalry officers, the very people he aimed to influence.

That the basic argument was considered to be important and deserving of attention can be seen by the fact that no less a man than Lord Roberts was prepared to write a preface to it. He was full of praise for the book, describing it as an important work. But he also offered a warning to potential readers:

> I would ask you, my brother officers ... to read this book with an unbiased mind, and not be put off by the opening chapters, or to throw the book on one side with some such remark as, 'This is written by a civilian, and what can he know of the subject'.

Despite Lord Roberts's plea, it is a safe assumption that many officers in the cavalry were not just put off by the opening chapters; they were put out by them as well. There is for instance Erskine's bland statement, 'The only difference between a cavalryman and an infantryman is his horse'. Physically of course he was perfectly correct. But that is not how the remark would have been read by an officer in the Dragoon Guards or the Lancers. And it was not how it was meant to be read, for by now the opportunity to take a sideswipe at the British establishment was something that Erskine found irresistible. To such men in class-ridden Britain the cavalry was the *crème de la crème* not only of the army, but of society as well. Any suggestion that an officer in the Lancers was no different to an officer in, say, the Suffolk Regiment was pure socialism, not to mention a personal insult.

Similar examples of assertions in the book that were guaranteed to offend are easy to find: 'There has grown up what is known as "the cavalry spirit". This consecrates the past, and entrenches the type behind an impregnable rampart of sentiment.' And Erskine's fondness of using the word 'religion' to mean an obsolete belief would without doubt have

1. Erskine Childers with his brother Henry. (*Courtesy of the Board of Trinity College Dublin*)

2. Erskine Childers. (*Courtesy of the Board of Trinity College Dublin*)

3. Erskine and Molly Childers, Flensburg 1906. (*Courtesy of the Board of Trinity College Dublin*)

4. Erskine Childers aboard the *Sunbeam*, with his sisters Constance and Dulcibella and others. (*Courtesy of the Board of Trinity College Dublin*)

5. Molly Childers, with rifle, and Mary Spring Rice aboard the *Asgard*. (*Courtesy of the Board of Trinity College Dublin*)

6. Glendalough House, Annamoe, County Wicklow. (*Courtesy of the Board of Trinity College Dublin*)

7. Molly Childers with her son Erskine. (*Courtesy of the Board of Trinity College Dublin*)

8. Erskine Childers talking to Eamon de Valera. (*Courtesy of the Board of Trinity College Dublin*)

9. Under Irish arrest. (*Courtesy of the Board of Trinity College Dublin*)

offended a completely different set of people: 'The *arme blanche*, indeed, is a religion in itself, comparable only to the religion of sail and wood which, in the affections of the old school of sailors, long out-lived the introduction of iron-clads.'

The following year a book by a German general, von Bernhardi, contradicting much that Erskine had written, was published in English translation. It carried a preface by Sir John French, who took the opportunity thus presented to him to criticise Erskine's opinions, although without naming him:

> Some prominence has lately been given in England to erroneous views concerning the armament and tactics of cavalry.
>
> In all theories, whether expounded by so eminent authority as General von Bernhardi or by others who have not had his claims to our attention, there is, of course, a great deal that must remain a matter of opinion, and a question for free and frank discussion. But I am convinced that some of the reactionary views recently aired in England concerning cavalry will, if accepted and adopted, lead first to the deterioration and then to the collapse of cavalry when next it is called upon to fulfil its mission in war. I therefore recommend not only cavalry officers, but officers of all arms and services, to read and ponder this book, which provides a strengthening tonic for weak minds which have allowed themselves to be impressed by the dangerous theories to which I have alluded. Those who scoff at the spirit, whether of cavalry, of artillery, or of infantry, are people who have had no practical experience of the actual training of troops in peace, or of the personal leadership in war. Such men are blind guides indeed.

Erskine, possibly stung by being called 'reactionary', immediately produced a second book, entitled, *The German Influence on British Cavalry*. Ostensibly this new book was a refutation of von Bernhardi's views. In it Erskine argued that German cavalry tactics, based as they were upon experiences gained during the Franco-Prussian War, had been made completely out of date by accurate, quick-firing guns such as the Mauser and Lee-Enfield rifles. However, more than a third of the book was given over, not to criticism of Bernhardi, but a violent attack upon General French's nineteen page preface: 'This curious little summary of the war shows to what incredible lengths of self-delusion a belief in the *arme blanche* will carry otherwise well-balanced minds.'

French had clearly committed the unforgivable crime of disagreeing with Erskine Childers. If the tone of the first book had been dogmatic, the second was so intolerant as to be almost hysterical. No religious extremist could have reacted with more ferocity. For the first time we see Erskine the fanatic, the least pleasant aspect of his character; an aspect that was to become all too dominant when his naturally obsessive nature became involved with Ireland. But for the moment it was military matters that obsessed him, an obsession that caused him to forget his normal good manners. At one point in his long diatribe against Sir John French he wrote: 'We go a long way towards dissipating the whole of the *arme blanche* myth, which in the opinion of our greatest living soldier, Lord Roberts, is as mischievous a superstition as ever fettered a mounted military force.' That particular sentence was inexcusable. On which occasion the field marshal made or wrote the quoted remark we have no way of knowing. But what is quite certain is that, in writing the preface for Erskine's book, Lord Roberts had been extremely careful to avoid upsetting anyone. Knowing, as he undoubtedly did, that he was dealing with a delicate question, Roberts had taken great care to be both reasonable and diplomatic. Erskine should have had the decency not to have dragged him into the argument, but unfortunately, when he climbed onto one of his hobby-horses, all of Erskine's best qualities became submerged beneath his current obsession.

In October 1910 Erskine, finally making the move that he had pondered for years, gave up his job at the House of Commons to embark upon the risky course of a political career. By now he was Senior Clerk to the Chairman of Committees, on a salary of £800 per year. Had he chosen to stay on he might well have become head of the department within a few years. But that was not what he wanted; he had long found the job a bore. If he was ever going to escape from it, now was the time, even if he would find the income difficult to replace. True, he did still have his investments, but they provided him with less than half his requirements.

That autumn his finances received an unexpected boost. *The Riddle of the Sands* had continued to sell ever since its first publication in 1903. There had been editions in 1904, and one each in 1907 and 1908. Now, just as sales were showing signs of running out of steam, they were given a new impetus as a result of activities in the Frisian Islands in which life followed art.

On the night of 21 August 1910 two British amateur yachtsmen were arrested by the German authorities. At Borkum, Lieutenant Vivian Brandon RN was caught by a sentry within a wired enclosure containing a coastal battery. A few hours later, his colleague, Captain Bernard Trench of the Royal Marines, was arrested in an hotel room at Emden. Beneath the mattress in Captain Brandon's room were found twenty photographs of coastal areas and defence installations, together with maps of Kiel, Wilhelmshaven and a number of the Frisian Islands. The next morning, more charts, suspicious papers and photographs of Cuxhaven were discovered on board their yacht. Also seized were a camera and sextant. Both men were charged with spying for British Intelligence.

Elements of the German press promptly erupted in violent anti-British hysteria. The most extreme newspaper, the *Berliner Neueste Nachrichten*, in commenting upon the men's impending trial, made a particularly outrageous demand. Remarking upon the vital secrets that the men might have discovered, the paper demanded that 'the English prisoners should be made incapable of reporting what they have seen. They carry in their heads what may not be written down on paper. They should therefore be subjected to a long period of detention in Germany, with appropriate mental treatment so that upon their release they may not retain too clear a memory of what they had seen'.[2]

More responsible people in Germany took a calmer view of the affair, arguing that the men were not traitors; they were British officers acting in British interests. They were simply doing their duty. Every country spied upon every other country, Germany being no different than Britain in that respect. This argument took on considerably greater force when, shortly afterwards, a German naval officer was arrested in Portsmouth harbour while engaged in collecting information about the British fleet. Erskine, unimpressed by the alleged evidence of the men's spying activities, intervened by writing a letter to the *Daily News*, which they published on 29 October:

> Captain Trench, for example, is charged with having measured depths of water while bathing at Sylt and Amrun, two of the North Frisian islands. Well, that is within the right of all bathers, whether at Eastbourne, Sylt or anywhere else. For my part, I should be content to rely for my measurements

on the extraordinary accurate and detailed large-scale charts of the German North Sea coast published by the German Admiralty and obtainable at stationers in London, which give depths whose accuracy I have myself tested down to a tenth of a metre.

Lieutenant Brandon and Captain Trench were finally brought to trial, at Leipzig, on the 21 December 1910. Much of the first day of he trial was taken up by cross-examinations of the two men by both counsel and judge. They were particularly interested in the relationship between the defendants and someone they called 'Reggie'. Lieutenant Brandon told the court that he had been collecting information to be passed to a third person. 'I will call him Reggie, though that is not his real name.' Questioned further, he replied, 'Reggie is a personal friend of mine; "Sunburnt London" is his private telegraphic address'. Prosecution Counsel asserted that the mysterious 'Reggie' was attached to Royal Navy Intelligence, but produced no evidence to that effect.

To illustrate the prisoner's criminal activities, the judge showed the court a sextant, which he said had been discovered on board their yacht. He seemed to consider it a cunning instrument devised by British Intelligence specifically for the purpose of espionage. Brandon, agreeing that it was his, said that he had bought it in London for £3 10s. od. The next day, Captain Trench was questioned at length as to the precise route that they had followed during their cruise. Trench replied that they had been to Kiel, Brunsbuttel, Bremen, Sylt, Fohr, Heligoland and Nordeney. At the mention of Nordeney, a sixpenny edition of *The Riddle of the Sands* was held aloft by defence counsel, who described its contents to the court. Trench was asked if he knew the book. He confirmed that he did. Brandon, upon being asked if he had read it, caused laughter in court by replying, 'Yes, I've read it. I've read it three times'.

Throughout the trial counsel for the defence based his arguments upon the proposition that 'it is impossible for something that anyone can see can be declared secret'. This argument came especially to the fore when a Captain Tagert was called to give evidence for the prosecution. Asked to comment upon the value to an enemy of the information collected by the defendants, he became especially passionate about their alleged measuring of the length of the pier at Sylt by pacing its length. This he described as 'of the utmost military importance'. Defence counsel pointed out that every year tens of thousands of people walked the length of the pier, it being the only means of access to the island, an island that had long been a popular destination for holiday-makers. How then, he asked, could its length possibly be regarded as 'a secret of the utmost importance'? This point was however considered entirely irrelevant, the court apparently accepting with Germanic logic Captain Tagert's assertion that anything he said was secret was secret, however many people knew about it. At the end of the two day trial both men were found guilty and each sentenced to four years imprisonment. In May 1913 the Kaiser granted them both a pardon, enabling them to resume their naval careers, although not without a bitter dispute with the Admiralty over the reimbursement of the defence costs.

Their exploit had been inspired partly by reading *The Riddle of the Sands* and partly by visiting Kiel as officers on the training-ship HMS *Cornwall*, whose captain had been Reginald Hall. While at Kiel, unofficially encouraged by their captain, they were involved in spying upon German naval ships and installations. When Captain Hall became Director of Naval Intelligence in 1914 they joined him in the famous Room 40. Captain Hall was widely known as 'Blinker Hall', except to his friends, who always called him 'Reggie'. Naturally the case generated a great deal of interest in Britain, giving a significant boost to sales of *The Riddle of the Sands* and leading to a new edition of the book. In 1913 there was another edition, plus the first of numerous American editions. The beginning of the war in 1914 coincided with yet another edition. It has continued to be in print ever since. There has also been a film that, from time to time, makes its appearance on television.

When Erskine told his friends in the Liberal Party of his wish to enter Parliament as a Liberal, they were at first sceptical, commenting that he had left the decision rather late. He had to agree with them, having just celebrated his fortieth birthday. Walter Runciman, however, then a government minister with responsibility for education, promised to contact the whip's office on his friend's behalf.

The reason for Erskine's decision to enter politics at that particular time is obvious enough, although it is probably not the reason that he gave the Liberal Party. Had he told them the truth it is unlikely that they would have welcomed him quite so warmly. For, as was invariably the case with Erskine, there was now only one subject that interested him, his latest and greatest obsession, Ireland. For the rest of the party's policies, for social reform within Britain for instance, a subject close to the true Liberal's heart, he cared not a jot. Thanks to Gladstone, the Liberal Party had been theoretically in favour of Irish Home Rule for a generation. From time to time they had even tried to do something about it. But always they came up against the fact that any Parliamentary Bill introduced to implement it was bound to be defeated in the House of Lords. Being practical politicians, they had therefore put the issue to one side to await a more favourable time. It now appeared that the favourable time might be coming at last.

This change of political climate had not of course been brought about with the intention of helping the Irish, although it did have a strong Celtic ingredient, in the form of the Welsh Wizard, Lloyd George. It was his determination to carry through his reformist policies, despite House of Lords opposition, that now gave Home Rule at least some chance of success.

When the Liberals returned to power in 1906, they had optimistically planned to finance social reform by cutting expenditure on armaments. But, like many politicians before and since, they discovered that in government the world was not quite so simple as they had imagined it to be. They were hardly in office when they became involved in a naval arms race with Germany. Instead of being able to make slashing cuts in defence spending, they were forced to find ever larger amounts of money to finance bigger and bigger battleships.

Undeterred, on 29 April 1909, Lloyd George put before the House of Commons a budget designed to raise enough money both to build three extra battleships and to finance a social security programme. He proposed increasing income tax, introducing a super-tax on incomes above three thousand pounds a year, raising tax rates on alcohol, tobacco and motor vehicles; and most audacious of all, he planned to introduce a tax on property. To the opposition Conservative Party it was seen as a declaration of war.

Despite ferocious opposition, on 4 November the budget was approved by the House of Commons by 379 votes to 149. Only three days later, the House of Lords, against all precedent, rejected it by 350 votes to 75. On 2 December the House of Commons passed a motion, by a huge majority, declaring the House of Lords' action, 'a breach of the constitution and a usurpation of the rights of the Commons'. The following day Parliament was dissolved and an election called for 15 January. During the resulting campaign the Liberal Party worked hard to portray the election as 'the Lords versus the People', but inevitably not everyone saw it that way. Some voters for instance regarded the Lloyd George budget as dangerously socialist. Others were alienated by a speech by the Prime Minister, Asquith, in which he declared his party's intention of introducing a Home Rule Bill in the next Parliament.

When the votes were counted they produced a result that, while giving the Liberals victory, deprived them of their overall majority. Whereas before the election they had had a clear seventy-six seats over all other parties, they would now be dependent upon Irish Nationalist support to get their policies through. The figures were Liberals 275, Conservatives 273, Irish Nationalists 82, Labour 40. The implications appeared to be quite clear. As a result of the election, the Liberal Party could claim a mandate to remove the Lords veto, but could do so only with Irish support. And once that veto was gone there would be nothing to prevent a Home Rule Bill being pushed through. Needless to say, it did not quite turn out that way. But that was the situation that brought Erskine into politics as a prospective Liberal Party candidate.

Meanwhile, within the government there was nothing but disagreement and indecision. Some cabinet ministers wished to abolish the House of Lords altogether; others wanted to merely reform it, although how and to what extent they could not agree even among themselves. As for the opposition, they argued that the election gave the government a mandate to push through its budget, but not to remove the Lords' veto. To further confuse the issue, no one was quite sure how the King would react if the Lords simply rejected any reform package; a state of affairs that became even more of a puzzle when King Edward suddenly died early in May.

By now at least one contentious issue had been settled. At the end of April the Lloyd George budget passed through both Houses without major difficulty. The Irish, having kept their side of the bargain, now looked forward to the government keeping theirs by forcing through a measure of Home Rule. But would they? Or indeed could they?

In an attempt to clear the political impasse the new King, George V, proposed a Constitutional Conference. Throughout the summer months and well into the autumn the leaders of the two main parties argued behind closed doors. But always there was the same sticking point – Ireland. The opposition would not agree to any settlement that would allow Home Rule, while the government could not accept a settlement that prevented it. The deadlock remained.

Hoping to strengthen their parliamentary position the government once more called an election. During late November and early December 1910, Erskine visited parliamentary constituencies where, he had been given to understand, suitable Liberal candidates were being sought. His travels took him from one side of the country to the other; from Sudbury in Suffolk to Shrewsbury. But all was in vain. Either the constituencies already had candidates, or they were not seriously looking for one.

When the General Election was held in December, not having a constituency of his own, Erskine roamed the country making speeches on behalf of his friends. In particular he did his best to support Basil Williams, who was standing for a seat in Warwickshire. Throughout the campaign the Conservatives concentrated upon the issue of Home Rule, clearly believing that their opposition to it would give them victory. They were wrong. Although Basil Williams was defeated, the final result was almost identical to that of the previous year.

During the spring of 1911, Erskine visited both Belfast and Dublin, where he had talks with leading industrialists, politicians, churchmen, government officials, Home Rulers of all persuasions and independently minded men like Sir Horace Plunkett. Despite all these conversations, he seems to have returned to London with no more understanding of the political implications of the religious divisions within Ireland than when he went. Not that he was alone in that. Hardly anyone outside Ulster was aware of the dangerous emotions waiting to be let loose, not even those in England who were already planning to release them. As for the Nationalists in Dublin, they continued for some time curiously unaware that the historic northern fear of Roman Catholicism was far stronger than any wish for Irish independence.

Following his tour, Erskine published a book dealing with the Irish problem under the title of *The Framework of Home Rule*. It was a typical Childers production, thoroughly researched, well written, its arguments impeccably logical and reasonable. His proposed solution, a united Ireland, with Dominion status, would indeed have been ideal had the peoples of Ireland, and indeed of Britain, been equally logical and reasonable. But they were not, any more than people normally are. There was too much history, too much emotion, too much religion, too much distrust. All of which Erskine chose to either underestimate or ignore completely.

The first half of a long, closely written book, was given over to a comparison of Irish history with the histories of the United States and of the self-governing British dominions of Australia, South Africa and Canada. Most of the second half was largely economic. The most important part of the book was in the middle, where he laid down his own deductions and solutions. It was there that he showed his failure to understand the power of emotions and beliefs, rational or irrational, over the minds of men.

> The political habits formed in dealing with Ireland have disastrously in-fluenced Imperial policy in the past. Cannot we, by a supreme national effort, reverse the mental process, and, if we have always failed in the past to learn from Irish lessons how not to treat the colonies, at any rate learn, even at the eleventh hour, from our colonial lessons how to treat Ireland? Must we forever sound the old alarms about 'disloyalty' and 'dismemberment' and 'abandonment of the loyal minority to the tender mercies of their foes'?
>
> We have a mighty rival in Europe and we need the cooperation of all our hands and brains. On a basis of mere profit and loss, is it sensible to maintain a system in Ireland which weakens both Ireland and the whole United Kingdom, clogs the delicate machinery of Parliamentary government and, worked out in real figures of pounds, shillings and pence, has ceased even to show a pecuniary advantage.
>
> The purpose of the Irish Unionist party in the Commons is purely negative, to defeat Home Rule. It does not represent North East Ulster, or any fragment of Ireland, in any sense but that. It is passionately sentimental and absolutely unrepresentative of the practical, virile genius of Ulster industry. The religious question I leave to others, with only these few observations. It is impossible to make out an historical case for the religious intolerance of a Roman Catholic tyranny in the future.
>
> ... it is hardly to be conceived that Ulster Unionists really fear Roman Catholic tyranny. The fear is unmanly and unworthy of them.
>
> Intense, indeed, must be the racial prejudice which can cause Ulstermen to forget the only really glorious memories of their past. Orange memories are stirring, but they are not glorious beside the traditions of the Volunteers.

The Orange flag is a symbol of conquest, confiscation, racial and religious ascendancy. It is not noble for Irishmen to celebrate annually a battle in which Ireland was defeated.[3]

The unnamed critic of the *Times Literary Supplement* commented with commendable astuteness:

Mr Childers is a clear thinker who deals honestly with facts and is not afraid of his own conclusions. His intellectual vice is perhaps to be a little the slave of his own logic. Statesmanship is not wholly nor even mainly an affair of logic.

If it were possible to hold Ireland at arm's length like a colony, we can imagine that after a period of something like civil war equilibrium would be established under his solution; but apart from the danger of civil war, the thing is not possible.

Nowhere in his book does Mr Childers show any consciousness of the depth or significance of the opposition of Ulster.

In Parliament, meanwhile, a long, bitter, fight took place as the government slowly but inexorably pushed through their Bill restricting the powers of the House of Lords. The most extreme Conservative lords fought every inch of the way until, faced by the threat of 250 new peers being appointed, they finally surrendered. In August 1911 the Parliament Act at last cleared the House of Lords and received the royal assent. The Lords still held the power to delay a government measure, but only to delay it.

On 11 April 1912 the government prepared to pay their debt to the Irish Nationalists by placing before Parliament a Bill designed to give Ireland a large degree of Home Rule. With the inevitable Irish support in the House of Commons, there seemed to be nothing that could stop it. Under the new parliamentary rules, even if the Bill was rejected by the Lords, it would still automatically become law in the summer of 1914. The 'problem of Ireland' at long last appeared to be approaching a solution.

But already storm clouds were building up in Ulster. Only a month after the passage of the Parliament Act, Sir Edward Carson addressed an audience of 100,000 people in Belfast. He told them that they should defy any government established in Dublin. That 'the morning Home Rule passes', they should 'become responsible for the government of the Protestant Province of Ulster'. In January 1912 Protestant leaders formed an Ulster Volunteer Force. Two days before the Home Rule measure appeared in the House of Commons, 80,000 men marched through Belfast. The precise purpose of this new army went undeclared, but its implications were clear enough.

The Prime Minister, Asquith, reacted with characteristic indecision. Unable to decide what to do, he did nothing. Opportunities for compromise came and went unheeded. But if the Liberal Party showed indecision, the Conservatives were totally irresponsible. Unable to prevent the government's social reforms by parliamentary means, they set out to destroy their opponents by playing the 'Orange Card'. On 27 July 1912, their leader, Andrew Bonar Law, himself an Ulsterman and therefore well aware of the forces he was prepared to unleash, declared, 'I can imagine no length of resistance to which Ulster will not go, which I shall not be ready to support, and in which they will not be supported by the overwhelming majority of the British people'. Releasing the genie from the bottle was easy enough, getting it back in again would be another matter altogether.

Erskine, meanwhile, viewed most of this with indifference. Like many ardent supporters of Home Rule, he found it inconceivable that Ulster would allow a personal thing like religion to get in the way of national independence. On the 2 March, at the invitation of the Young Ireland branch of the United Irish League, he gave a public lecture in Dublin's Mansion House. He called it, *The Form and Purpose of Home Rule*. He began with a review of the state of Ireland, which he found greatly improved, even if the improvements were long overdue:

> A great change has taken place in the condition of Ireland during the last nineteen years, We all know its main characteristics and I need only summarise the result. By contrast with her situation in 1893, Ireland may be said to be completely tranquil and comparatively prosperous. More than half of the tenants of Irish land are on the road to freehold ownership; the rest have their rights guarded and their rents limited by law. The great cardinal land reforms, late, terribly late, though they came, laid the foundations of a new social order and rendered possible a change for the better in every phase of national life.[4]

He then went on to economic matters, during the course of which he reminded his audience of the extent to which the people of Ireland were being subsidised by the British tax-payer. He acknowledged that a truly independent Ireland would have to be economically self-sufficient. But, he argued, despite the recent improvements to Irish life and the inevitable costs that Home Rule would bring, the desirability of Irish Home Rule remained:

> We want Home Rule in order to get a legislative organ for the expression and realisation of Irish views upon Irish needs. We want to elicit conscious responsibility for departments of government now conducted by Boards and officials and autocratic as those which exercise power in the most dependent of the Crown colonies.[5]

He finally moved logically on to recommend Dominion status as being the best solution for the long-standing Irish problem:

> We arrive at a Constitution not pedantically copying, but closely resembling, that of the self-governing Colonies. It would resemble theirs in that Ireland would have fiscal autonomy without representation at Westminster.[6]

By now his hoped for, but long delayed, political career at last showed signs of coming to life. In May 1912 the Liberal Party found Erskine a suitable constituency, the west country town of Devonport. His old boss at the House of Commons, Sir Courtney Ilbert, was not impressed, commenting sourly, 'MPs are ten-a-penny, and none worth the price'.

The supposed attraction of Erskine as a candidate for Devonport are obvious enough; the town was dominated by its naval dockyard. For the people of Devonport, as for people in the rest of the country, Erskine was famous only for writing *The Riddle of the Sands* and for his campaign for a bigger Royal Navy. Nothing was more desirable to the people of Devonport than a bigger Royal Navy; it meant work and prosperity. Hence the eager welcome they gave him. They were not to know that Erskine's only real interest now, his sole reason for wanting to enter Parliament, was Home Rule for Ireland. The result of this fundamental misunderstanding was to be a disappointment for everyone.

It is safe to say that, throughout the long, trouble-strewn association between Britain and Ireland, the connection has been viewed by the vast majority of the people of England with indifference. Even for British governments, the subject has rarely been of anything but peripheral importance. Occasionally, over the centuries, when nothing much else was happening, the problem has come to occupy the minds of the government at Westminster. Not usually for very long; invariably some more urgent issue, such as a military threat from a continental neighbour, has appeared to once more relegate Ireland to the back burner.

But to the ordinary people of England the Irish problem had long been viewed as nothing much to do with them. If they thought about it at all, which was rarely, they usually concluded that it was insoluble. And, with their well-known pragmatism, they saw no point in wasting their time looking for solutions that didn't exist. From time to time, misguided Irishmen have attempted to force the English public to take the problem seriously by threatening them with bombs or bullets. The reaction had always been the complete opposite to that intended; it had produced a public even more distrustful of the Irish and therefore more opposed to change than their government.

In all this, the people of Devonport were no different to anyone else in England. Their primary concerns were strictly parochial: local employment prospects, old age pensions, education, taxation. As for Ireland, they had no real interest in the subject at all. So far as they were concerned, they cared little more for the problems of Ireland than they did the problems of China.

To Erskine, this indifference was incomprehensible. One January evening in 1913 he spoke 'to a very small audience in a stony cold schoolroom hung with big, obvious texts'. After speaking, for a short time, about local issues, he then went on to talk, at some length, about Irish Home Rule and was, he thought, eloquent about the subject. He was therefore angry and baffled when the local newspapers, in reporting his speech, printed not one word about Ireland. The truth was that they understood his constituents much better than he did.

In the circumstances, the association between Erskine and Devonport was not one that could last for long. In September 1913 Erskine resigned, ostensibly over the long-established custom of local charities extorting cash from parliamentary candidates. He made a great fuss about the issue, claiming corruption. But the real reason for his departure was that of incompatibility between his obsession with Ireland and the interests of any English constituency. The Liberal Party, puzzled both by his arguments and his behaviour, went to a great deal of trouble to find him an alternative constituency. He was offered several, including St Pancras and Kidderminster. But he turned them all down.

The fact was that he was as disillusioned with the Liberal Party as he was with the people of Devonport and for much the same reason. When he learned that the Liberal Party were seriously interested in giving Ireland some form of Home Rule, he jumped to the conclusion that they would give the issue priority over everything else, in the way that he did. But the Liberal Party was a British political party with many interests and a variety of policies, many of which their supporters considered more important than Ireland.

Towards the end of September 1913 he made another visit to Belfast, where he met Roger Casement for the first time. As always, he was easily open to influence, even when he recognised the limitations of the source of that influence. He wrote to Molly:

> These last days I have been more and more in the back of my mind accustoming myself to the idea of giving up a political career in England. I spent most of the morning with Casement, climbing a lovely mountain just behind the town. He is a Nationalist of the best sort and burning with keenness but, I fear, unpractical.[7]

As a consequence of all this, Erskine turned his back upon British politics, of which he knew a great deal, increasingly involving himself in the politics of Ireland, of which he knew little and understood less.

While Erskine had been concerning himself with the possibilities of a parliamentary career, Gordon Shephard had been combining his military duties with his new passion for sailing. By the summer of 1911 he was as proficient a sailor as his old mentor. He was also now a frequent visitor to Erskine's old haunts around the Frisian Islands and the adjacent German coast. His interest in sailing those waters was not, however, simply a matter of enjoying lonely places; he had developed close links with Admiralty Intelligence. Although unpaid for the work, he regularly supplied the Admiralty with photographs and maps of German installations, an activity not without risk. Since the Brandon and Trench trial the Germans had so become suspicious of British yachtsmen as to be almost paranoid.[8]

In September 1911 Shephard, together with a Ramsgate fisherman,

Robert Nowell, spent some weeks taking photographs of new German activities at Nordeney and Borkum. Satisfied with their work, they returned to the Dutch port of Delfzijl, from which town Shephard posted his discoveries to his associates in London. Delfzijl, however, he found a dull place. His spying activities completed for the moment he felt in the mood for somewhere larger and more interesting. He decided to spend a day in the German town of Emden, on the other side of the estuary, and connected with Delfzijl by a ferry.

He passed a pleasant day in Emden, roaming about the streets, buying postcards, pausing for the occasional beer or coffee, and generally behaving like the tourist that, on this occasion, he was. In the late afternoon, strolling down the pier to catch the ferry back to Holland, he stopped for a moment to photograph two Dutch barges as they entered harbour. He was immediately arrested for suspected espionage, his camera and other personal belongings being taken away for inspection.

Shephard was held by the German police for three days, being questioned repeatedly and at length. At his suggestion the film in his camera was removed and developed. Its contents proved to be entirely innocuous, but the Germans were not convinced. They sent agents over to Delfzijl, where they watched the yacht and tried to obtain incriminating evidence from Nowell. He, however, like most seamen, was too wily a bird to be caught that easily, especially as the indignant local people tipped him off as to the real identities of his visitors. In the end, faced by growing diplomatic protests and not a shred of evidence, the Germans were forced to let their prisoner go. But their suspicions remained.

On 26 June 1913 Gordon Shephard once more left England bound for German waters, this time on *Asgard* with Erskine and Molly. Also on board were Robert Nowell, sailing as a paid hand, and two Americans, Barthol Schlesinger and Samuel Pierce. Whether Erskine was aware of Shephard's spying activities is not known. In all probability he wouldn't have cared anyway. But it was a risk.

This was to be Erskine's most ambitious and successful cruise. The early stages of the voyage, however, did not go quite as planned. They had intended to enter the Baltic by way of the Kattegat, but bad weather, and the sickness of everyone on board, except for Shephard and Nowell, forced them to take shelter in Texel. Entering harbour the mizzen mast was broken when Erskine 'ran into a battleship'. As a result, they were

forced to remain there for three days. When they got underway again
they decided to make up the lost time by using the Kiel Canal, which
they reached without further incident. Once clear of the canal, instead
of taking the old familiar route up the coast of Jutland, they set an
easterly course designed to take them across Lübeck Bay and on towards
the German island of Rügen:

> Just then the western sky brightened, with a momentary fleck of blue in the
> racing clouds. The leaden vapours rolled away to leeward, revealing a vast
> shallow mere through which straight as an arrow runs the double line of
> buoys marking the dredged channel, in a far perspective of tiny dots.
>
> Behind us the mere is locked by the banks we have threaded, as it were
> blindfold. On the left are green islands with here and there the vivid red spot
> of a village or farm, and far ahead, where the mere narrows to a slender
> sound, Stralsund, dominating all the low wooded country around with its
> three mighty spires, and already beginning to glow and sparkle in the sun.[9]

Beautiful it might be, but it also had its dangers. Upon entering
Stralsund harbour *Asgard* was invaded by customs men. What happened
then is best told in Gordon Shephard's own account, written to his
brother, Jack:

> Here seven customs officials came on board and declared that their signal to
> stop the yacht outside the harbour had not been obeyed. They proceeded to
> search the yacht, opened all the books, and in fact made themselves as
> annoying as possible. They then took away a camera and films and had them
> developed. The whole business lasted four hours. I was pleased they did not
> ask for my name.[10]

His relief is understandable; his own name was suspicious enough. But
had they found him on the same boat as Erskine Childers, author of
the notorious anti-German book, *The Riddle of the Sands*, the consequences could have been serious. But, to their considerable relief, the
customs men eventually went away, enabling them to leave Stralsund
behind them. Departing from Rügen they left German waters, turning
north eastward, heading past Bornholm and the Swedish island of
Gotland, to the coast of Estonia. Their navigation was greatly helped by
the long hours of the Scandinavian summer.

> In fine weather indeed there is only an imperceptible transition from the
> warm afterglow of evening to the paler radiance of dawn, with blendings of

colour in sea and sky which the benighted cruiser in Western Europe has hardly dreamed of.[11]

Although their primary objective had been Helsinki, when they reached it they allowed themselves only one day in the city before turning back towards the west. That day was spent 'shopping, bathing, sightseeing and feasting in this beautiful and interesting town'. Thoughts were turned, temptingly, in the direction of St Petersburg, less than two hundred miles to the east, but time was already pressing. Off the south-east tip of Finland they found their way, not without difficulty, through a sea studded with a myriad islands and islets. Always conscious of the jagged rocks that lined their narrow channel, they took great care to follow the buoys that marked the way:

> We turned into a lonely little stream between two low islands and then into a gorge, where you could throw a biscuit onto either shore. For the most part the rocks rose near sheer to the pines; but sometimes they were cleft by a little grassy strand with browsing cattle and a glimpse of farm buildings or by a creek with shady pools, bending out of sight. In and out from reach to reach we glided in utter silence, even the ripple at the forefoot stilled, only the loftiest angle of the topsail catching the breeze, our lifeless mainmast almost grazing the tall red and white spar buoys; till at last the sound widened, the mainsheet straightened, and we shot under a strengthening wind into more open lagoons.[12]

Upon reaching Stockholm, Gordon Shephard and the two Americans left, planning to catch a boat to Lübeck the next day. Shortly after his arrival back in England, Shephard received a letter from the Admiralty thanking him for the valuable information that he had provided. 'Your last report was full of good stuff', they assured him.

Erskine and Molly meanwhile, made the most of their visit to Stockholm: 'We dined luxuriously both nights at the Operahallen and sat on the upper terrace afterwards for coffee and music.' Two days later, with only their paid hand (thirty shillings a week) to help them, they sailed down the coast, through wind and rain, to Kalmar. Here they were joined by three new crew members; two of them, Alfred Ollivant and R. C. Woodhead, both complete novices and one, F. W. Maitland, a near novice. On 2 August they sailed once more, 'bound for anywhere we could get to'. Making for Bornholm, they came across the tiny Danish island of Christianso, 'A high rocky islet crowned by a huge dismantled fort and covered with the remains of massive fortifications'. They also watched the island children play 'an exciting game of rounders'. From Christianso they sailed via Bornholm to Copenhagen and on through Danish waters to the Jutland port of Fredericia. Ollivant later wrote a description of Erskine as he saw him at that time. It shows, as much as anything, his indomitable will: 'A little figure in a fisherman's jersey, with hunched shoulders and straining arms, the wind tearing through his thick hair, his face desperately set, he tugged, heaved, fought with hands, feet and teeth, to master the baffling elements and achieve his end.' Eventually they made their way to Oslo, where they left *Asgard*, before returning home on a Hull-bound steamer. Early in October, Gordon Shephard, fighting ferocious equinoctial gales, brought the yacht back to Britain. He finally left her at Holyhead.

7

Gun-Runner

In the autumn of 1913, while Erskine was busy sailing in the Baltic, the Home Rule Bill continued its leisurely way through the parliamentary process. Already the measure had been passed twice by the Commons, only to be rejected by the Lords. Unless something very remarkable happened, when the Bill next appeared before their Lordships the following summer Home Rule would become reality, whether the opposition liked it or not. With neither the natural fears of the Ulster Protestants nor their increasing belligerence receiving any serious attention from the government, the likelihood of a violent outcome loomed ever nearer.

As every half-hearted attempt to find a compromise foundered on the growing intransigence of both sides, Carson and Bonar Law became ever more irresponsible. Bonar Law even tried to persuade the King to dismiss the elected government. That the British public would almost certainly slaughter his party at the subsequent election apparently never to have occurred to him. Not content with that act of foolishness, at the end of November the Conservative leader made an open appeal for the army to mutiny should they be instructed to impose order in Ulster. That Bonar Law, himself an Ulsterman, could behave in such a manner is perhaps understandable; that the rest of the Conservative Party allowed themselves to be dragged along unprotesting in his wake is quite extraordinary.

Within the army his appeal fell upon potentially fertile ground. There were many officers, including some of very high rank, who were themselves Ulster Protestants. Their loyalties were inevitably divided between their own community and the oath they had taken to the King. It was only with difficulty that the government calmed the situation. That the leader of one of Britain's most important political parties should be inciting the army to mutiny, at the same time as Europe was drifting towards war, is a clear indication of just how blinkered politicians could become when the future of Ireland was on the agenda.

By the end of 1913 the Ulster Volunteer Force numbered 23,000 men, most of them armed. The authorities, on the other hand, had within the province only one thousand soldiers to support a largely demoralised and unreliable police force. It should have been clear to everyone that Ulster could not be coerced into a unified independent Ireland. Some form of partition was inevitable. But, although the Irish parliamentary leader Redmond recognised that fact, there were many who did not. Already he was being outflanked by more extreme elements. And there were still others who persisted with their belief that a United Ireland was possible without coercion. One of them was Erskine Childers. In September, nearly 250.000 people publicly signed a Solemn League and Covenant in Belfast. Erskine was there and saw it happen. But still he believed that a united Ireland could be obtained peacefully.

The successful formation of the Ulster Volunteer Force not surprisingly led to the creation of a similar force amongst the nationalist community under the name Irish Volunteers. Initially they were led by moderate nationalists, the most important of whom was Eoin MacNeill, a university professor and gaelic scholar. But inevitably more extreme men began to infiltrate and take over.

In April 1914 the UVF, as the result of a gun-running operation, acquired a further 25,000 rifles and three million rounds of ammunition. With more than fifty thousand armed men at their disposal, Ulster could declare its independence whenever its leaders felt so inclined. It might be imagined that the nationalists in Dublin would have been horrified at these developments. But they were not, they were delighted. Such was their blinkered anti-English view of the world that they saw the Ulster gun-running as a triumph for the Irish over the English. Their leaders congratulated the Ulstermen and invited them to join the Nationalists in driving the English out of Ireland. It was of course pure self-delusion. It was they themselves who were the potential target for all those weapons.

But there was also another nationalist response to the gun-running in the north. If Ulster could do it, they thought, why can't we. The idea also occurred to their supporters in England. Early in May 1914 an informal committee met at the London home of Alice Stopford Green in Grosvenor Street, Mayfair. Its members were almost all liberal-minded Anglo-Irish Protestants, with little understanding of the explosive situation building up in Ireland. Most of them saw rifles as purely symbolic. That they might be used to kill people did not occur to them. The committee included Roger Casement, who acted as a link with Dublin, Sir George and Lady Young, Lord Ashbourne, Sir Alexander Lawrence, Mary Spring Rice, Conor O'Brien and Erskine Childers. Darrell Figgis, who claimed to have contacts with continental arms dealers, was later added to the committee at Roger Casement's suggestion.

Between them, the eleven members of the committee and their friends raised a total of £1523 19s. 3d. for the purchase and transport of arms and ammunition. The name of Molly Childers appeared high on the list of subscribers, some of whom were understandably anxious that their names should not be divulged. The sum raised hardly compared with the financial resources available in Ulster, but that was not the point: they had no wish to start a war; they merely wanted to make a point.

Once they knew money was available, Darrell Figgis and Erskine went to the London agents of a Belgian arms dealer. They were shown weapons of various types. Although no decisions were made, both men considered the guns they were shown to be too expensive. Figgis assured Erskine that they could do better in Hamburg. But before the committee could proceed with the purchase of guns they had to find some way of smuggling them into Ireland. Mary Spring Rice offered the use of the *Santa Cruz*, a fishing-smack that she owned, which was the lying at Foynes, just down the Shannon from Limerick. Conor O'Brien, who knew the boat well, thought that some alterations would be needed and agreed to draw up plans for her conversion.

A few days later, Erskine and O'Brien travelled to Foynes to inspect the *Santa Cruz*. Erskine was not impressed. He thought that she was fine for pottering about the Shannon and had no doubts that she could be used. But he was concerned at the amount of work that would be needed to make her seaworthy and relatively comfortable for the five or six people who would have to spend at least two weeks aboard her. And it was not just a question of cost but of time. As an alternative, O'Brien suggested that his own yacht, *Kelpie*, could be used. But, quite apart from the fact that *Kelpie* was too small, it also raised the ticklish problem of command. Mary Spring Rice had made it plain that she had no confidence in O'Brien's qualities of leadership. He would, she felt sure, be useless in a crisis. She wanted Erskine in charge, which would be difficult to arrange on O'Brien's yacht.

Following their return to London, Erskine expressed his doubts about *Santa Cruz* to the committee and offered the use of *Asgard* as an alternative. He made the point that an Irish fishing-smack hanging about in the English Channel would appear highly suspicious, whereas nobody would give a yacht a second glance. O'Brien also offered his own yacht. Between them, it was thought, the two boats would have sufficient cargo space to serve their purpose. When the proposal was put to MacNeill in Dublin, he was delighted, being confident that no one would ever suspect Childers's yacht of involvement with gun-running. It was, however, a very risky undertaking for Erskine. As he explained to Molly, if they were caught he would face a prison sentence and *Asgard* would be confiscated. She, however, seems to have made no objection.

On 27 May Erskine and Darrell Figgis departed for the Continent on a mission to buy guns. They travelled first to Liège, then the principal centre for arms dealing. Several dealers were consulted, who showed them a variety of types and makes of rifles. But all the weapons offered they considered old and expensive. Figgis continued to believe that they could do better in Hamburg. Therefore, two days later, they caught the train northwards, to the Hamburg offices of a company called Moritz Magnus. The two brothers who owned the business showed them several types of weapons, from which they selected 9 mm Mauser rifles. They were old-fashioned weapons, but very reliable. Even more to the point, they were comparatively cheap. After a quick calculation, they offered the dealers a contract for the supply of 1500 rifles and 45,000 rounds of ammunition. But it quickly became apparent that there was some kind of problem. Although obviously interested, the brothers were strangely reluctant to accept the contract. Several times the Germans disappeared into a back room to confer. Figgis guessed that the difficulty lay with the German government's recently introduced ban on the export of weapons to Ireland. After the Carson gun-running the British government had applied a great deal of political pressure. The Germans were concerned that another consignment would be used as a pretext for war.

Looking for a way round the problem, Figgis told the Germans that he and his friend were Mexicans, a remark that caused the astonished Erskine to comment that nobody in his right mind could believe that. But Figgis told him to be quiet. He was soon proved right. The two Germans were well aware whom they were dealing with, but the story served their purpose well enough. Trading with Ireland was illegal, but there were no restrictions on sales to Mexico. The deal was quickly settled to everyone's satisfaction. It was now 12.30 p.m., the negotiations having taken three hours. With an agreement in principle the four men adjourned for lunch. Upon their return a formal contract was drawn up. According to Figgis, this turned out to be no easy task because Erskine insisted upon going through it word by word, clause by clause, frequently arguing about the use of a word or the position of a comma. When, at almost seven in the evening, he finally admitted himself satisfied that the contract was legally binding, he immediately destroyed its legality by signing with a false name. The next morning, before returning to England via the Flushing steamer, the two men went to a local branch of the Deutsche Bank, where they made arrangements for payment. The money was to be released upon delivery of the cargo.

The following week Figgis visited Antwerp to organise shipment. It was intended that the guns, which were held in a Liège warehouse, would be moved to Hamburg in close-boarded crates labelled 'machine parts'. On the chosen day they would be loaded onto a tug that would then rendezvous with the two yachts in the English Channel.

In June, Erskine went over to Dublin for discussions with MacNeill and Bulmer Hobson. Between them they thrashed out a plan for landing the guns in Ireland that was both ingenious and audacious. What Erskine did not know was that control of the Irish Volunteers was already being prized from MacNeill's grasp. Erskine and the London committee continued to believe that obtaining guns was simply a political gesture, that no one had any intention of using them. But others had very different ideas.

Returning to England, Erskine began the search for a suitable crew for the operation. He invited Gordon Shephard and a fellow officer from the Royal Fusiliers, Colonel Robert Pipon, to lunch at his Chelsea flat. He then told them of his intention to smuggle guns into Ireland and invited them to join him in the enterprise. The guns would, he said, be loaded at sea from a German ship off Terschelling and landed at Howth Bay.

Given the delicate and highly illegal nature of the proposed operation Erskine's total lack of security is quite extraordinary. Having warned Molly of the dire consequences for them should they be caught, he then proceeded to inform officers in the British Army of the entire plan. As it happened, Gordon Shephard accepted the offer without much hesitation. Colonel Pipon, however, reacted very differently; he wanted nothing whatever to do with it. In a letter written much later, he made his reasons quite clear. He considered the whole idea completely crazy, almost as crazy as the man who was planning it:

> He promised us there was no intention of using them other than as a gesture of equality. I refused. I recognised Childers as a crackpot. Something always happens to crackpots. Something always goes wrong. Shephard and I knew the Childers [sic] well. They had a little boy of nine whom they – chiefly she – wouldn't allow to be told any word of religion of any sort, until he was old enough to decide freely which he considered the best religion. Poor little devil. Crackpot, of course. It always comes out somewhere.[1]

Colonel Pipon therefore stayed at home but kept his mouth shut, no doubt out of regard for his fellow officer. In his absence, *Asgard*'s crew would comprise, in addition to Erskine and Shephard, Molly, who insisted upon taking part, despite her limited mobility, Mary Spring Rice, and two Donegal fishermen, who had not been told the nature of the voyage they had been recruited for. Conor O'Brien had meanwhile obtained a similarly makeshift crew for his own boat. He was taking his sister, a barrister friend, very knowledgeable about court procedure but ignorant of the sea, and two paid hands from western Ireland. They slipped quietly away from the Shannon, intending to meet up with Erskine at Cowes on 7 July.

Erskine had serious problems to overcome before he could get underway. In the middle of June he went to Conway, where *Asgard* had been laid up since Gordon Shephard's arduous return voyage from Denmark the previous year. He found the yacht in no fit state to put to sea. Her mainsail was split, much of her rigging needed renewing, and the clock, compass and barometer were all missing. Below deck everything was a hopeless mess. He wrote to Molly in a mixture of anger and despair.

Somehow, with his customary energy, even within the limited time available, Erskine prepared *Asgard* for sea. That, however, was not to be the end of his troubles. The intended sailing date came and went with most of his crew missing. Mary Spring Rice eventually turned up on the 1 July, but Gordon Shephard and one of the fishermen had still not arrived. Erskine, concerned that they would be late for the rendezvous with the tug, and anxious to make the most of the fine weather, decided that the would sail the next day, crew or no crew. That evening the weather broke, bringing a severe thunderstorm.

The following morning as Erskine prepared for sea, the barometer was falling fast and there was a complete absence of wind. They raised anchor and drifted around for a while, before giving up in disgust. The two missing members of the crew finally arrived the next day, Gordon Shephard only after the anchor had already been raised. Worried at the possible consequences to his military career should his involvement be discovered, Shephard adopted the alias of Mr Gordon. As they edged away from the land, with scarcely enough wind even for *Asgard*'s ample canvas, their main concern was the shortage of time. It was now 3 July. They were due to meet O'Brien's yacht at Cowes on 7 July and only three days later to rendezvous with the tug off the mouth of the Scheldt. Was that still possible?

When the sun rose the next morning, the wind was fresh, from the east and growing in strength. It brought with it an unpleasantly choppy sea, which soon had everyone but Mr Gordon violently seasick. For Mary Spring Rice, feeling awful, Gordon's frequent assurances that 'it wasn't really rough' were no help at all. In search of calmer water Erskine set a course closer to the shore, although it inevitably meant losing some time.

The following day, Sunday 5 July, produced improving weather, although the wind direction was not ideal. The crew gradually recovered from their seasickness. Erskine was able to eat and Molly sat on deck, enjoying the fresh air. While *Asgard* struggled against adverse winds and tides to clear Strumble Head, on the other side of the Irish Sea the volunteers were beginning the first of a series of Sunday morning route marches designed to lull the authorities.

In her diary for the next day, Mary wrote:

Monday 6 July. Got up to find us still struggling to get past the Smalls
Lighthouse; no wind and a great swell. We had now left the Welsh coast and
thankful we were to see the last of it. I never knew Wales went on so long –
we were making for Cornwall along the mouth of the Bristol Channel with
a big Atlantic swell rolling in and still beating with a wind about sou-sou-west.
To bed with the prospect of a very rough night; Mr Gordon assured me that
when we went about I should certainly be shot out of my bunk, so I moved
the water-can out of the way, thinking how painful it would be to fall on.[2]

Twenty-four hours later found *Asgard* working her way slowly along
the north coast of Cornwall, against a strong Bristol Channel tide.
According to Mary:

We had some thought of putting into St Ives, which looked most attractive
in the sunlight, and waiting for the afternoon tide, but this was strongly
discouraged by Erskine. I believe he was right, though Mr Gordon had got
so far as planning his lunch ashore.[3]

Late that evening they rounded Land's End. With a fresh breeze behind
them, they set every piece of canvas they possessed and sped up the
English Channel in style, dropping anchor in the calm, sheltered, waters
off Cowes in the early morning of 9 July, just forty-eight hours behind
schedule.

Barely had they finished breakfast, when Conor O'Brien came alongside in a flaming temper, shouting abuse at the top of his voice. In
between curses, he demanded to know where they had been and why
had they kept him waiting so long. Amongst the sedate and normally
peaceful anchorage of Cowes, they could not but feel conspicuous.
Concern for the secrecy of their mission was not lessened when they
learned that Conor had spent the last two days sending telegrams to
Alice Green asking where they were. When Conor eventually calmed
down, they prepared to go ashore, an experience that Mary, after almost
a week aboard a small yacht, found more difficult than she expected:

Meanwhile Mr Gordon had been struggling into his shore clothes in the
saloon, and finally appeared resplendent in blue serge and we went ashore.
I found that I could hardly stand so I tottered to a lamp-post and clung to
it regardless of Molly's protests. It might be quite true, as she said, that people

would think I was drunk, but if I stopped clinging to it I should certainly fall down which would be worse. So I clung till I felt a little more secure, but all that day I felt rather dizzy and fairly reeled along the streets of Cowes.[4]

They were greatly relieved when a visit to the local post office produced a letter from Darrell Figgis informing them that the planned meeting with the tug had been postponed for two days. This gave them three days to make the rendezvous. By way of celebration, they had a huge lunch at the Marine Hotel. Gordon Shephard took the opportunity to write to his father, keeping him informed about his holiday activities, but at the same time observing the necessary discretion:

I arrived at Deganwy at 9.30 and at 10 a.m. we started. They have this year two fishermen from Connaught for crew, so we consist of Childers and Mrs Childers, Miss Spring Rice, two hands and self. Miss Spring Rice is a wonder. She has never been far to sea before, yet she was hardly ill at all and looks and is most useful. We came round without stopping and arrived this morning. Good weather on the whole but head winds as far as Land's End and then a fair wind up Channel. The Childers [sic] had an appointment here with some Irish people on another yacht.[5]

Early the next morning, 10 July, Conor sailed *Kelpie* out into the Channel, with *Asgard* following in the afternoon, just as the tide was on the turn. They were met by an easterly wind, freshening all the time. This did not make for comfortable sailing, especially for the female members of the crew:

The wind got up a good bit and cooking supper was not an easy job. Or going to bed. Mr Gordon insisted on setting the topsail, much to Molly's disgust, and she went to bed protesting how much more comfortable we should have been without it. I rather agreed with her at the time as I struggled into my bunk, and sighed that all men were alike about setting topsails on all possible occasions, but we sped along, so perhaps it was as well.[6]

Saturday brought calmer weather, but with the wind still from the east. Time was running out fast; they had to be off the Scheldt by noon on the following day. However, for some people the calm weather did bring compensations:

Saturday 11 July. Much calmer, which made getting up and cooking pleasant, but it was a bad lookout for getting to Dover. All day long we had light winds, and 8 p.m. found us still struggling to get round Beachy Head. A roasting hot day, even on the sea, and my pink sun-bonnet was my one joy.[7]

When Mary came on deck the next morning it was to find Erskine 'steering in a calm sea with a light breeze only ruffling the water – a heavenly summer morning – if one had no gun-running appointment forty-five miles away at noon'. As the morning progressed, from down below there came the sounds of banging and sawing as Gordon, Molly and one of the fishermen busied themselves making more room for the guns by demolishing the two bunks in the saloon.

Noon, the intended time for their meeting with the tug, found *Asgard* still twenty-two miles short of the rendezvous point and completely becalmed, her sails hanging motionless, the sea showing barely a ripple. The big question, unasked, but in all their minds, was how long would the tug wait for them. Then suddenly, when it was least expected, there came a puff of wind from astern. The sails filled. *Asgard*, dipping her bow in response, edged slowly forward. The wind strengthened. The boat gained momentum. They were underway again. Almost immediately, as if to contradict the wind, a mist settled over the sea, blotting out everything. From somewhere nearby came the low mournful sound of the foghorn on the East Goodwin Lightship. But still *Asgard* slipped easily, quietly, forward; with everyone on board peering ahead into the grey gloom that now completely enveloped the boat.

Inevitably it was Molly, with those famous eyes of a sea eagle, who first caught sight of Ruylingen lightship, their intended meeting-point. But where was the tug? They edged onwards, straining their eyes in an attempt to see through the surrounding murk. There came a cry, quickly stifled, as a Belgian fishing-smack appeared momentarily, and was gone again. Once more it was Molly who was first to glimpse something. Something through the fog. Something so oddly shaped, that at first she couldn't quite make out what it was. Then she knew what it was. It was a tug, a tug with a yacht moored alongside. As they drew closer the yacht moved away, making room for them at the tug's side. The familiar figure of Conor lifted an arm in greeting; then the fog closed in on him, and *Kelpie* was gone.

Asgard moved alongside the tug and was quickly made fast. Erskine felt grateful for the greyness that enveloped them, hiding them from the prying eyes of passing ships. From the larger vessel's deck, Darrell Figgis called out to him. Conor had taken only 600 rifles, instead of the 750 expected and less than half of the intended ammunition. Erskine was stunned. That meant they had to find room on *Asgard* for 900 guns and 25,000 rounds of ammunition. Was that possible? They could only try.

Already the rifles were coming aboard. Across the narrow gap between tug and yacht a human chain took them, passing them over the yacht's deck and down through her main hatch. Other eager hands grasped them, passed them on, and stacked them below. The guns came aboard in bundles of ten, carefully wrapped in straw and canvas. But the yacht's crew couldn't handle them like that; it was impossible; they were too unwieldy. The packing was torn off, the guns handed down, the straw being left behind to litter the deck and the surrounding sea. Mary wrote later:

> I wish you could have seen the scene. Darkness, lamps, strange faces, the swell of the sea making the boat lurch, guns, straw, everywhere, unpacking on deck and being handed down and stowed in an endless stream – the vaseline on the guns smeared over everything; the bunks and floors of the whole yacht aft from the fo'c'sle filled about 2′ 6″ high even from side to side, men sweating and panting under the weight of twenty-nine ammunition boxes – a German face peering down the hatch saying, 'they will explode if you knock them or drop them'. A huge ship's oil riding-light falling down through the hatch, first onto my shoulder and then upside-down into a heap of straw – a flare-up, a cry, a quick snatch of rescue, the lamp goes out, thank God, work again, someone drops two guns through, they fall on someone, no room to stand save on guns, guns everywhere. On and on and on.[8]

It was long, messy, exhausting work. Work that lasted until half past two in the morning. By now the wind had dropped completely and the fog was thicker than ever. An offer from the tug's skipper to tow them as far as Dover was accepted with gratitude. Not that it enabled the yacht's crew to rest, not just yet. First the deck had to be cleared of rubbish, and of the odd gun left lying in the scuppers and of ammunition boxes. Erskine, faced with the last two boxes of ammunition, but with nowhere to stow them below, ordered them thrown over the side; then instantly regretted it. Only then could they begin to think of rest and refreshment.

We all drank cocoa and beef-tea and then shifted down the mattresses and bags of clothes, which had been stowed aft of the mizzen, and lumped them down on the guns anyhow – and lay down on them as the grey light of dawn was breaking. I remember thinking how absurd it was to go to bed in daylight and then went off into a deep sleep.[9]

By the time Mary came back on deck, two or three hours later, the sun was beginning to break through the fog. Off the starboard bow the chalk cliffs of Dover shone brilliantly. The tug cast them off, they set the sails and *Asgard*, catching the freshening easterly breeze, headed down Channel, homeward bound. Over the next few days, with un-usually favourable winds, *Asgard* made good time; by early Tuesday morning she was clearing Beachy Head. But below deck life was far from easy, in spite of determined feminine attempts to tidy up.

We sorted provisions etc in those lockers which were still get atable, and now things really look ship-shape, but its terribly easy to lose one's pos-sessions in the cabin; they drop between the mattresses into the rifles and disappear. There will be a lot of hairpins found among them when they are unloaded.[10]

A couple of nights later, off Plymouth, in the pitch dark, they suddenly found themselves surrounded by warships in some kind of night exer-cise. Huge, black, menacing shapes towered over them, seemingly unaware of their puny presence. At one point, a destroyer bore down on them at full speed, looking all set to run them down, before changing course at the last moment, leaving the yacht rolling wildly in its wake. The next day Mary was offered relief from the constant struggle to cook under difficult conditions: 'Mr Gordon said he would cook the supper tonight, and produced a wonderful dish, which he called a sweet ome-lette; it was really buttered eggs with golden syrup, but it tasted better than it sounds.'[11]

On Saturday 18 July, on a particularly lovely morning, with bright sunshine glinting on the sea and with a fresh breeze filling her sails, *Asgard* once more rounded Land's End. Later in the day the wind eased, leaving them wallowing uncomfortably in an Atlantic swell 'which upset everything, including our tempers'. Not for the first time, nor the last, they began to be concerned about delay. Gordon Shephard's leave was almost up. He simply had to catch the train from Milford Haven the next day. Some consideration was given to the possibility of putting him ashore on the north coast of Devon. But, towards evening, the wind once more picking up, they held their course for Pembrokeshire and spent a busy night:

> Every stitch of canvas was being set and reset throughout the night to catch all the wind there was which was constantly shifting and everyone but me was up from 2 a.m. I, having been up two nights, slept the sleep of the just, and only just heard through my dreams the shifting and setting of the spinnaker, etc, though my guns are not as comfortable for sleeping on as they were, especially on the starboard tack.[12]

Early in the morning *Asgard* dropped anchor in the calm waters of Milford Haven. After breakfast Gordon Shephard was put ashore to catch his train, Mary going with him to do some shopping. But it turned out that there was no train until the afternoon. Gordon therefore helped Mary with her shopping, then took her to lunch at an hotel. When she eventually returned to the yacht it was to face an angry Molly, left waiting for supplies, and possibly just a little bit jealous.

In Dublin, meanwhile, for the third consecutive Sunday, the volunteers were setting off on a route march; the police barely giving them a second glance. There was now just one week to go before delivery of the guns. Everything appeared to be going according to plan.

It had been Erskine's intention, as a reward for all their recent exertions, to spend a second night at Milford Haven, perhaps with the luxury of a meal ashore. But Monday brought a gale from the east. Early in the afternoon, *Asgard*'s anchor began to drag, forcing Erskine to change the yacht's position. The sails once set, his natural inclination not to let a favourable wind go to waste overcame his desire for rest. He swung over the wheel and set the yacht's bow for the harbour entrance. Out in the Irish Sea, *Asgard* was put onto a northerly course, bound for Holyhead. But they might as well have remained at Milford Haven because, almost at once, the wind dropped. For the next twenty-four hours the yacht made little progress, as short periods of gentle breezes alternated with longer periods of flat calm. Then the wind at last returned. By noon on Wednesday they lay peacefully anchored at Holyhead.

Erskine, having been up all night, went below to catch up on his lost

sleep, while Mary sat in the saloon sewing. Suddenly the concentration
on her work was broken by hearing one of the men on deck call out,
'*Asgard*, Yacht'. Quickly she awoke Erskine, who wasted no time in
getting on deck. They could not afford visitors, whoever they were.
Climbing up through the main hatch and looking about him, Erskine
saw, only a few yards from the yacht's side, a rowing-boat containing
several coastguards. He hailed them as calmly as he could, asking what
they wanted. They began by asking the usual routine questions. Last
port of call? Destination? Registered tonnage? Owner? Erskine called his
answers back, some true, some false. The coastguards appearing satisfied,
thanked him and rowed slowly away. He breathed a sigh of relief. Mary
turned her mind back to domestic matters:

> Erskine is a most appreciative person to cook for, but he has the habit common
> to everyone on board, of starting to do something else just as the food is hot
> and ready. Molly generally begins to do some elaborate cleaning, Erskine
> disappears on deck, or, worse still, gets out the charts all over the breakfast
> table and takes a bearing of the course, and back has to go the food into the
> oven again.[13]

Thursday morning arrived, bringing with it a strong wind and driving
rain from the west, together with a barometer that continued to fall
rapidly. Once more they began to worry about timing. Just three days
to go now, with only the Irish Sea to cross. But what about the weather?

> To bed tonight with the usual howling wind through the rigging, and rather
> dismal forebodings of the morrow, for we ought to start for Howth unless
> there was an absolute gale. The excitement is almost too great as the time
> gets near, and I have a horrible vision of being weatherbound here. Still
> I know Erskine will get across if it is humanly possible to do so. It's a pity
> Mr Gordon is not back with us for this final venture.[14]

On Friday morning, with two days to go, there was more wind and
rain, as bad as ever. And still the barometer fell. Nevertheless, the anchor
was raised and the mainsail set. *Asgard* sailed out into the raging storm,
everything securely battered down, the crew almost unidentifiable in
their heavy yellow oilskins. Within the hour, the mainsail, unable to
withstand the pressure, split. They turned back, back to Holyhead and
anchored. Molly and Mary sat out on the open deck, the rain pouring
over them, repairing the mainsail, struggling to direct their cold, wet

fingers over the heavy, unyielding, canvas. Two hours later *Asgard* sailed again. The wind veered, eased and dropped for a while; and then, as evening set in, returned, with renewed vigour. 'It was an awful night. Erskine stayed on deck the whole time; the waves looked black and terrible and enormous and though everything was reefed one wondered if we should ever get through without something giving way.' [15] Despite the appalling weather, daybreak found *Asgard* within sight of the Irish coast, and less than ten miles from Howth. An impressive piece of navigation. By now the storm had at last blown itself out. They worked their way closer to the shore and hove to. Once more it was a matter of timing, but it was nice to be early for a change.

The next day was a Sunday. The Irish volunteers from Dublin would be on the march again, just as they had been on the previous three Sundays, except that this week their march would bring them to Howth, which they would reach at 1 p.m., the time of high water. This was vital because *Asgard* needed all the water she could get. With her big keel, her normal draught was seven feet six inches, but heavily laden with guns as she was nine feet would scarcely suffice. And Howth was a harbour that dried up completely at low tide. The possibility of *Asgard* being caught by a falling tide, and of sitting perched helplessly on her keel waiting for the police to arrive, didn't bear thinking about.

Towards evening, with only the bare minimum of canvas set, they cruised slowly up the coast for a few miles. Then they slowly cruised back again, a procedure they continued to perform all night. Daybreak found them still on patrol, making use of a fresh north-westerly breeze. At least they wouldn't be becalmed. According to the plan, at ten o'clock a motor boat would come out of Howth to tell them that it was safe to enter. But ten o'clock came and went without any such boat appearing. As did eleven o'clock. And twelve. Edging down on their southerly tack, they had a clear view of Dublin Bay, with nothing there to cause them concern.

Moving once more northward they gazed with interest into Howth harbour. There was little to see. The whole place looked deserted, the quay empty. Mary came on deck, wearing a bright red skirt, the signal of their approach. She stood on the most prominent spot she could find, staring ahead, looking for a reaction. Molly took the wheel, leaving the men free to handle the sails. She turned the wheel hard over. *Asgard,* a strong breeze filling her sails, responded, and swept through the harbour entrance, on course for the quay. Her jib dropped, then her mizzen. Finally her mainsail came down with a sudden clatter. With momentum still on her the yacht held to her course; reaching the seaward end of the quay just as a group of men suddenly emerged from behind it.

One at least of the figures was instantly recognisable. It was Gordon Shephard, who now stepped forward to catch the coiled rope that flew unerringly towards him. Quickly he slipped it round a bollard, eased it for a moment, and then allowed it to tighten again. *Asgard* soon lay motionless against the quay. It was 12.45 p.m. From the other end of the harbour came the sound of marching feet. The Volunteers were arriving precisely on time. The unloading of the guns began chaotically, with too many over eager men and not enough organisation. But Erskine and Gordon between them soon changed that; before long the rifles moved from ship to shore in a steady flow. There was only one interruption, when four coastguards came rowing across the harbour towards them. But, faced with hundreds of armed men, they wisely chose discretion and rowed away again. A short time later, having discovered that the telephone lines between Howth and Dublin had been cut, they tried to summon help by firing distress rockets into the air.

Within an hour the work was complete. *Asgard*'s mooring-ropes were cast off and she edged away from the quay. Her mainsail caught the wind, she turned, and slipped quietly away, a mysterious 'white yacht with a woman at the wheel', as newspapers all over the world were soon describing her. The Volunteers, meanwhile, began their march back to Dublin, with a new jauntiness in their step, and rifles over their shoulders.

Asgard once more crossed the Irish Sea, her decks littered with rubbish, her skylight broken, her cabins a shambles of straw and broken woodwork, and everything covered in grease and dirt. With all the excitement over, a reaction set in amongst her crew. They no longer felt triumphant, just exhausted and filthy. On their approach to Anglesey, with the weather worsening, they put into Bangor. It was 27 July 1914. The next day Austria declared war on Serbia.

Erskine paid little attention to those far off events. With his usual single-mindedness, his thoughts were still upon Ireland. Once *Asgard* was safely anchored, he went first with Molly to London, then returned to Ireland, where he lay up, awaiting events. Were the authorities aware of his involvement in the smuggling? And what would they do if they found out? He need not have worried. London, as so often in the past, had put the problem of Ireland to one side. They now had a bigger game to play, one that did not just threaten British rule in Ireland but the continued existence of the entire Empire; perhaps even of Britain itself.

Early in August the headquarters of the Irish Volunteers in Dublin were astonished to receive a telegram from London asking for their help. If, it said, they knew the whereabouts of Erskine Childers, would they please ask him to contact Admiralty Intelligence as soon as possible. Their reaction to the telegram is not difficult to imagine. Who, they thought, is Childers really working for? Us or the British? Once asked, it was a question that remained at the back of many Irish minds for years to come. It is a question that some still ask today. It was also a question that, for Erskine Childers, was to have dire consequences.

8

The Cuxhaven Raid

While many people in England were taken by surprise by the outbreak of war between Britain and Germany in August 1914, the British Admiralty was not. As we have seen, mutual spying and the drawing up of contingency plans had been going on since the turn of the century. Even the precise timing of the outbreak of war had been accurately forecast.

When he was appointed First Lord of the Admiralty, in October 1911, Winston Churchill inherited contingency plans for dealing with the threat of German invasion. These had been produced, at least in part, in response to the publication of *The Riddle of the Sands* in 1903. But Churchill was not long content with an entirely defensive strategy. In January 1913 he instructed Rear Admiral Bayly to investigate the possibilities of Britain seizing territory in, or near, the Frisian Islands. The intention was to establish a forward base close to the German naval ports. This it was believed would either compel the German fleet to come out and fight, or enable the Royal Navy to bottle it up completely.

To assist him in his work, Bayly was joined by Rear Admiral Leveson, the Director of Operations, and Major-General Sir George Aston, of the Royal Marines. They were asked to produce plans for the possible seizure of Borkum, Sylt, Heligoland, the Dutch island of Ameland and the Danish port of Esbjerg. They were also asked to consider occupying the western end of the Kiel Canal. Rear Admiral Bayly submitted his report at the end of June. Churchill passed it to the Prime Minister a month later. It got no further. Quite apart from the practicalities of the schemes, the suggested seizure of neutral territory in Holland or Denmark was enough to give the Foreign Office nightmares.[1]

Churchill bided his time. In July 1914, conscious of the drift towards war, he resurrected the scheme. This time he began by deliberately bypassing Asquith, sending the plans direct to the War Office, no doubt hoping for their support in dealing with the Prime Minister. They, reacting cautiously, played the ball straight back to the bowler. General Harrer, in his reply to Churchill, dated 1 August, commented:

> It is impossible to give an opinion on the practicality or otherwise of this scheme in the absence of more detailed information as to landing facilities and nature of the locality. There has also been no time to submit the details of the scheme to technical experts.[2]

If that was intended to keep Churchill quiet, they did not know him well. He immediately pressed Sir Henry Oliver, the Director of Naval Intelligence, to obtain the details of the German coast that the War Office had found lacking. Oliver's department said that they knew the ideal man for the job. A man who was intimately familiar with the German coast and who had provided them with valuable information in the past. His name was Gordon Shephard. By now Britain was at war. What had been not much more than an academic exercise now took on a new urgency. A telegram was sent to Shephard's home in Scotland. It arrived too late. Having volunteered for transfer to the Royal Flying Corps, he had left to take up his new post the previous day. Was there anyone else who could help them? Anyone else who was familiar with the German coast and the Frisian Islands? Yes, there was. There was Erskine Childers. But where was Erskine Childers? No one seemed to know. Pressed by an impatient Churchill, Oliver's department sent out telegrams in all directions. Did anyone know where he was? Would they please ask him to report for an interview at the Admiralty? Several of the telegrams finished up with Molly, living quietly at home in Chelsea. One was sent to the headquarters of the Irish Volunteers in Dublin.

About a week later Erskine finally reported to the Admiralty, no doubt wondering whether he was going to be recruited or arrested. His mind was soon put at rest when he found himself being interviewed by an old friend, Captain Herbert Richmond, Assistant Director of Naval Operations. On Erskine's behalf, all the usual rules and regulations were swept away. After a series of interviews and a quick medical, he emerged a few hours later, a First Lieutenant in the RNVR.

Early the next morning he once more reported to the Admiralty, where he was given a small office, a desk and a chair. His task was to produce a draft plan for one of Churchill's pet projects: the invasion of Borkum, in the German Frisian Islands. This does seem to be a curious way of going about things. Erskine did know a great deal about Borkum and its surrounding waters. But, despite his military studies, he was hardly qualified to produce an invasion plan entirely on his own. What did he know of the effectiveness of naval gunfire? Of the availability of suitable landing craft? Or of the logistical problems involved in landing and supporting an army?

Surely the obvious way of making use of his talents and knowledge would have been to make him a member of a committee comprising a variety of experts, of which there was no shortage at the Admiralty. The same kind of group that Churchill himself had set up with Admiral Bayly only a few years before.

However, in the usual Childers style, Erskine threw himself into his allotted task with total commitment. The world about him seemed barely to exist. He worked long hours, greatly resenting the time lost in eating and sleeping. Molly hardly saw him and, when she did, he seemed to be present only physically, his mind far away, amongst those old familiar sands and tides. By the end of the third day, his report was complete. It bore the simple title, 'Seizure of Borkum and Juist'. Characteristically, when he submitted the plan to his superior officers, he pinned a personal note to it: 'The writer ventures to hope that he may have the honour of being employed, if the service permits, whether in aeroplane work or in any other capacity, if any of the operations sketched in this memo are undertaken.'[3]

The report was circulated amongst the naval planning staff, who quietly stifled it. Churchill continued throughout his period in office at the Admiralty to hanker after just such a project. From time to time during the war it was taken off the shelf, dusted down, and then put back again. It was never adopted. The War Office had always been against the idea, as indeed, with more circumspection, were most senior Royal Navy officers. As for Captain Richmond, who had given Erskine the task of drawing up the plan, he made his own opinion on the idea clear enough: 'It is quite mad. The reasons for capturing it are NIL, the possibilities about the same. I have never read such an idiotic, amateur piece of work as this outline in my life.'[4] But surely he cannot have been surprised that the outline plan was amateurish, as he himself had asked an amateur to produce it. Why had he done so? Why had he not given Erskine expert help in preparing it? Probably because he wanted to kill it; because he wanted the whole scheme to be rejected, just as he plotted the rejection of many Churchillian ideas. In his published diary Richmond appears as a professional naval officer, contemptuous of the amateur meddling of his political master. A master who, he believed, had no understanding of naval strategy, and whose madcap ideas would, he feared, bring disaster on the navy. He describes his reactions to that earlier plan of Churchill's to seize Amelund: 'I did not argue. He was vehement in his desire to adopt an offensive attitude. I saw that no words could check his vivid imagination and that it was quite impossible to persuade him both of the strategical and tactical futility of such an operation.'[5] So he kept his mouth shut, but did his utmost to prevent any such scheme from being adopted.

Sir Roger Keyes, in his own memoirs, describes what happened when he first reported to the First Sea Lord, Sir John Jellicoe, upon being appointed Director of Plans in September 1917:

> He handed me a sheet of notepaper, with a list in his own handwriting of every conceivable offensive operation, from the capture of Heligoland and Borkum to the blocking of Zeebrugge and Ostend. In fact, as someone remarked to me, every wildcat scheme that had ever been suggested to the Admiralty.[6]

His planning work at the Admiralty complete, on 18 August Erskine reported to the naval air base at Felixstowe. Two days later he joined the crew of HMS *Engadine*, then being commissioned at Chatham. *Engadine* was one of three former Channel ferries that had been requisitioned from the South-East and Chatham Railway by the Royal Navy for conversion into aircraft-carriers. The other two were a sister ship of *Engadine*, HMS *Riviera*, and an older, slower, ship, HMS *Empress*.

The extent of the conversion from ferry to aircraft-carrier can be fairly gauged from the fact that it took the dockyard precisely one week to carry the work out. The title 'aircraft-carrier' was literally correct. There was no kind of flight deck. Three seaplanes were carried in a canvas hanger constructed towards the stern of the ship. The space below deck was divided up between accommodation for the men, repair workshops, and storage space for spare parts, for which there was an unceasing demand.

Before a seaplane could take off, it needed first to be manhandled out of the hanger, then lifted by crane into the water. And that was the easiest part of the operation. For an aircraft to take off from the open sea was a difficult trick to perform. It was relatively simple from the sheltered waters of an estuary, but from the sea was another matter altogether. To be successful it required an unlikely combination of circumstances. First, if the aircraft was not to be wrecked, it required a calm sea. But, if it were to get airborne, it needed the kind of lift that could only come from a stiffish breeze. And there was also the unfortunate fact that the primitive engines of the time often simply refused to work in cold or damp conditions. Given that the North Sea is notoriously cold and frequently rough, it is perhaps surprising that seaplanes ever succeeded in taking off from it at all.

Erskine's primary function on board was teaching navigation to pilots and observers; navigation not only by the use of charts but also by the stars. But only a week after joining the ship he took on further responsibility when he volunteered to be *Engadine*'s Intelligence Officer. Amongst other duties he had the delicate task of censoring the men's letters home. In the wrong hands it was an activity that made an officer very unpopular. But not Erskine, indeed rather the reverse. It was his custom never to simply reject a letter out of hand. He always discussed the offending words with the man concerned and suggested an alternative, acceptable version. Indeed, quite often he wrote entire letters for men less gifted with words than himself. As with the army in South Africa, he felt very much in sympathy with the ordinary seaman and they quickly learned to respect him. At forty-four, he was twice the age of most of the men on board. Inevitably, they nicknamed him 'Uncle'.

Two days after he joined the ship, *Engadine* was visited at Sheerness by Churchill and Admiral Jellicoe. On 1 September, she embarked her three seaplanes and just two days after that she sailed for Tynemouth, which she used as a base for full-scale training. Every day they put to sea and practised take off and landing procedures. Her pilots were also usefully employed in searching for floating mines.

Towards the end of the month, while Erskine was flying with a Lieutenant Gaskell, the aircraft developed engine trouble twenty miles from land. They were forced to land on the sea, where they bobbed about for hours, unable to attract the attention of passing ships. The arrival of darkness found them still adrift, without food or water, apart from one bar of chocolate. At two in the morning, seeing the lights of a steamer, they managed to draw her attention by burning and holding aloft pages from their signal book. The ship, a Swedish cargo boat, took them in tow until, with the return of daylight, she was replaced by a tug off Hartlepool.

When *Engadine* and her sister ships were first taken over by the Royal Navy and converted, it was intended to attach them to the Grand Fleet at Scapa Flow, where they were to act as 'the eyes of the fleet'. But that was not to happen, at any rate not yet. Instead, Erskine once more became caught up in a Churchillian plan, and once again it involved the north German coast. The intention this time was to deal with 'The Menace of the Airship'. In the years immediately prior to the outbreak of war, the earlier fear, that of a sudden German invasion, had been replaced by a new fear, that of the Zeppelin. Popular magazines and newspapers published frequent stories featuring Zeppelin attacks upon England, in which whole fleets of airships, of monstrous size and bristling with cannon, roamed freely over the defenceless countryside, dropping bombs at will.

But it was not only the general public who were concerned with the perceived threat. The authorities were also worried, with some justification. In 1914, the only way in which an aircraft could destroy a Zeppelin was by dropping a bomb on it. But a Zeppelin had a rate of climb greater than any aircraft. It could also fly higher than any aircraft, a height well above the range of any artillery. It followed that, once in the air, a Zeppelin was invulnerable. In point of fact, the threat was not anywhere near as serious as even the government believed. For one thing British estimates of Zeppelins available to the Germans at the outbreak of war were wildly inaccurate. Whereas the British put the figures at thirty or forty, the true figure was eight. And the Germans had no plans to use them for bombing England. Like *Engadine*'s aircraft, they were intended solely for fleet reconnaissance.

There was also the fact that Zeppelins had very real limitations, in particular the weakness of their engines. They might be invulnerable to aircraft or ground artillery, but they were all too vulnerable to the elements. Later in the war, when they were used to attack England, one of them spent most of the day cruising above London, in perfect safety. But during its return journey a storm blew up. The Zeppelin, completely helpless, was swept as far south as Morocco before the crew was able to bring it back under control and return home. But in the London of 1914 that was not appreciated. To British minds, and to Churchill's mind in particular, if Zeppelins in the air were invulnerable, the obvious answer was to hit them while they were on the ground. During August and September 1914 several attacks were mounted by ground-based aircraft against Zeppelin sheds in Germany, but with only very modest success. Soon afterwards there took place a particularly audacious raid against the Zeppelin factory at Friedrichshafen, on the shores of Lake Constance.

The centre of Zeppelin activity, however, as would be expected given their attachment to the High Seas Fleet, was the north German coast, in particular the vicinity of Cuxhaven. Under Churchill's urgent prodding, plans were drawn up to use the seaplanes from *Engadine* and her sisters to bomb the Cuxhaven Zeppelin sheds. Erskine's task, given his knowledge of the area, was to instruct the pilots in navigation.

When, on the 10 October, all three aircraft-carriers were declared operational, instead of joining the Grand Fleet at Scapa Flow as originally intended, they were sent to join 'Harwich Force' under Commodore Tyrwhitt. At that time Tyrwhitt had under his control four light cruisers and about forty destroyers. Also based at Harwich were the ten submarines and two command destroyers, *Lurcher* and *Firedrake*, of the Eighth Submarine Flotilla under Commodore Roger Keyes. In this way Erskine came into contact with two of the Royal Navy's most audacious and aggressive officers. Both men were natural inheritors of the Nelson spirit, ready at any and every opportunity to 'engage the enemy more closely'. Whenever there was a possibility of action neither man was happy to sit behind a desk and wait for reports; always they were at sea, leading from the front.

On 22 October Tyrwhitt was called to the Admiralty to take part in a planning session. He returned to Harwich with an agreed plan for an attack upon a reported Zeppelin base south of Cuxhaven. Its precise location was at that time unknown, but was later found to be approximately eight miles south of the port. Under the plan, the three carriers, protected by cruisers and destroyers, were to proceed to the Heligoland Bight, where they would release their aircraft. Meanwhile, another cruiser, HMS *Fearless*, together with attendant destroyers, would operate off the mouth of the Ems to repulse any German ships that might emerge from there.

At 5 am on 24 October, Harwich Force set off for the Heligoland Bight in fine weather. But the good weather didn't last. At dawn the next day, at which time the seaplanes were due to be launched, the ships were thickly shrouded in fog and soaked by pouring rain. Under such conditions take off was impossible. The operation was postponed and the ships returned to port.

Two further attempts were planned, one in late October, the other in early November. Both were cancelled without the ships even leaving harbour. Weather conditions were just too bad. The next planned attempt was scheduled to begin on 22 November. On this occasion it was hoped that the presence of Royal Navy ships in German waters might have the additional merit of tempting out units of the High Seas Fleet.

Early on the morning of 23 November a force of three carriers, three cruisers and eight destroyers left Harwich, intending to reach take-off point by dawn the following day. However, code-breakers in the Admiralty read an intercepted German message which suggested that enemy cruisers were already active in the area. The carriers and their escort were recalled, while Tyrwhitt's own cruisers pressed eagerly on, hoping to see some action. They observed distant smoke and were attacked by enemy aircraft but found no ships.[7]

In the middle of December, German battle-cruisers staged a sudden raid against the English coast, during the course of which they shelled the towns of Hartlepool, Whitby and Scarborough, before returning to their bases unscathed. The British press and public, greatly enraged by these German attacks on entirely civilian targets, naturally demanded revenge. So did Churchill. A new attempt against the Cuxhaven Zeppelin sheds, codenamed 'Plan Y', was scheduled for Christmas Day. In addition to Tyrwhitt's Harwich force, it was intended to employ Roger Keyes's submarines in support.

At 10 a.m. on 23 December, the cruiser, HMS *Fearless*, with eight destroyers left Harwich bound for German waters north of Heligoland.

The following night, two destroyers and nine submarines, with Keyes himself present on the destroyer *Lurcher*, slipped quietly out of Harwich. Another submarine, *E7*, was already in position between Heligoland and the entrance to the Elbe, Weser and Jade rivers, watching for any German movements. The submarines were to operate in a dual capacity; as both a defensive screen for the surface ships and as rescue vessels for any aircraft that ditched inside the ring of islands. Because the radios carried by the submarines could be heard only over a short distance, *Lurcher* acted as a command vessel, relaying their messages to both Tyrwhitt and the Admiralty.

At 5 a.m. the following morning, the three carriers, *Engadine*, *Riviera* and *Empress*, left harbour. They were escorted by the cruisers *Arethusa* and *Undaunted*, together with eight destroyers. All were under the direct command of Tyrwhitt himself. More than one hundred ships of the Grand Fleet were also at sea, but too far away to offer any real assistance should the operation run into serious trouble.

At first everything went according to plan. At 6 a.m., just before daybreak, the carriers reached their intended take off position about twelve miles west of Heligoland. They spread out in line abreast and stopped engines, the escort vessels forming a protective ring around them. According to Tyrwhitt, 'conditions were perfect for flying, light airs from the east, sea calm and great visibility, but bitterly cold'. No time was wasted in getting the aircraft into the water. By 6.30 all nine of them were bobbing about on the sea, their pilots already seated, while mechanics stood precariously on the floats, unfolding the wings. Tyrwhitt had instructed that each seaplane was to carry enough fuel to last for three hours. It was a question of weight. The more weight an aircraft carried, the more fuel it used up, especially in getting off the water. But, on HMS *Riviera*, Commander Robertson chose to ignore the instruction, each aircraft from his ship being fuelled for four hours.

The decision as to whether or not to carry an observer was left to the individual pilots. Once again it was a matter of weight. Each pilot had to decide for himself whether an observer was literally worth his weight in fuel. The result was that, whilst all three aircraft from *Empress* carried observers, none of *Engadine*'s did. On *Riviera* two of the pilots had chosen to fly alone. The pilot of the third *Riviera* seaplane, C. F. Kilmer, now sat waiting for take off, with wings spread and the engine running. But he was puzzled. Where was his observer? Where was Childers? At their final briefing, before leaving Harwich, Kilmer had approached Childers and asked him if he would like to come along. Childers had seemed to jump at the chance and been enthusiastic. But where was he now? Surely he hadn't got cold feet?

It says a great deal for Erskine's nerves that, on the very morning that he was planning to fly in a small, fragile aircraft, taking off from the sea, in the middle of winter, and going deep into enemy territory, over an area bristling with guns, that he overslept. Now, at the last possible moment, he was rowed across from *Engadine* to clamber awkwardly into the unsteady seaplane.

There were several different types of aircraft taking part in the raid; precisely which type each carrier or each pilot was allotted being simply a question of luck. Kilmer and Childers were fortunate that day in being given probably the best type then available. The Short 200 horsepower seaplane was a biplane, with an engine that pulled rather than pushed, by no means a universal arrangement in those early days. The observer sat immediately behind the fourteen cylinder engine, with the pilot behind him.

By now the time was approaching 7 a.m., the hour scheduled for take-off. Everyone was anxious to see the aircraft depart, not least the ship's captains, who felt all too vulnerable sitting stationary in the water, the perfect target for any passing submarine. But there were problems: because of the intense cold, most of the pilots had difficulty in getting their engines to start.

At 7 o'clock *Engadine* gave the signal for take off. One by one seven small aircraft sped across the calm sea, faster and faster, leaving a widening creamy wake behind them. They were not helped by the conditions: there was too little wind, but one by one they lifted gently above the surface of the sea, banked cautiously, and then headed off towards the German coast, invisible beyond the misty horizon. Two aircraft, one each from *Engadine* and *Empress*, were left behind, their engines silent and lifeless, while preparations began for lifting them back on board the carriers.

By 7.25 a.m., in seaplane no. 136, Erskine could clearly see Heligoland, about nine miles away, on their port beam. If Tyrwhitt had considered the weather to be bitterly cold on the deck of his cruiser, conditions in the open cockpit of an aircraft flying at 80 mph can only be imagined. A few minutes later they passed over a seaplane sitting on the water, apparently damaged. They assumed it to be British, as did some of their colleagues who also saw it. But they were wrong. It remains one of several mysteries of that day's operations; neither British nor German records account for it.

At 7.34 they passed over two German destroyers, steering north. By now, continuing to climb, they had reached 3000 feet. Shortly afterwards a Zeppelin was spotted ahead, a large and tempting target. They closed on it rapidly, steadily gaining altitude, reached it and began to circle, still climbing. If they could only get above their target they could drop one of the three 20 pound bombs they carried. The only other armament on board was the pilot's revolver. But the Zeppelin's rate of climb was too great for them. At 4500 feet, giving up the attempt as hopeless, they turned once more towards the German mainland.

At 8.17 they crossed the German coast north of Bremerhaven, only to encounter thick fog, which drifted in the slight breeze. Visibility continued to worsen; the cold to intensify. They dropped down to 250 feet, but could still see no more than half a mile. Below the worst of the fog the atmosphere was dull and dark, beneath them nothing but open fields, thickly covered with hoar frost. As if their situation was not difficult enough already, the engine began to misfire badly, which it continued to do intermittently for the rest of the flight. But still they pressed on, hoping to find the Zeppelin sheds that were their intended target. A village was spotted, which Erskine believed to be Cappel, the nearest settlement to the supposed sheds. They circled, the fog now worse than ever. Edging lower, they were at times down to no more than 100 feet. The engine coughed again. Below them lay nothing but empty fields. The engine spluttered. They gave up the search, turning away, back towards the coast and open water.

At 8.35, as they recrossed the coast, relieved to have water beneath them once more, the fog cleared and the engine ceased to cough. Now feeling much happier, they began to regain altitude. Having failed to find their primary target, perhaps their secondary objective might be achieved. At a height of 1500 feet Kilmer turned his aircraft towards Schillig Roads, the main anchorage of the German High Seas Fleet, outside the port of Wilhelmshaven. Their task was to discover the number and types of ships anchored there. As they wrote in their joint report:

> On entering Schillig Roads we turned west until we reached the middle of the fairway and came under fire from several ships. The weapons used against us were anti-aircraft guns firing a bursting shell of a shrapnel type. The fusing was excellent, bursts occurring frequently just at our level, and in some cases the direction was very nearly accurate. Two drift wires were severed and a chassis strut damaged.[8]

During the course of this exciting flight down the fairway, despite the considerable amount of metal being thrown up at them, Erskine was still able to count seven battleships, three armoured cruisers, three light cruisers and ten destroyers. They made no attempt to bomb the anchored ships. As they turned away from the German coast, one objective remained, to which they now turned their minds. According to intelligence reports, the Germans had established a depot for submarines on Erskine's old haunt of Nordeney. Seaplane 136 had been given the task of discovering whether or not such a base existed and, if it did, of bombing it. By 9.53 they were circling the east end of Nordeney, unable to find anything that even remotely resembled a submarine base. Their engine, which luckily had behaved itself under fire, now began to cough alarmingly. Deciding not to push their luck any further, they turned towards the point where they hoped their ship would be.

While the aircraft had been away, the carriers and their escort had seen action themselves. Luckily they had been undisturbed by enemy activity while getting their aircraft away. The Germans had expected trouble, but not from seaplanes. Their own intelligence service knew that *Engadine* and her sisters had been taken over by the Royal Navy. They also knew that the ships were at Harwich. But what, the Germans asked themselves, were the former ferries to be used for? In the absence of more accurate information, it was assumed that the ships were intended to be used as blockships, to be sunk in the narrow channels leading to the German ports. The sudden appearance of British seaplanes over their principal naval base took the Germans completely by surprise.

After the departure of their aircraft, the carriers were delayed by the necessity of recovering the two seaplanes whose engines had failed. That done, the carriers and escort vessels moved off on a northerly course designed to take them further away from the enemy coast, out of range of German aircraft. There was also the hope that their presence would tempt German surface ships out into the paths of waiting British submarines.

Almost immediately a Zeppelin appeared, closely followed by an enemy seaplane, which mounted a determined attack upon HMS *Empress* which, being slower than its sisters, tended to lag behind. Four bombs were dropped, all of which fell 200 to 300 yards off the starboard bow. A second aircraft then appeared, which dropped two larger bombs, straddling the ship. One bomb fell only twenty feet off the port beam, shaking the vessel severely, but causing no damage. The second bomb dropped forty feet off the starboard beam. Gunfire from the other ships then drove the aircraft away. The Zeppelin meanwhile had been edging closer, at the same time gaining height. Now it too attacked, diving down towards *Empress* and dropping three bombs, one of which fell off the port quarter, the other two astern. None did any damage. *Empress* then brought her twelve pounder gun into action. The Zeppelin sheared away and didn't bother them again.

At 9.30 the ships changed course to the south. Almost immediately HMS *Fearless* with her accompanying destroyers came into sight, giving the carriers extra protection. Shortly afterwards the first seaplane, no. 119, landed close to the destroyer HMS *Lurcher* and was taken in tow. At 10.15, seaplane no. 136, with Kilmer and Childers aboard, landed safely close to *Riviera* and taxied over to her. A few minutes later a second aircraft, no. 811, flown by Flight Lieutenant Edmunds, joined her. Ten minutes after that, with both aircraft safely aboard and stowed away, the ship was underway again. Lieutenant Commander Robertson's gamble had paid off. His seaplanes were the only ones with sufficient fuel to return directly to their ship; all the others were forced to land on the sea well short of the carriers. At 11.00 a.m. four aircraft were still unaccounted for, all by now certainly out of fuel.

Three of them, two from *Empress* and one from *Engadine*, all out of fuel, landed close to the submarine *E11*, six miles north east of Nordeney. Although under attack from a Zeppelin, the submarine rescued all three pilots. The aircraft had to be abandoned. The one remaining seaplane,

Riviera's third aircraft, failing to find the ships, landed on the sea, its pilot eventually being picked up by a Dutch fishing boat. The ships meanwhile all returned safely to Harwich. The results of the operation were meagre. None of the aircraft had found their intended target. Although one seaplane had attempted to bomb the German ships, no damaged was done. The official German report stated, with rare accuracy: 'They threw bombs at an anchored ship and a gasometer in the vicinity of Cuxhaven without hitting them or causing damage.'

But the failure of the raid wasn't known at the time. Intelligence reports spoke of warships seriously damaged and of warehouses successfully bombed. The raid also had valuable effects on morale, both in England and Germany. In England it helped to maintain the Royal Navy's confidence in itself. In Germany it went towards inducing a feeling of vulnerability and to strengthen further the inferiority complex felt by many men in the young and untested German Navy when faced by their opponents' long and glorious history.

The raid itself had other useful side-effects. It went some way, for instance, in demolishing the perceived threat of the airship. Tyrwhitt, in his report, was contemptuous of the 'stupid great things', which were, he thought, 'ridiculously easy to avoid in spite of their speed'. He also believed that 'a ship with anti-aircraft guns would always bring a Zeppelin down in daylight, should one attack'. His own vision of the future was very different, even if he was ahead of his time: 'One can well imagine what might have been done had our seaplanes, or those that were sent out to attack us, carried torpedoes. Several of the ships in Schillig Roads would have been torpedoed and some of our force might have been sunk as well.' Erskine, for the first of numerous occasions, found himself mentioned in despatches. The report from Lieutenant Commander C. L. Malone, HMS *Engadine*, read:

> At the same time I should like to bring forward the valuable assistance rendered by Lieutenant Erskine Childers RNVR whose knowledge and experience connected with the navigation of the German coast proved invaluable in instructing the pilots, and the success attained is largely due to the energy expended by him in preparing charts and collecting topographical data. He also accompanied Flight Lieutenant C. F. Kilmer in 136 and was to a large extent responsible for such an able reconnaissance.[9]

That by Lieutenant Commander Robertson, HMS *Riviera*, stated:

> With regard to the flights of Flying Officer Kilmer and Flight Lieutenant Edmonds, although they failed in locating the airship sheds, yet I think that the reconnaissance results speak for themselves. To carry on overland in a seaplane at a height of 200–300 feet, with an engine giving only 800 revolutions instead of 1300, as in the case of Flying Officer Kilmer, requires considerable nerve and coolness. Although they do not say much about it in their reports, both officers were under fire for considerable periods.
>
> I would also draw your attention to the service of Lieutenant Erskine Childers. His knowledge of the German coast and landmarks, which has been imparted as far as possible to the pilots, has proved invaluable to them. In actual flight he went as passenger to Flight Lieutenant Kilmer and this officer speaks highly of his knowledge and assistance.[10]

Following *Engadine*'s arrival back at Harwich and the usual de-briefings, Erskine was able to take a week's well-earned leave. He saw little of Molly; she was being kept very busy helping Belgian refugees at Crosby Hall, not far from their Chelsea home. But, in any case, Erskine's way of using his leave was unusual. Other men might choose to try to forget the war, to put their feet up, or to meet a few friends for a pint or two. But Erskine was not made that way. He gave himself little opportunity to become bored. His mind was still centred upon that string of sandy islands off the German coast. Two days of his precious leave were spent at the Admiralty, searching for maps that he knew they had but which they couldn't find. He also had several long talks with Captain Murray Sueter, Director of the Air Department, officially known, not inappropriately, as DAD.

Shortly after reporting back for duty, Erskine was invited to dine with Commodore Tyrwhitt on the cruiser *Arethusa*. Other guests included *Engadine*'s captain, Lieutenant Commander Malone, Commodore Roger Keyes and two of the seaplane pilots. Much of the talk centred around the raid on Cuxhaven. Tyrwhitt, who had at one time been doubtful of the value of aircraft, was by this time one of their strongest advocates. Keyes was if anything even more enthusiastic about the future of sub-marines. Working together they made a formidable combination. In their minds, the concept of submarines and aircraft working closely together offered immense possibilities. But it was an idea that would remain effectively unused until adopted by Germany in the Second World War.

Twice during the month that followed the seaplane-carriers revisited the German coast. On both occasions bad weather prevented their aircraft from taking off. At the end of January *Engadine* and *Riviera* sailed for Liverpool, where it was intended to improve their efficiency by replacing their canvas hangers by something more substantial.

Upon their arrival at Liverpool, *Engadine*'s captain, Commander Malone, taking Erskine with him, inspected the former Isle of Man ferry, *Ben-My-Chree*, then being converted into an aircraft-carrier. She was being equipped with a large hanger aft, together with a strong derrick on her mainmast for lifting aircraft in and out of the water. She was also to have a trackway fitted forward, from which it was hoped to fly off aircraft directly. Below decks there were workshops, engine-testing facilities, extensive storage areas and crew's accommodation that made *Engadine*'s own personnel envious. Both men were impressed. Shortly afterwards Malone was delighted to hear that she was to join *Engadine* and *Riviera* under his command, as a replacement for *Empress*. Since the new ship was obviously the pick of the bunch, he transferred his flag to her, taking Erskine with him. Towards the end of April, their renovation complete, the three carriers sailed for Harwich to resume operations against the German coast.

On 3 May the three carriers, escorted by three heavy cruisers, four light cruisers and eight destroyers, made an attempt to raid enemy installations. As so often in the past, the plan was foiled by adverse weather conditions, on this occasion by heavy seas. Yet another attempt was made on 6 May, only to be prevented by thick fog.

Meanwhile, within the confines of the Admiralty, the possibility of seizing Borkum had once more risen to the surface. In assessing the practicalities of such a scheme it was considered necessary to obtain up to date information on the island's defences. A plan was therefore devised for a secret reconnaissance. It was decided that the carriers would launch a bombing raid against the Frisian Islands, under the cover of which two of the aircraft would photograph defence installations on Borkum.[11]

The operation was scheduled for 11 May. As the carriers and their escort approached the proposed take-off point, a Zeppelin was spotted in the distance. An attempt was made on *Ben-My-Chree* to launch a Sopwith Schneider aircraft, fitted with wheels, from the forward platform. Unfortunately the engine backfired, wrecking the starting equipment. At the same time, *Engadine* successfully hoisted out her three seaplanes, which swiftly took to the air. While they were away, vainly chasing the Zeppelin, thick fog descended and enveloped the ships. Only one of the aircraft returned safely to the carrier. One, for some unknown reason, suddenly spun out of control into the sea, its pilot not being seen again. The third aircraft, suffering engine failure while trying to land, also crashed, but luckily the pilot was successfully fished out of the water by a destroyer.

That was to be the last occasion that the carriers operated out of Harwich as a squadron. Shortly afterwards *Riviera* was transferred to Dover, while *Engadine* moved north to join the Battle Cruiser Fleet based on the Firth of Forth. As for *Ben-My-Chree*, later that month she, with Erskine on board, sailed for the Mediterranean. Once more he was caught up in one of Churchill's projects, this time the most famous of them all: the Dardanelles.

9

The Dardanelles

The story of the ill-starred Dardanelles campaign is too well known to need much description here. The original idea stemmed from an understandable desire in the British cabinet to bypass the bloody deadlock in Flanders, which was costing so many lives for so little return. It offered them that prospect which so often seduces politicians, a quick and easy victory. Unfortunately, the product of a divided cabinet and divided service departments, the whole campaign was ill-conceived, ill-planned and ill-executed.

The idea that Churchill sold to the cabinet was that of an entirely naval expedition which, they believed, could easily be aborted should it fail to offer rapid success. When it did fail, however, Churchill reacted like a gambler on a losing streak by raising the stakes, and then raising them again. All too soon the entirely naval operation had been replaced by an almost entirely military one, with the War Office showing even less foresight than had the navy.

By the time *Ben-My-Chree* dropped anchor in Iero Bay, Mytilene, on the 12 July 1915, the campaign already bore the same features of stalemate as existed in Flanders. Men had died, and were still dying, in their thousands. And yet the British positions still amounted to little more than a bridgehead. Meanwhile the Turkish army grew in strength by the day.

Churchill had been forced from office on 17 May. A more prudent government would have taken the opportunity to withdraw then, blaming everything on him. But prudence is not a quality often found amongst politicians, nor is a willingness to admit to past mistakes. And so, in the continued pursuit of the quick victory, the stakes were raised once more. The continuous stream of ships and men heading for the battlefields soon built up to a new peak. Amongst them were *Ben-My-Chree* and Erskine Childers. The reason for their inclusion is not hard to see. When operations began, back in February, Keyes found himself desperately short of aircraft; many senior offices at the Admiralty still regarded them as a waste of money. All he was given was the carrier *Ark Royal*, old and slow, and six aircraft, all of obsolete design, and no trained observers. By the middle of April, Commander C. R. Samson had established an airfield on Mudros. But his aircraft were just as obsolete as the seaplanes and even less suitable for conditions in the eastern Mediterranean. Modern aircraft and experienced personnel were badly needed.

Back in his days at Harwich, Keyes had found that, 'in the carrier squadron, two people particularly impressed me, the Squadron Commander, C. Le Strange Malone, a young naval lieutenant who had been given command over the heads of many seniors, and Lieutenant Erskine Childers, an observer on one of the seaplanes'.[1] In the circumstances it was not surprising if Keyes specifically asked for *Ben-My-Chree*. Much more surprising is the fact that he was given it; generally speaking, the Dardanelles force was only given equipment that nobody else wanted.

The arrival of *Ben-My-Chree* was especially opportune. In the early days of the campaign the Royal Navy had had the luxury of the complete freedom of the Aegean Sea, with little threat from the enemy. Now the appearance of German submarines in the area had ended that happy state of affairs for good. No ship felt safe from sudden torpedo attack, and *Ark Royal*, with her abysmally slow speed, was considered to be particularly vulnerable. The original plan, which was to have *Ben-My-Chree* operate north of the Straits and *Ark Royal* south of them, was quickly discarded. *Ark Royal* now functioned solely as a depot ship, rarely leaving harbour. *Ben-My-Chree*, capable of steaming at twenty-five knots, now roamed freely, ranging from northern Greece to the coast of Syria. Her complement of aircraft comprised at this time of five Short seaplanes with 225 h.p. Sunbeam engines, the same type of aircraft used in the Cuxhaven raid; and three single-seat Sopwith Schneider biplanes. Seaplanes were rarely used to fly above the battlefield, their low flying height making them vulnerable to artillery. Instead they were used on reconnaissance missions or bombing raids deep into enemy territory and anti-submarine work. They were also frequently employed as spotter aircraft for naval guns.

Ben-My-Chree's arrival in Aegean waters coincided with the appearance there of Colonel F. H. Sykes, a senior Army officer on secondment
from the Royal Flying Corps. Colonel Sykes had been sent out by the
Admiralty to report upon the efficiency of RNAS operations and to
recommend changes in methods and equipment. He was immensely
thorough, visiting every unit and having discussions not only with senior
officers but also with pilots and ground staff. His lengthy report was
dispatched to the Admiralty on 9 July. They were so impressed by his
work that, on 24 July, he was appointed to command all RNAS units
in the eastern Mediterranean. Colonel Sykes made few criticisms of
personnel but many more of equipment and organisation, which he
found unnecessarily complex and inefficient:

> Many of the units had only recently been formed and had no experience of
> service away from good sheds and other conveniences. The heat, flies and
> dust have rendered the work of officers and men on shore very laborious.
> Though the atmosphere is wonderfully clear for aerial observation, the glare
> from the sea and the large areas of sandy country cause severe strain to the
> eyesight of the observer.
>
> Amongst the eleven seaplanes on HMS *Ark Royal* there are five different
> types of machine and three different types of engine.
>
> On the whole the results gained by seaplanes are disappointing and experi-
> ence points to the fact that it is wasteful to employ seaplanes for work which
> can be carried out by aeroplanes. The engines employed are not so reliable,
> the machines are more frequently prevented from flying by weather
> conditions and they are more difficult to keep efficient order.
>
> It will be extremely interesting to see whether the seaplanes of *Ben-My-Chree*
> are able to effect a great concerti or moral result by means of their torpedoes.
> One has not yet been fired against the enemy.[2]

The answer to that question would not be long in coming. But first
there was preparatory work to be done as the ship's crew, and the
aircrew in particular, came to terms with their new surroundings.
Theoretically, Erskine's function on board, in addition to teaching
navigation, was to train pilots and observers in the difficult arts of
artillery spotting, photo-reconnaissance and bombing. His primary value
to the service was considered to be his experience, his knowledge and
his teaching ability. He was not intended to take part in dangerous
missions, as there were plenty of younger men who could do that.

But in practice things were very different. By now Erskine was forty-six, an age at which most men are learning to be cautious, becoming aware of their own mortality. Erskine, however, was showing signs of returning to his behaviour as a young man, before the arrival of Molly into his life tamed his need for danger and physical discomfort. From now on Erskine was only happy when taking risks. The greater the risk, the more eagerly he sought it. Colonel Sykes was only the first of a string of senior officers with whom he was continually in dispute over their attempts to restrict his activities. Repeatedly he was banned from flying on anything but routine training missions, but always he broke the rules and went anyway. The more dangerous the mission, the more likely he was to be on it. As Colonel Sykes, was later to write: 'While Childers was with me, our chief difficulty was to prevent him from taking flights out of turn; on two occasions when he crashed into the sea it was found that he had no business to be on that patrol at all.'[3]

The cause of this reversion can only be speculated upon. It may have arisen simply from his enforced separation from Molly, or it may have happened anyway. Certainly even when, in the following year, he and Molly were reunited by his transfer to London, her power to control his desire for physical danger no longer existed. He exerted every effort to return to the fighting, continually pleading and pestering his superiors until they eventually grew tired of him and found him a posting where he stood a reasonable chance of being killed. For the remainder of the war it is difficult to say which was more damaging to Erskine's mental condition, the severe stresses of action against the enemy or the (for him) unbearable periods of enforced inactivity. Between them they slowly ground down a man who became ever more dependant upon his indomitable will.

On 22 July, *Be-My-Chree* was ordered to Mukro Island, a forty foot lump of bare rock forming part of the Rabbit Islands group, off the coast of Asia Minor, just south of the Straits. Soon after arrival they were joined by two monitors, *Roberts* and *M19*, together with supply ships. Conscious of the threat posed by German submarines, they wasted no time in surrounding themselves with protective nets. Their task was to assist in silencing Turkish guns situated near Kum Kale, which were firing across the Straits at troops on the Gallipoli peninsula. From where the ships were anchored at Mukro Island, the enemy guns were out of sight, well beyond the horizon, hence the necessity of spotter aircraft to plot the fall of shot.

Ben-My-Chree remained at Mukro Island for the next two or three weeks, her aircraft constantly in the air. Hour after hour was spent circling the Turkish positions, reporting on the accuracy or otherwise of the monitor's guns as they lobbed shells from ten miles away. The biggest problem was maintaining communication between ship and aircraft. The seaplane's radio could be heard easily enough by the ship, but the amount of wire used in the construction of the aircraft made it almost impossible for the crew to hear the replies. Eventually they adopted a combination of methods. The seaplane radioed to the ship, which then replied by means of its searchlight, which was clearly visible over ten miles, even in bright sunshine.

Despite these difficulties, several Turkish guns were destroyed and others damaged. Even more useful was the psychological effect upon the Turkish troops caused by the heavy shells landing amongst them from beyond the horizon. They became more and more reluctant to man their own guns and their accuracy was clearly diminished. When *Ben-My-Chree* was eventually called away for duties elsewhere, she left one of her aircraft behind, together with mechanics, to continue the good work.[4]

During the first week of August the new gamble of landing 20,000 men at Suvla Bay, coinciding with an offensive at Helles, kept *Ben-My-Chree* busy. On 3 August, in an attempt to confuse the Turks as to Allied intentions, an elaborate bombardment, supported by mock landings, was staged at Sighajik, a small port about twenty miles south of Smyrna. *Ben-My-Chree* was one of many ships that took part, under the command of a French admiral. Her aircraft worked hard all day, providing continuous air cover and reporting enemy movements. That job done, they returned to their usual operational area just north of Gallipoli. They were kept active on reconnaissance duties, watching for submarines and attacking enemy troop concentrations during the main army offensive. By the time fighting calmed down, some days later, the Allies had achieved only another bridgehead, at the cost of 40,000 casualties. The Turkish dead numbered more than 70,000. The quick and easy victory remained a mirage.

On 11 August, *Ben-My-Chree* sailed into the Gulf of Xeros to spot for a monitor that was shelling Turkish reinforcements as they headed for the front. Later in the day her seaplanes mounted attacks against the same troops. The following day, Erskine's star pupil, Flying Officer Edmonds, flying one of the carrier's Short seaplanes, crossed the neck of the Gallipoli Peninsula to attack enemy shipping in the Sea of Marmora. He soon spotted a large cargo ship lying motionless close to the shore. Having glided his aircraft down until he was only fifteen feet above the sea, he sped across the water, oblivious of fire from the shore, and released his torpedo at a range of 300 yards. Looking back over his shoulder, he had the satisfaction of seeing the ship apparently going down by the stern. Only later did the pilot learn that the ship had been deliberately beached by the Turks several days earlier after being torpedoed and shelled by a submarine. Five days later, Edmonds made up for his previous disappointment by torpedoing another large steamer, leaving it a blazing wreck.[5]

Shortly afterwards other aircraft from *Ben-My-Chree* attacked two smaller vessels. One of them, loaded with ammunition, instantly exploded with a satisfying display of fireworks. The other was set ablaze by Flying Officer Dacre. Forced by engine trouble to land on the water, he saw the ship on the other side of the Straits. Forgetting his own troubles, Dacre taxied towards the target and successfully torpedoed it. He then taxied his seaplane for two miles under continuous rifle fire until, the aircraft's weight reduced by the release of the torpedo, he managed to lift it into the air.

Clearly *Ben-My-Chree* and her seaplanes had more than proved their worth. On 25 August the most senior naval officer present, Admiral De Robeck, reported to the Admiralty: '*Ben-My-Chree*'s recent performances have been remarkable and truly Lieutenant Edmonds has confounded all our opinions by his success.'[6] But, despite this brilliant achievement, *Ben-My-Chree*'s seaplanes were not really suited for carrying out torpedo attacks; their engines were simply not powerful enough. The extra weight of a torpedo severely restricted the amount of petrol they could carry, which in turn greatly reduced their operational range. As a result flights were limited to a mere forty-five minutes; rarely sufficient to reach the target and return safely.

Flying in the vicinity of Asia Minor had advantages and disadvantages for both pilots and aircraft. Pilots familiar with North Sea conditions relished not only the unaccustomed warmth, but also the amazing degree of visibility in their new arena. As the Turks were soon to discover to their cost, almost nothing could be hidden from overflying aircraft, either on land or at sea. It seemed that almost no amount of camouflage could hide a field gun, and submarines could often be seen sitting on the ocean floor at depths of sixty feet or more, just waiting to be attacked. As for disadvantages, they came principally from the climate. Sand and dust, often swept along by strong winds, were a constant threat, choking engines, making maintenance an endless struggle, and shortening the life of every piece of equipment. The burning heat of the summer sun was another cause of trouble, drying out and warping the woodwork that made up much of the seaplane's superstructure. The RNAS never had sufficient aircraft in the area to carry out all the tasks allotted to them, and only rarely were more than half of them fit to fly. Very precise instructions were issued to aircrew as to what equipment they should carry with them on operations:

> Pilots must always be armed with a revolver or pistol; to carry binoculars; some safety device, either waistcoat, patent lifebelt or petrol can.
>
> Observers should always carry a rifle; proper charts for the journey; binoculars; life-saving device or petrol-can; watch, if not fitted to aeroplane.[7]

On the 2 September a transport ship, the *Southland*, carrying almost seven hundred Australian troops from Egypt, was torpedoed in the vicinity of the small island of Efstratis. This was about thirty miles south of Mudros, the port on Lemnos where the Royal Navy had their main base. Almost immediately the ship developed a list and orders were given for the troops to take to the boats. Even as they were being lowered a second torpedo only narrowly missed the ship.

Ben-My-Chree was just leaving Mudros on a routine patrol when she picked up *Southland*'s Mayday call, giving her position as ten miles south of Efstratis. As there appeared to be few other ships within range, Lieutenant Commander Malone ordered his ship south and they sped to the rescue at twenty-six knots. At this stage, although they knew *Southland* to be a transport ship, they had no idea that so many lives were at stake. They found the stricken ship five miles east of Efstratis, well away from her reported position. Only one other ship, a small naval vessel, HMS *Racoon*, was present, her crew helping with attempts to prevent *Southland* from sinking. The sea for miles around was dotted with lifeboats packed with men, often full of water and close to capsize. Malone stopped engines and ordered the launching of the ship's two motorboats to tow lifeboats to the ship and pick men out of the water. Luckily the sea was calm and everything went smoothly, except when soldiers in one boat, excited at their imminent rescue, stood up to cheer and wave. The boat promptly overturned, throwing everyone into the water, but all were eventually fished out, safe but more subdued. By the time their work was complete, *Ben-My-Chree* had picked up 694 soldiers and 121 members of the *Southland*'s crew.

Thanks to members of *Racoon*'s crew, assisted by a number of Australian volunteers, *Southland* was kept afloat and taken to Mudros. Almost all her own stokers had left the ship without permission after the torpedo struck. Of the nine hundred or so men who had been aboard her, all but twenty were saved, almost all the dead having been killed in the initial explosion.[8]

Ben-My-Chree, following a refit at Mudros, spent much of September in the Gulf of Xeros, north of Gallipoli, conducting reconnaissance and bombing missions against Turkish lines of communication. The art of accurate bombing was still in its infancy, with only the most primitive of bombsights available. While every bombing mission was exciting and dangerous for the pilots involved, their effects upon the enemy were often more psychological than physical. The pilots of the day had a favourite rhyme, which expressed it perfectly:

> There's a game that some play for the whole of the day
> Of dropping a bomb from the air,
> And men grin with delight if they drop it aright
> A contingency only too rare.[9]

On 2 October, spotter aircraft provided by *Ben-My-Chree* assisted monitor *M16* in an attempt to destroy a large flour mill in Gallipoli town. The mill was considered to be of great military importance because it was the sole supplier of flour to the Turkish army in Gallipoli. The attack, however, achieved little. The mill was situated amongst numerous other old buildings, the unintended destruction of which created such clouds of dust that the aircraft's observer could see almost nothing of the real target. A second attempt the next day, with a different monitor, was no more successful.[10]

21 October saw great activity around Fener Point, where a feint landing took place. No troops were put ashore, but a naval bombardment was made of Turkish defences, both there and at Dedaegatch. Seaplanes from *Ben-My-Chree* also played their part, chiefly in photo-reconnaissance which, thanks to Erskine's training, was rapidly becoming their speciality. They also performed spotting work for the naval guns. Much damage was done, especially to railway and harbour installations. Locomotives and railway trucks were wrecked; and store-houses, a factory, an oil store and the harbourmaster's office were all left blazing fiercely.

During the month of November, Bulgaria's entry into the war on the German side saw the chances of a British victory in Gallipoli recede considerably. Within only a few weeks, Serbia was overrun by the Central Powers, which had the effect of totally changing the supply situation. All kinds of munitions and equipment now began to pour into Turkey completely unmolested. Until now the advantage had rested with the British, whose control of the sea gave them a long, but safe, supply line. The Turks, on the other hand, had been entirely dependant upon small ships hugging the Black Sea coast, under constant threat from Russian warships. The new situation was that the British line remained just as long as it had always been, but now liable to submarine attack. The Turks, in contrast, now had direct rail communication with Germany through the Balkans.

The entry of Bulgaria into the war thus gave *Ben-My-Chree*'s pilots and observers an entirely new operational area to explore. Before long her seaplanes were regularly overflying southern Bulgaria on reconnaissance missions. And that was just the start. On 26 October she went into action supporting monitors shelling Bulgarian railway installations at Bodamo Junction.

With the new supply situation in mind, the Admiralty instructed Colonel Sykes to interrupt the flow of munitions from Germany by attacking the key railway bridge across the Maritza River in Eastern Thrace. The destruction of the bridge would assist not only the campaign in Gallipoli but also the newly opened Allied front at Salonika. Enemy forces on that front were supplied by the same railway line, which divided just south of the river. The bridge, which carried the railway line thirty feet above the river, consisted of two sections. The eastern section comprised fifteen spans, each about fifty-five feet long, with iron girders forming a box through which the railway ran; the whole structure being supported by stone piers. It was this section that was felt to provide the most tempting target.

The first attack, performed by three aircraft, took place on 8 November. One of the aircraft was land-based, being flown by Wing Commander C. R. Samson from the airfield on Imbros. The other two were Short seaplanes from *Ben-My-Chree*. Erskine, typically, broke regulations by going as navigator in a seaplane flown by Flying Officer Edmonds; the other seaplane being flown by Flight-Lieutenant Dacre. Each of the three aircraft carried two 112 pound bombs. For the purposes of the raid *Ben-My-Chree* moved close to the island of Enos, giving her seaplanes a round flight of about eighty miles. Samson's Henri Farman had been fitted with an additional fuel tank for its round trip of almost two hundred miles.

The outward flight presented the pilots with no problems, the weather being fine, with visibility excellent and the machines operating perfectly. Samson spent much of the flight making mental notes of possible future targets. There seemed to be plenty of them, especially troop concentrations, just asking to be bombed. But not this time. As they approached their target, Samson, as lead aircraft, chose to go straight into the attack. The other two circled above, providing cover against the unlikely eventuality of enemy aircraft appearing. Although the bridge was protected by anti-aircraft guns, their arrival took the Turks completely by surprise. By the time they had woken up to the threat, Samson was well into his attacking run.

Sweeping down low, he released both bombs from a height of 800 feet, missing the target by only a few yards. One bomb landed close to the base of one of the supporting columns, on a small island in mid-river. The damage done was sufficient to interrupt rail traffic for several weeks. Edmonds and Dacre then each attacked in turn, diving in low, despite the now lively anti-aircraft fire. But they succeeded only in hitting the railway track, the resulting damage being easily repaired. Over the next few weeks five more attempts were made to destroy the bridge by bombing, all by land-based aircraft. The first two were foiled by bad weather over the target. From then on each successive raid ran into continually strengthened Turkish anti-aircraft fire.[11]

In December the government, which had for two months been dithering over whether or not to admit the defeat of the Dardanelles campaign, finally decided to withdraw. The army's evacuation of the Gallipoli peninsula was planned to begin on 19 December. Secrecy was absolutely essential. Should the Turks discover British intentions, the withdrawal could end in disaster. It followed that for the operation to stand any chance of success enemy ships and aircraft must be kept away. Beginning several days before the intended withdrawal, every available aircraft was kept continually in the air. The land-based aircraft flew over and around the battlefields, chasing away any enemy aircraft that ventured too close. Meanwhile, *Ben-My-Chree*'s seaplanes maintained a constant watch for surface ships or submarines, easily spotted in the clear Mediterranean waters. This they continued to do until the last soldier was safely aboard one of the supporting ships.

Even before the military withdrawal from Gallipoli had been completed, a new task was being planned in the Admiralty for *Ben-My-Chree* and her crew. Following their successful defence of Constantinople, it was feared that the Turks might be tempted to try their luck elsewhere. On 6 December the War Office wrote to the Admiralty requesting their assistance in providing air support for the army defending the Suez Canal: 'We are of the opinion that the Turkish lines of communication are specially vulnerable to attack and that valuable assistance could be given by seaplanes under Naval escort operating off the coast of southern Syria.' [12]

It was not until after 8 January, when the last of the troops were evacuated from the Gallipoli peninsula, and the armada of ships began to disperse, that the Admiralty felt able to release *Ben-My-Chree* for operations elsewhere. Towards the end of that month, the carrier sailed quietly southwards to establish her new base at Port Said. There she met up with two smaller carriers, *Anne* and *Raven II*, which had been in the area for some time. Soon afterwards they were joined by *Empress*, fresh from England. Together they made up the grandly titled, 'East Indies and Egypt Seaplane Squadron'. The new force was allocated a huge operational area and a wide range of tasks. Their area stretched from the coast of Syria in the north, down through the Lebanon,

Palestine and Sinai to Egypt, and on to Cyrenaica in the west, while in the south they were expected to cover the whole of the Red Sea and the Gulf of Akaba. They were also responsible for wide expanses of desert in between. As for tasks, these included routine patrols over the desert approaches to Egypt through Sinai. They also did reconnaissance, photo-reconnaissance and the bombing of Turkish positions and supply lines, together with spotting for both land based and naval guns. And anything else the army or navy could think up.[13]

Over the early months of 1916, *Ben-My-Chree* spent much of her time to the east of Egypt, her aircraft continually in the air watching for any Turkish threat to the Suez Canal. From time to time, seeing signs of enemy troop concentrations, they returned laden with bombs with which to cause the maximum disruption. The railway running down from Syria through Palestine was a regular target. On 29 January, Erskine wrote, in eager anticipation, 'We sail tonight to carry out flights to Beersheba and the railway northwards'.

The next day, he sat in the observer's seat as his seaplane circled low over the outskirts of the town. He was not in a good mood, having failed to persuade Wright, his pilot, that the danger of being hit by rifle fire at 800 feet was negligible.

All we did, was to make one sweep south of the town then home again. However, we did obtain some important results; verifying the fact that the railway does not go beyond Beersheba, though the embankment and a light construction railway alongside it do; that the bridge across the Wady al Saha, a splendid viaduct, is incomplete; that 200 or more camels were leaving the town for Auja by the direct route; that there are a large number of troops at Beersheba on both sides of the Wady; and big barracks, shown in half a dozen pictures; that the approaches of the town from Gaza are entrenched for miles out; that three hitherto unreported bridges exist, two of them being broken or uncompleted as well as one of the deviation bridges on a loop at this point so that traffic is blocked.

We flew low over Gaza and I gazed in rapt attention at a beautiful mosque and courtyard, showing an exquisite pale green colour, with delicate fretted arches and porches.[14]

In the middle of February, by way of a change, *Ben-My-Chree* sailed westwards to assist the army against Senussi tribesmen making a nuisance of themselves in the Western Desert. In this way, place names that were to become famous in a later war became familiar to Erskine and his friends; names such as Sidi Barrani and Martruh. In the first week of November a German submarine had successfully torpedoed two merchantmen off the North African coast. They removed the crews before sinking the ships, but then handed them over to the Senussi in the port that later became known as Tobruk. Demands to their Sheik for the men's immediate release were met, first, by claims of ignorance, then by procrastination, finally by blunt refusal. Offers of bribes were no more successful than threats of action.

The Senussi, stirred by declarations of a holy war emanating from Constantinople and encouraged by German submarine activity off their coast, became increasingly belligerent. Soon they took to attacking Egyptian border posts. On 18 November Sidi Barrani was raided. A state of undeclared war then developed rapidly, as exposed Egyptian border posts were evacuated; the British falling back to more easily supplied Mersa Metruh. By the time *Ben-My-Chree* headed that way three months later, large-scale British reinforcements had effectively seen off the threat. For all their courage and religious zeal, the Senussi had discovered that camels and rifles were no match for armoured cars and artillery. The time had now come to re-establish the Egyptian borders by retaking Sollum.

On 11 February the old team of Edmonds and Childers once more took off on a reconnaissance mission, this time to discover Senussi positions around Sidi Barrani and Sollum prior to the intended British advance. At first everything went according to plan. Flying conditions over the desert were ideal, with visibility excellent. Erskine was able to take photograph after photograph of Senussi encampments, oblivious of ill-aimed rifle fire. The problems began when they turned for home. Over the desert visibility remained perfect, but the moment they crossed the coast they found the sea smothered in fog. Reaching the point where they thought *Ben-My-Chree* ought to be, they circled; then circled again, wider. Nothing. Nothing but empty sea. They continued the search, round and round, straining their eyes, peering into the fog, seeing nothing. With their fuel now rapidly running out, they had no choice but to land on the sea, despite a nasty swell. Edmonds can now take up the story:

> The port wing rose high in the air and Erskine shouted, 'Run out on the wing', which we both did and she righted. In another moment the tail began

to sink and the floats rear up vertically so that the whole of the observer's seat was submerged. Erskine stayed where he was on the end of the wing, knee-deep in water. I nipped back to the floats and stood on the cross-bar between them, dry except for my feet.[15]

Drifting slowly further out to sea, the two men were eventually picked up, several hours later, by a fishing-boat, the half-submerged aircraft being towed to *Ben-My-Chree*. Erskine's only complaint about the incident was typical of his single-mindedness: 'I was bitterly disappointed at the loss of twenty-nine negatives – all good, I'm sure, as conditions were perfect.'[16]

By early March *Ben-My-Chree* was back in familiar waters east of the Canal. On the 7 March, Erskine was once again detailed to reconnoitre Gaza and Beersheba, this time in the company of Edmonds, a pilot much more to his taste than the cautious Wright. Reading Erskine's operational reports, there is always the suspicion that he judged the relative success of a mission not just by the information gained but by the number of bullet-holes acquired by his machine. Early that morning, *Ben-My-Chree* had reached her designated position, to the south of Gaza, safely out of sight of land. At 9.18 the aircraft sped across the calm, blue sea, lifted off the water and turned eastwards. Their first destination was Bir Suleinean, where Erskine found little of interest, except for a few camels. They then headed for Beersheba, which they reached at 10.30. They circled low over the town's outskirts, while Erskine peered calmly downwards before writing in his notebook. His official report reads:

> Animals. Camel and horse lines observed at numerous points especially one or two miles NW of the town.
>
> Troops. Numerous scattered groups in and around town. Rifle and machine-gun fire. Several hits. No damage
>
> Anti-aircraft guns. Two fired from a point two miles NW of town. Aim bad.
>
> Possible aerodrome. Four miles NE of station. Two large sheds and arched roofs. Largest about 200 feet x 60 feet.[17]

After ten minutes they left Beersheba for Kalasa, which they were able to observe unmolested:

> East of Wady Khalasa, two sheds about 100 feet x 40 feet, three small stone buildings, one apparently a partly roofed well. One possibly an engine-house.

A few camels near a well. Twelve moving on road to Beersheba. West of Wady two camps of Arab tents, 50 and 30 apiece.[18]

One final reconnaissance was made, at Beni Seleh, which had nothing to interest them apart from a handful of Arab tents and a few camels. They then turned away and returned to the ship, which they reached without incident at 11.43. A careful inspection of the aircraft revealed a disappointing score of only two bullet-holes.

For Erskine flying over Palestine was always a fascinating experience. Although he had no religious beliefs, so many of the places that he now saw brought back memories of biblical stories heard at school or from his mother. And there were the occasional surprises. During the course of a reconnaissance flight with Dacre, he saw his first kibbutz, at what was then an obscure place called Tel Aviv:

> I was much struck by what I took (rightly as it turned out) to be a Jewish colony, just north of a river. A splendid wood, densely planted, the only one I have ever seen in the East, make it a large area of beautifully cultivated land ringed by an enclosure and skirted by a mile long avenue of trees. These led to what I should call a model village laid out in regular streets, each house with its garden – a garden city indeed, with large separate farm buildings. Behind it, as we faced the sea, ran a dazzling golden belt of sand dunes, and beyond, the vivid blue ocean.[19]

Early in 1916, the War Office, which had requested the presence of aircraft-carriers in the Suez Canal and Palestine areas, wrote to the Admiralty again, expressing their appreciation of the work being done by the Seaplane Squadron:

> Reconnaissance and bomb-dropping work has been carried out by seaplanes in this area with the greatest success, and has allowed of our obtaining knowledge of the enemy's whereabouts.
>
> The bombing raids have had a most beneficial effect upon Turkish and Arab forces who dislike very much this form of attack and have been driven out of many encampments thereby.

Throughout this period, *Ben-My-Chree*'s aircrew had enjoyed the luxury of having uncontested control of the air. Over the Dardanelles there had been the occasional enemy aircraft to watch out for, even if they invariably flew away the moment they saw a British aircraft in the same patch of sky. But since the ship's move south there had been no enemy aircraft in their area at all. Not that is until March 1916, at which time the Turks could be seen preparing runways and building aircraft hangers. It seemed that the days when aircrew had nothing more to worry about from the enemy than the occasional sniper's bullet were coming to an end. Towards the middle of the month Erskine, once more in the sky over Beersheba, for the first time saw enemy aircraft parked in neat lines. But, no doubt to his disappointment, he was not destined to fight them. Only a few days later he was called home to take up a post in the Air Department of the Admiralty. His colleagues were sad to see him go, but hoped that, with Erskine in the Air Department, they might at last stand some chance of being sent the right aircraft and the right men.

10

Sea and Sky

At the end of March 1916 Erskine arrived back in England to take up a post in the Admiralty. Throughout his period there he kept no diary and made no reference in his letters to his official activities. Inevitably there have been suspicions that his duties were in some way involved with espionage and Ireland, especially as his return to London coincided with the Easter Rebellion.

But the British Admiralty in the spring of 1916 had much more on their minds than a little local difficulty in Dublin. The Germans were conducting a U-boat campaign which, given the lack of adequate counter-measures, was proving extremely difficult to contain. Their High Seas Fleet, while reluctant to come out and fight, was a permanent threat to Britain's control of the seas.

As for Erskine, he spent the next nine months sitting at a desk in Section M of the Air Department in a former hotel in the Strand which had been requisitioned 'for the duration'. His task was mundane, the allocation of aircraft to the various squadrons and ships. This was not an occupation likely to appeal to a man of his temperament. What he longed for was action. Tying Erskine to a desk was like keeping a seagull in a cage. He longed to be free; to be once more in an aircraft over enemy territory, with bullets coming up at him. Almost at once he began pestering his superiors to let him go.[1]

He arrived home just in time to watch horrified as the Irish Volunteers, whom he had helped to arm, mounted a pointless rebellion against British rule. Once again the old doctrine so beloved of Irish Nationalists, 'England's peril is Ireland's opportunity', had been resurrected. The fact that, over the centuries, it was precisely that attitude which had been the biggest obstacle to Irish independence was ignored. Seen through British eyes, it proved once again that the Irish could not be trusted, that giving them independence would be like going to bed in a crime-ridden city and leaving the back door open.

Shortly after the outbreak of war, an Irish Home Rule Bill was passed by the British Parliament, but suspended for the duration of the war. Irish independence, now inevitable, was simply a matter of time. But the more extreme elements in the Republican movement were not content either to wait or to have independence given them on a plate – preferring poetic visions of desperate heroism and blood sacrifice. It was with these aspirations in mind that preparations were made for an Easter Rising in Dublin in the spring of 1916.

The plans for the uprising were very detailed and highly ambitious. They also bore remarkably little resemblance to reality. It was intended that the rebels would occupy all the key strategic positions in the city. They would then hold them against determined attacks from the British while the rest of Ireland, inspired by their example, would enthusiastically rise in sympathy. That the rest of Ireland might simply think that they were mad and stay at home never entered their heads. It was believed that they could achieve all of this thanks to generous support from their allies, the Germans, who would readily supply them with all the armaments they needed. In their more optimistic moments the Republicans envisaged the Kaiser and his generals, inspired by Irish heroism, rushing to their aid with thousands of troops. This picture of the Kaiser's Germany as one overflowing with kindness and concern for small nations was not one that came readily to the minds of most people in Europe, or indeed to Roger Casement, who had been sent to negotiate with them.

The two men mainly responsible for the planned uprising, Patrick Pearse and James Connolly, distrusted one another, cooperating as little as possible and keeping the moderate leader John MacNeill in the dark as to their real intentions. It was only on the Sunday before Easter that MacNeill was told that a route march of the Irish Volunteers planned for the following Sunday would mark the beginning of the Rising. On Good Friday Roger Casement was landed from a German submarine only to be immediately arrested. A ship carrying 20,000 obsolete German rifles, the only support that they were prepared to give, was scuttled when intercepted by the Royal Navy. That the British knew all about the planned revolt in advance was due to a weakness not of Irish but of German security, their naval code having been broken long before.

So what was to be done now? It had been Casement's intention to urge that the rising be stopped, but he was already in British hands and in no position to do or say anything. MacNeill, who had never liked the plan anyway, placed an advertisement in a newspaper declaring that the intended manoeuvres had been cancelled. The British read it with great satisfaction and relaxed. It seemed to justify their policy of taking no action against the Volunteers. But Pearse and Connolly were infected by that curious blindness that affects anyone who plans military operations and makes them mentally incapable of cancelling a pet project, no matter how badly they know things are going. They therefore chose to proceed anyway; but a day later than originally intended.

On the morning of Easter Monday, hundreds of young men, most of them teenagers, some as young as fifteen, left home in the fond belief that they were going for a march and would be back in time for dinner. Many of them never returned. Instead of a pleasant march, they found themselves in occupation of the General Post Office, besieged by professional troops armed with artillery. Volunteers they may have been, but they had not volunteered to commit suicide. In this way Dublin came to be one of the first European cities to experience the horrors of street fighting with modern weapons. This was something that was to be a recurrent feature of the twentieth century. Dublin was the very modest overture to the much greater dramas of Stalingrad, Warsaw and Berlin.

Initially everything went according to plan. The various strategic positions were occupied without opposition, although there were moments of pure farce when elderly ladies wanting stamps resolutely refused to be bullied by men with guns. There were also casualties in the form of unarmed policemen and off-duty soldiers who were ruthlessly gunned down. Young men were taught the pleasures of committing cold-blooded murder; lessons that Ireland would learn to regret in the years to come.

With their first objective achieved, the rebel leaders triumphantly declared the creation of an Irish Republic and confidently awaited a national acclamation. It didn't come. The only reaction was one of bafflement. At Jacob's Biscuit Factory, one of the strategic positions occupied by the rebels, they were jeered at by local people and urged to 'go and fight the Germans'.

As would be expected on a Bank Holiday, the British authorities took a while to become organised. Hardly had the rebels established themselves in the Post Office before a troop of English cavalry, with their customary foolishness, chose to trot prettily down the road, right through the rebels line of fire. The rebels could hardly be expected to miss such an opportunity. Seven men died. The rebels, however, were not to have things their own way for very long. General Lowe, in charge pending the arrival of General Sir John Maxwell, soon had a cordon thrown round the occupied zone. Within it, in the absence of normal law and order, looting had already begun. This was to be a feature of the siege and a cause of many casualties as men and women carrying carpets or bed linen ignored shells and bullets in their eagerness to gain something tangible from the uprising.

Over the next few days the British army brought in more and more men; they were soon to number twelve thousand compared with sixteen hundred rebels. With them the British first closed the cordon and then slowly tightened their grip. But, as other armies were to discover, street fighting was difficult and dangerous. The city streets were blocked with improvised barriers continually swept by gunfire from prepared positions. Day followed day with little to show for their efforts but lengthening casualty lists. At one point they brought up the River Liffey the *Helga*, a vessel that Irish historians delight in calling 'a gunboat'. It was in fact a fishery-protection vessel. Its gun did make a very satisfying 'Bang', but, apart from dislodging a few roof slates and the odd chimney-pot, it was never likely to have much impact upon the tide of battle.

What did decide the battle were two 18 pounder field guns, which began rapidly to demolish the General Post Office about the ears of its defenders. Pearse, who had belatedly discovered that a blood-sacrifice using real blood, far from being poetic, was messy and brutal, finally negotiated a surrender on the Friday. The rebel losses numbered sixty-four killed and 116 wounded, compared with British casualties of 132 dead and 397 wounded. More than three hundred non-combatants died.

In the hours immediately following the surrender a number of junior army officers had the good sense to tell captured teenage rebels to go home to their mothers. Unfortunately the man at the top showed considerably less intelligence. Instead General Maxwell decided to 'teach the Irish a lesson' by sentencing to death not just the leaders of the rising, which would at least have been understood, but scores of their followers as well. By the time the government in London exerted themselves and brought pressure to bear, ensuring that the vast majority of death sentences were never carried out, the damage was done.

The Easter Rebellion was an act of criminal foolishness that should have been suppressed without too much difficulty. Unfortunately, the British officer responsible for the operation was Maxwell. He had begun the war by successfully defending Egypt against a Turkish attack. He had, however, then been heavily criticised for his failure to follow up his victory and for allowing the Turkish army to withdraw unmolested. The War Office, concerned at his lack of zeal, chose to transfer him to a nice, quiet, out of the way place, where he wouldn't get in the way of more aggressive-minded officers. They sent him to Ireland. Naturally, when the rebellion broke out in Dublin, he determined not to make the same mistake twice. If his masters wanted zeal and aggression that would be what he gave them. The result was, as was usual in Ireland, violent stupidity from one side met with violent stupidity from the other. In the process, Maxwell turned a minor military problem into a political disaster.

The mishandled suppression sent waves of reaction in all directions. Shortly after Easter, Erskine was shocked when Robert Barton told him that he had resigned his commission in the army. Posted to Dublin immediately after the rebellion had been crushed, Barton had been appalled by the number of death sentences pronounced and the general air of military reprisal. Erskine joked that, the way Robert was talking, he would soon be supporting Sinn Fein. It did not remain a joke very long.

As for Erskine himself, his reactions were no different to those of many thinking people on both sides of St George's Channel. In a letter, dated 23 May 1916, he wrote:

My opinion about Ireland is a simple one, based on cause and effect as observed for all white races and many coloured ones, and indeed as old as man himself, for ought I know; namely that peoples denied freedom will rebel, the responsibility for the tragic results resting on those who deny the freedom and resting most heavily when they sin against the light, as most assuredly all British Governments do, or they must look at our Empire with blind eyes.

The typical rebel is often half-crazy and half-starved, a neurotic nourished on dreams. We shoot a decent number – again a venerable convention, probably justified – the wiser then say, 'Yes, but we must now do something'.

There is no moment in history that I know of when it would not have been best for England and Ireland that Ireland should govern itself. One of the most urgent of all was when war broke out – a war whose noblest justification was the freedom of small nationalities.[2]

Also concerning him was the fate of his former associate in the Howth gun-running, Roger Casement. Erskine's judgement of Casement, as a man whose ideas were hopelessly impractical, had proved all too accurate. He had been under close scrutiny by British intelligence ever since the start of the war. They had seen him attempting to persuade Irish members of the British army, captured by the Germans, to change sides and fight for them. None did. They knew of his constant urging for a German invasion of Ireland which, given the strength of the Royal Navy, could never be anything but a pipe-dream The Germans, in fact, regarded Casement much the way Erskine did; they never really took him seriously.

Shortly before Easter, Casement had been captured while landing on the coast of Tralee from a U-boat. A few days later a German ship loaded with arms was scuttled off the Irish coast. Casement's fate was sealed. His only defence, that he was not a British traitor because he was not British but Irish, convinced very few outside Ireland, and not many there. His argument might have been more convincing if he had not been employed for many years by the British Consular Service, had not accepted a knighthood from the King, and was not still drawing a British Foreign Office pension.

Molly was among those who pleaded for his life. Many of her literary friends also signed the petition: Conan Doyle, Arnold Bennett, G. K. Chesterton, John Galsworthy and Jerome K. Jerome. But given the time, in the middle of a particularly bitter war, his execution was inevitable. Almost every family in Britain had a husband or son fighting in the trenches of Flanders. To them there could be only one fate for a traitor.

Throughout the summer and autumn Erskine struggled to break free from his office-bound existence. But it was not until December that, helped by Captain Richmond, he at last escaped from the accursed desk and rejoined the real war. Even then he didn't get what he really wanted, which was to return to flying. With his new posting, although he remained in the Royal Naval Air Service, there were to be no aircraft involved, at least not officially. Instead, on 13 December 1916, he reported to Queenborough, on the Isle of Sheppey, where he joined a Coastal Motor Boat Squadron.

The squadron that Erskine joined was equipped with twelve motor-boats, each forty feet long, fitted with 250 hp Thorneycroft engines capable, in favourable conditions, of a speed of thirty-five knots. That was, of course, the big snag, as 'favourable weather conditions' were unusual in the North Sea, which was their normal hunting ground. To quote the commander of operations in the Dover Straits, Admiral Bacon: 'as their trim when steaming at speed was always with the bow up and the stern down, they jumped from sea to sea, landing with a thud on the water which, when accentuated by particularly unfavourable conditions, was injurious to them'. And not, presumably, very comfortable for their crew, which comprised only two men, a lieutenant and a midshipman.

Their intended use was in sudden attacks, at night, on enemy coastal shipping, especially submarines and destroyers caught close to their bases. The usual armament carried by a CMB was one torpedo, one depth charge and two Lewis guns. They were also employed in planting mines, of which they were capable of carrying just two. Given the difficulties Second World War destroyers equipped with ASDIC and scores of depth charges had in sinking U-boats, it is hard to believe that the CMBs stood much chance of success with only one depth charge, even if they did hunt in pairs.

As for their torpedoes, the manner in which they were fired was decidedly peculiar. The torpedo was carried and released from the stern of the boat, stern first. This meant that the moment the rear of the missile touched the water its propeller began to work, driving it straight ahead, towards the boat that had just released it. Clearly some very smart work with the boat's wheel and engine was necessary if disaster was to be avoided.

Early in the new year, Erskine, newly promoted to Lieutenant Commander, led the first batch of four boats across the Channel to their new base at Dunkirk. Nine more followed later. Only a few miles up the coast, in the Belgian ports of Ostend and Zeebrugge, lay German destroyers and submarines. Erskine, straining at the leash, could hardly wait to attack them. But he had a cautious commander, whose ideas of 'favourable conditions' for small boats were not Erskine's. And there was also another reason for waiting. Vice-Admiral Bacon was anxious that the CMBs first attack should take the enemy completely by surprise. For that he wanted very specific conditions:

> The CMBs were useful mainly at night. In daylight – and bright moonlight nights may be looked upon as daylight – the German destroyers could hunt them down. On very dark nights the visibility is so poor that they were not suitable for purposes of attack, as craft low in the water like CMBs cannot see their prey. The best nights therefore on which to use the boats were about the first and last quarters of the moon.[3]

Unfortunately, it soon became apparent that in the North Sea, especially in winter, when the moon is right the weather is probably not. Erskine therefore spent day after day, week after week, sitting in a hut near the beach, playing bridge, studying maps and gazing at a sea that he was not allowed to venture out upon. Much of the winter passed in this frustrating manner. Just occasionally, on the rare fine day, he and his men were allowed to put to sea; but only for practice; they were strictly forbidden to go anywhere near the enemy. They must wait.

At last, with the improvement in the weather that came with the approach of spring, an offensive operation was mounted against the German destroyers based at Zeebrugge. As with all of the more successful operations performed by the CMBs, it was done in association with naval aircraft; either land-based planes from St-Pol or seaplanes from Dunkirk. The operation had the advantages that come with simplicity. Under cover of darkness the CMBs positioned themselves close to the entrance to Zeebrugge harbour, but sufficiently far from it not to risk being seen from the shore. The aircraft then mounted a bombing raid on the harbour, concentrating their efforts on the area close to the mole where the destroyers were moored. Everything went according to plan. Within only a few minutes of the start of the air raid the destroyers hurriedly left their heavily defended positions against the mole and headed for the supposed safety of the open sea. This led them straight past the waiting motorboats. One destroyer was sunk and a second badly damaged.

From then on, regular night patrols set off from Dunkirk. Many hours were spent lurking just off the Belgian coast in the hope of catching an enemy ship off guard. It was wet, cold and frequently dangerous work. It was also rarely successful. The boats lay so low in the water that visibility was very short, and the chances of seeing a ship, other than close by, remote. On 19 April Erskine was at sea on an unusually calm night. Off Zeebrugge they caught sight of a U-boat on the surface. They closed in for the kill, but it submerged before they could make their attack.

Finding the long periods of inactivity almost unbearable, Erskine made friends at the nearby airbase and began making regular unofficial flights over enemy territory. On 26 April he was invited by Squadron Leader Fellowes, CO of 1st Wing RNAS at St-Pol, to go with him on a recon-naissance trip over Zeebrugge in a DH4. Naturally he leapt at the chance. They took off and climbed to 20,000 feet. It was a beautiful day, offering perfect visibility although bitterly cold at that altitude. At the end of a most enjoyable flight, Erskine dashed off in a car to his own base, having just enough time for a quick meal before going out in a CMB on night patrol.

Only a few days later, on the 30 April, another attempt was made to drive German destroyers into the path of waiting CMBs, this time from Ostend. Erskine was not included in the planned attack. But he couldn't be kept out of the action quite that easily. Once more he took to the air without permission, on this occasion in a Short seaplane. Meanwhile two CMBs, numbers 7 and 13, had also left Dunkirk to take up their ambush positions. They spent an hour and a half slightly to the eastward of the port waiting for the air raid to begin. When heavy firing and the sound of explosions indicated the start of the raid they moved closer, peering into the darkness.

On *CMB 7*, Lieutenant Commander Wellman caught sight of a ship silhouetted against the moon. It was about a mile away and appeared to be a destroyer, moving out to sea. He sped towards it, his boat bouncing off the wave tops in the exciting but uncomfortable way characteristic of CMBs. His colleague on *CMB 13* joined eagerly in the chase. When the distance between his boat and the enemy ship had been reduced to half a mile, Wellman stopped to check the ship's course and speed and to plan his line of attack. The two boats then edged further out to sea and separated, intending to attack the enemy from different angles. They moved in on their quarry hoping not to be seen, but were spotted and fired upon. The destroyer turned away, increasing speed. The two boats chased after her, edging out either side, until she had one on each beam. They were now heading straight for the nearby coast. Sooner or later the destroyer would have to turn. Suddenly the enemy's helm was put hard over; she swung violently to starboard. Wellman fired a torpedo at a range of 400 yards and sped away at full speed; the usual practice after mounting an attack. Watching over their stern they saw a flash, followed immediately by a rising cloud of thick, black smoke; then the sound of an explosion. Wellman slowed and turned. All enemy firing had ceased; the destroyer's position was now marked by a dull red glow, seen through a cloud of dense smoke. The glow died; the smoke drifted away; the sea was empty.

Meanwhile, hundreds of feet above them, Erskine gazed down at the sea, watching the criss-cross tracks of vessels etched on the water, clearly visible in the moonlight. He saw a flash, warm orange in colour, indicating an explosion; one of the white tracks ended and was seen no more. A few days later Erskine was ordered to report to Vice-Admiral Bacon, who had apparently heard of his flight in the seaplane. He went prepared for trouble, expecting to be disciplined for unauthorised flying. But there came no word of criticism, or any comment on his unusual off-duty activities. He was required purely as a witness. The admiral had received Wellman's report on the destroyer sinking and didn't believe it. Erskine was able to assure him of its accuracy.

On 2 May there took place a larger sea-battle involving the Dunkirk CMBs. Following a report of an enemy destroyer patrolling off Ostend, four boats were sent out to attack her. Unfortunately, the report was inaccurate; there was not one German destroyer but four. And the Germans found them before they found the Germans. The hunters quickly became the hunted. In an attempt to confuse the enemy, the boats scattered in all directions, like a covey of partridges, relying on their speed, manoeuvrability and small size to keep them out of trouble.

Choosing *CMB 7* as their main target, the destroyers set off in hot pursuit, firing machine-guns and driving her out to sea. By the time the destroyers had been shaken off, there were two bullet-holes in her carburettor, three in the induction pipe, one in the water-jacket of the engine and two in the steering compass. Amazingly her crew remained completely unharmed. Other boats also had their troubles. The skipper of *CMB 2* had been wounded, effectively putting his boat out of action. The engine of *CMB 10* was misfiring badly, giving her insufficient speed to catch the enemy. As for *CMB 13*, her steering-gear had been damaged, causing her to circle out of control. Twice she circled through the middle of the group of destroyers, while they fired at her from both sides. In retaliation her skipper launched a torpedo at an enemy ship; but it was too close and the torpedo passed beneath it. Luckily, by the end of her second circle the boat was sufficiently distant from the enemy to enable the crew to stop her engine and to become lost to view in the wide expanse of sea. Eventually all of the boats made it back to port, but disaster had been avoided only narrowly.

On 21 April 1917, it was officially announced that Lieutenant Commander Erskine Childers had been awarded the Distinguished Service Order in recognition of his services with the RNAS; specifically for his activities in the Mediterranean. The citation said, 'he acted as observer in many important air reconnaissances, showing remarkable aptitude for observing and for collating the results of his observing'. During the first six months of 1917, Erskine played his part in thirty-nine operations directed against the enemy-occupied Belgian coast. Virtually all of them were a complete waste of time. Only very rarely did he even catch sight of a German ship; when he did it seemed never to come within range of his boat's meagre armament. Under North Sea conditions CMBs were almost completely ineffectual. Again and again Erskine applied for transfer to flying duties. Always his attempts failed. Admiral Bacon had little faith in the new-fangled aircraft and was not prepared to waste a first-class seaman on them.

Escape from an activity that he considered pointless came on 27 July, when Erskine was called to the Admiralty. He met Sir Graham Greene and the Fifth Sea Lord, Commodore Payne, who told him that they intended to send him to Dublin as assistant secretary to a convention on the future of Ireland. His pay would remain that of a Lieutenant Commander, but he could wear civilian dress if he wished. He was of course delighted. Not only was it a new opening, but also a chance to do something useful for Ireland. Immediately upon leaving the Admiralty he hurried home to tell Molly the exciting news. That same day he caught the night boat for Ireland, full of optimism. Molly, he hoped, would follow him over, but she had responsibilities of her own; she could not desert the Belgian refugees who depended so much on her.

In that summer of 1917 Britain's new Prime Minister, David Lloyd George, faced problems wherever he looked. The introduction of convoys was in the process of solving the U-boat menace, but that was not yet apparent and remained a major worry until the end of the war. The army in Flanders was about to mount a new offensive, destined to go down in history as Passchendaele, an operation as appalling and as ineffectual as any of its predecessors. And, to add to his worries, Russia had collapsed into revolutionary chaos, releasing vast German resources to strengthen their position in the west.

The one source of encouragement for the beleaguered government was the entry into the war of the United States. But even that would take time to produce concrete results on the battlefield. Meanwhile his new ally was only adding to Lloyd George's workload by pressing him to do something about Ireland. The Prime Minister responded with the technique long favoured by British governments under pressure and playing for time: he set up an enquiry. He gave it an impressive title, calling it the Irish Convention. Naturally the last thing the government wanted from the Convention was a quick result. They therefore proposed that it should be composed of 101 members representing every conceivable shade of opinion. The chances of such a body agreeing on anything, least of all the future of Ireland, were not so much remote as non-existent. But meanwhile it kept the Americans from bothering Lloyd George.

Of the 101 delegates invited, ninety-five accepted. Of these fifty-two were Nationalist followers of Redmond, twenty-four were Ulster Unionists and nine Southern Unionists. Although Sinn Fein had been invited to take part, they refused to attend, sending only one observer, and even he officially unofficial, in the person of Edward MacLysaght. Trinity College, Dublin, was chosen as a suitable venue, with Sir Horace Plunkett as chairman. As for Erskine himself, according to Basil Williams: 'Childers himself was hardly a force for conciliation by this time, for he was already so fully convinced that anything less than a completely united Ireland with full self-government was the minimum that would be of any use in bringing peace.' In the absence of Molly, he stayed at the Harcourt Terrace home of Diarmid Coffey, the young lawyer who had been a member of O'Brien's crew on *Kelpie* during the Howth gun-running. Coffey, who was also serving on the secretarial staff, expressed his doubts to Erskine about the chances of the Convention becoming a success. Without the involvement of Sinn Fein, he considered them remote. The Sinn Fein observer, MacLysaght, soon became a regular visitor to Harcourt Terrace. Molly, who met him during her occasional visits to Dublin, took an instant dislike to him. Knowing her husband as well as she did, she could not but be concerned at the growing influence of this charming man, who could make the most extreme of policies sound reasonable.

Early in 1918 came the news that Gordon Shephard had been killed while taking off on a routine flight from an airfield in northern France. Molly was the first to hear and immediately wrote to his mother: 'I can't find words to tell you what this will mean to Erskine and myself. If Gordon had been our own son or brother, I don't think the blow could have struck closer.'[4] The next day, Erskine also wrote, in much the same vein:

> I have just heard of Gordon's death from Molly, and am full of sorrow for ourselves and deep sympathy for you and his father. We had thought of him as not in special danger now, but he was always as brave as a lion and loved to challenge all difficulties and to take any risk that presented itself in the course of duty, and often out of pure love of achievement of something difficult and worth doing. He is one of my heroes and always will be so. Molly and I loved him. We saw great things and lovable things in him from the very first, and the friendship has grown closer all the time.[5]

Erskine's home leave in February 1918 found his marriage under stress. For the first time he and Molly had a serious disagreement about their future together. In common with many married couples in wartime, the combination of dramatic events and long separation had caused them to move in opposite directions; to see things differently. Erskine told his wife that, when the war was over, he intended to live permanently in Ireland and to commit himself completely to the Nationalist cause. This intention arose, of course, partly from his own character, a continuation of his political drift to the left that had begun during the Boer War, and partly through the influences of Robert Barton and Edward Lysaght.

Molly had other ideas. She had come to England with the usual Boston suspicions and prejudices. No doubt she had found life in England difficult at first, having to penetrate the reserve of the English, a reserve so easily mistaken for coldness. But she had now lived in London for twelve years and she felt at home there. Most of all she had lived in England throughout the war; she had seen the English at their best, when they had their backs to the wall. She had shared their hardships, the food shortages, the bombings, the apparently endless bad news and, most of all, the continuing lists of dead and maimed young men. And they had taken it with a stoicism that she could not help but admire. She had also spent the war helping Belgian refugees, and had heard their stories of German occupation; heart-rending tales of brutalities to women and children that seemed to her inhuman, almost unbelievable. It would not be surprising if she had concluded that worse things could happen to a country than to be ruled by the British. She still supported Home Rule, but saw no reason why it could not be achieved peacefully.

There were also more simple, personal reasons for wanting to stay in London. She had always lived in cities. She liked the bustle and the convenience, and the ready access to theatres and concerts. Above all, she was a woman: she liked to have lots of people around her, friends and acquaintances to meet and talk to, a normal social life. To Erskine such things did not matter, but to her they did; for her rural Ireland was fine for holidays, but not to live in. And what of the children? They were without question English. What was to become of them? At the end of Erskine's leave, they parted sadly, with their disagreements unresolved.

Meanwhile, at the Convention, from time to time some signs of progress did appear. The moderate Nationalists and Southern Unionists edged closer together, encouraged by some gentle nudging from Lloyd

George. But always the Ulster Unionists resolutely refused to give an inch. This, coupled with the absence of Sinn Fein, prevented any real possibility of success. On 5 April the Convention ended, with a 176 page report, written by Erskine, but without any agreement. Erskine, disappointed and influenced both by MacLysaght and by Robert Barton, with whom he had spent Christmas and who was now a dedicated Sinn Fein supporter, continued his long drift towards a violent solution for Ireland:

> The collapse of the whole Convention, and the attempt to enforce conscription, convinced me that Home Rule was dead, and that a revolution, founded on the rising of 1916, was inevitable and necessary, and I only waited till the end of the war, when I had faithfully fulfilled my contract with the British, to join the movement myself.

With the ending of the Convention, Erskine returned to London to find himself transformed from a Lieutenant Commander in the Royal Navy into a Major in the Royal Air Force. On 1 April the Royal Flying Corps had merged with the Royal Naval Air Service; he had been part of the merger. Having begun his service in the Artillery, he now had all three services in his record. He had every reason to be pleased; perhaps they would allow him to return to flying. Molly too heard good news that April, news that she found both thrilling and unexpected. She received a letter from Buckingham Palace informing her of the King's wish to award her the MBE, 'for outstanding services to the Belgian refugees'. The award, and even more her obvious delight in receiving it, led to an exchange of letters with Robert Barton that was far from friendly.

Erskine resumed his intelligence work, now for the RAF, by being posted to the old RNAS base at Felixstowe. He was almost back to where he had begun the war on HMS *Engadine*, at Harwich, just the other side of the estuary. Invariably, when Erskine took over a new post, he reported finding it a complete shambles. Felixstowe was no different. Presumably this means that it was not organised to his own meticulous standards. He often struck his fellow workers as being unnecessarily fussy and precise. Curiously, they also found him untidy, with papers scattered everywhere.

Erskine set about organising his new office with all his customary thoroughness, but he didn't want an office; he wanted to fly. When he heard that his old boss from the Dardanelles campaign, Sir Frederick Sykes, had been appointed Chief of the Air Staff, he saw a possible opportunity and wrote to him. He extended his congratulations and tactfully offered his services.

In due course Sykes sent for him with the offer of a job. But once again Erskine was destined for disappointment; the job did not involve flying. Instead, he was asked to write the history of the Royal Air Force. Regretfully he turned the offer down. He didn't want to write. What he longed for was proper war work. Preferably with a strong element of danger in it.

He had to wait for another six months before a chance came to escape from his desk. And it didn't come from Sykes. Instead it came from Trenchard, who at this time was busy creating what he called an 'Independent Air Force', a curious and misleading name for an entirely new concept of aerial warfare. Until now aircraft had been used solely as a tactical weapon, in support of military or naval activities. Now they were to be used strategically and independently, as a separate fighting arm. For the first time aircraft were to be employed in strategic attacks, night and day, against enemy industries and communications. As part of the rapid expansion of this new force, in September 1918 Erskine was posted to Bircham Newton, not far from King's Lynn, in Norfolk. Everything about Bircham Newton was new: a new type of base, for a new type of aircraft, for a new type of operation. When Erskine arrived it was to find a vast empty field, surrounded by scores of empty, often only half-built huts. But before anything effective could be done, Erskine needed to consult Trenchard, to discover precisely what the great man required him to do. A colleague at the Air Ministry, a Colonel Davidson, suggested that he fly to Trenchard's HQ, at Autigny, near Nancy, in a Handley Page bomber which was being ferried out to join one of Trenchard's squadrons. Erskine did not need asking twice. He flew out on 19 September:

> Paris looked gorgeous from the air. We flew over the eastern suburbs, the Sacré Coeur a great landmark with its fine facade high up at Montmartre while, of course, the Eiffel Tower could be seen long before any sign of the city was visible.[6]

Erskine spent four days at the Autigny HQ, where he met Tenchard for the first time, having three interviews with him. He struck Erskine as being 'a bluff man, unintellectual I should think, but with great driving power and energy'. A man very much to Erskine's liking; a man who knew what he wanted and expected to get it.

> He did not anticipate our starting operations till November at the earliest, possibly January. Otherwise he appeared to me unduly optimistic, talking lightly of Berlin and seeming to think the machines will rise to 17,000 feet with bombs.[7]

During their discussions, Erskine learned that at Bircham Newton he was to be in charge of Intelligence. His operational area was designated as being all of Germany north of Latitude 52 degrees. South of that line would continue to be handled by Trenchard's own staff at Autigny. Communications between the two offices were to be direct, not via the Air Ministry. Relations between Trenchard and the Air Ministry were often strained as they wrestled to control his ambitions and he struggled to be free of their bureaucratic ways. As for priorities, the first target areas designated were Berlin, Hamburg and that perennial favourite, Borkum.

Visiting Trenchard's airfields in northern France, watching the heavy bombers taking off on raids into Germany, Erskine longed to go with them; his need for danger was now stronger than ever. He approached Trenchard, arguing that he could perform better as an Intelligence Officer if he had operational experience. But Trenchard would have none of it; Erskine was strictly forbidden to fly over hostile territory. On the homeward journey, using more conventional transport, he paused for a few days in Paris. He had some shopping to do. First, he went to Bon Marché for Molly. She wanted various items that were difficult to obtain in wartime London, including safety-pins. He then went to the French Army cartographic department 'to get an invaluable French catalogue of maps'.

Once back in Norfolk, he concentrated his efforts into making 27 Group, as his charge was now officially called, fully operational. Much needed to be done, even before the aircraft arrived. Not that he considered there to be any real hurry; in his view the war looked likely to drag on for at least another year. They might as well take their time and do the job properly. On 18 October he had a meeting with

Lord Weir at the Air Ministry, where he was informed that the first of the new aircraft would shortly be delivered to Norfolk. He was also told that the ministry wished to celebrate the plane's arrival by mounting the first ever bombing raid on Berlin. Erskine was instructed to prepare the necessary maps. A few days later, the two pilots intended to take part in the operation, Majors Darley and Digby, arrived at Bircham Newton. They spent the morning studying maps.

But all this planning had been done without Trenchard even being consulted. When he heard about the proposed operation he immediately ordered its postponement. As Erskine wrote in his diary, 'we are to wait for the next moon which means about the middle of November and do the thing in a thorough and well-prepared way, after proper tests of the machines'. He approved of the delay, as it gave him more time to produce the maps without which the pilots would never even find Berlin, let alone bomb it. Erskine, like Trenchard, always preferred to do things properly.

When the first two of the new Handley-Page aircraft arrived in Norfolk, Erskine wasted little time in getting up on a practice flight. They were huge four-engines bombers, the first in the world and the only ones the RAF were to have before the Lancaster arrived in the Second World War. Erskine, however, was not impressed. As usual his mind was on his job. He thought the navigational facilities were 'very bad. No room to handle maps in the front observer's cockpit and practically none in the seat next to the pilot, an amazing thing in a machine with fourteen hours' endurance, after four years of war'. A week or so later, he learned more of the way the intended raid was to be carried out. He was greatly shocked:

> The question of crossing Holland in raids on Germany has been raised and, to my great regret, Colonel Mulock [the station commander] and of course the pilots, were strongly in favour of it. I hoped Trenchard would turn it down, but not so. The answer was a smile. It is utterly unsportsmanlike and immoral.[8]

There cannot have been many people left in England after four years of war, after the endless slaughter of the trenches, the use of poison gas and of U-boat attacks on defenceless shipping, who still believed that war could be conducted in a sportsmanlike manner. But Erskine apparently did. Although how he squared that belief with a bombing raid on the civil population of Berlin is far from clear. He also had another reason for being unhappy. After Trenchard's refusal to allow him to fly on operations from France, he had thought that in Norfolk it would be different. That, as in the Mediterranean and at Dieppe, he would be able to ignore orders and fly unofficially. But now came a clear directive from Trenchard himself: all staff officers, including Erskine, were strictly forbidden to fly operationally. 'This is very disappointing, as in joining the Group I intended to take up active service. I had put in an urgent claim to be allowed to go on the special flight, feeling I had a right as Intelligence Officer.' [9]

Orders for the Berlin raid to go ahead came at last on 10 November. The attack was scheduled for that same night. At midday Erskine gave the crews their final briefing. Only a short time later, however, despite a favourable weather report, the attack was postponed for twenty-four hours. The reason for delay is not known, but it proved fortunate, because, despite the encouraging weather forecast, that night brought strong winds and pouring rain. The following day, 11 November, preparations once more began for the long-planned raid. Orders were issued for the aircraft to take off that afternoon. It was not to be: 'At eleven o'clock we were called to fire stations and addressed by the Colonel, who said that the war was over and the armistice signed. There was a great cheer.' [10] Although the war was over, the Air Ministry still had one final task for Erskine to perform. They asked him to lead a team of experts to inspect bomb damage in Belgium. Waiting in London for the rest of the team to be assembled, he was able to view the capital's celebration of the peace, but with a jaundiced eye:

Mafficking in London each day since the 10th – a rather sordid business; hoards of flappers and young sailors rioting vacuously. Bonfires in Trafalgar Square. No sign of national dignity. [11]

11

Sinn Fein

The First World War, like most wars, saw a swing towards more radical politics throughout Europe. Almost all governments, eager to encourage national fervour, made promises of a better world to come once the war had been won. The promises were usually vague but inspiring, 'a land fit for heroes', for instance. Now people expected those promises to be met and quickly became impatient when they were not. Amongst the Irish Nationalists and their sympathisers, the constant claim from the British government that the war was being fought to preserve the rights of smaller nations was taken seriously. And it was thought to include Ireland and to point towards their own independence. Similarly, President Wilson's constant reference to 'the right of self-determination' was thought, not unnaturally, to include the Irish.

Within Ireland itself, the same swing towards radicalism became evident in the 1918 election when Sinn Fein, a party with little popular support before the war, now won seventy-three of the 103 seats contested. The old Irish Parliamentary Party virtually disappeared overnight, their number of seats falling from eighty to a mere eight. Only in Ulster was the pattern totally and dangerously different. Sinn Fein reacted to their spectacular success by immediately declaring a republic, by refusing to take up their seats at Westminster, and by setting up their own administration in Dublin. Eamon De Valera was declared President. They also levied taxes and established their own republican courts, which quickly left the official, British-controlled courts, silent and empty. The British government reacted with more than constitutional propriety by immediately releasing from prison those Sinn Fein members who had been elected to the new Parliament.

The pre-war Home Rule Bill, originally set to become law in 1914, had, with the approval of all parties, including the Irish Parliamentary Party, been suspended for the duration of the war. Now, with the end of the war, there seemed to be no reason why Ireland too should not have a peaceful future. But there were difficulties. For one thing, Lloyd George, the only man in the British government with either the imagination or the political skill necessary to carry through such a measure, was busy in Paris. Once more Ireland had a low priority in British minds. The end of the war presented the victors with countless problems to resolve, not least the question of what to do about Germany.

Also on the agenda was the division into their constituent parts of the Austro-Hungarian and Turkish Empires. The fact that, in the case of Austria-Hungary, those constituent parts frequently overlapped and conflicted with one another did not make the task any easier. As for the former Turkish possessions, the problem there was a question of dividing the spoils amongst the victors rather than satisfying the wishes of the inhabitants. Compared with these map-drawing games the future of Ireland appeared almost trivial, and as something that could wait. It was left neglected and festering.

But not everyone in Ireland wanted peace anyway. The old Irish Volunteers were now tightly controlled by hard-line extremists led by Michael Collins and Cathal Brugha. While the rest of Europe revelled in the unaccustomed peace, Armistice Day was celebrated in Dublin by violent attacks on off-duty soldiers. Collins himself described the consequences with particular callousness, a callousness that did not augur well for the future of Ireland:

> As a result of the various encounters there were 125 cases of wounded soldiers ... Before morning three soldiers and one officer had ceased to need any attention and one other died the following day. A policeman too was in a very precarious condition up to a few days ago when I ceased to take any further interest in him.[1]

In January 1919 the Irish Volunteers were renamed the Irish Republican Army. Already the seeds of future disaster had been sown; Ireland now had a republican government and a republican army, but the army owed no allegiance to the government, or indeed to anyone. And the reason for that perilous arrangement was simple enough; it came from personal jealousies and mutual distrust, elements that would be the curse of Ireland for years to come. Collins was commander of the army and a minister in the government, but far from being in a position of

strength he straddled the two organisations uncomfortably, with powerful enemies in both camps. For the moment both sides needed his
abilities, and would find survival difficult without him. But neither
trusted him and both plotted against him, their dislike founded on
precisely those qualities of intelligence and personal charm that made
him so popular with less ambitious men.

Without bothering to consult either the new republican government,
or their new President, Collins launched his army into war against
Britain. The nature of that war was the cold-blooded murder of policemen, both on and off duty. The fact that the policemen were Irish,
frequently Roman Catholic, and doing no more than normal day to day
police work, was not considered important. They had ceased to be men,
becoming instead 'symbols of oppression'.

Erskine Childers, meanwhile, had problems of his own to cope with. In
March 1919 he returned home from his survey work in Belgium a
physical and mental wreck. Few men who went through the whole of
that war to end all wars the way that Erskine did returned home
undamaged by the experience. His nature was one that relied more on
willpower and mental energy than physical strength to see him through.
After four years of war both were at a very low ebb. As if that was not
enough, like millions of others, he became a victim of the influenza
epidemic that swept an exhausted continent, an epidemic that claimed
even more lives than the war itself. For almost a month he lay in a
hospital bed, hovering precariously between life and death. That he
survived at all was a tribute to his indomitable will.

But the illness only added to the damage done during the years of
war. The Erskine Childers who soon committed himself once more to
the cause of Ireland was a new Erskine, an Erskine who had lost the
most attractive elements of his character. His sense of humour, his good
nature, his courtesy, his sense of proportion, all were effectively gone
or distorted beyond recovery. At the same time, those other elements
of the Childers character, the tendency towards obsession, the intoler-
ance of other people's point of view, the sheer pigheadedness that
prevented him from changing a course once set, all were now dominant.
Above all, he developed an addiction to danger that amounted almost
to a death-wish. Together they led him inevitably to destruction.

When Erskine returned from hospital to a relieved, but still greatly concerned Molly, his doctors ordered rest and quiet, preferably in the country. At night his terrible bouts of coughing caused his wife to fear the tuberculosis that had killed both his parents. Only very slowly did he edge back from the brink. Early in March, when he appeared fit enough to withstand the journey, she sent him off to Glendalough, hoping that the clear Wicklow air would bring him back to health. She herself remained behind in London, partly because both their sons were now at school in England, but also because, despite the peace, there was still work to be done for the Belgian refugees. Molly, like her husband, could not leave a job unfinished. But, just as they had always done when separated, they wrote to one another every day.

In the peaceful surroundings of his old home, Erskine slowly recovered his strength. From time to time, when he felt up to it, he worked on the long-overdue report to the Air Ministry on bomb damage in Belgium. But his favourite pastime during that period was gardening; the activities of weeding and digging not only helped his physical recovery but also had a calming effect upon his mind. But even at Glendalough the disturbed state of the country outside broke in upon his quiet solitude. Robert Barton was arrested in Dublin, leaving Erskine with the responsibility of running the house. And Molly suspected that he would not be content for very long with doing only that. Any lingering hopes she had of living a well-earned peaceful life in London were shattered by a letter from her husband in which he declared ominously, 'I have been growing more and more to dislike compromise'. She would have been even more concerned had she seen his letter to Alfred Ollivant in which he wrote: 'No one dies for Home Rule. Freedom is the thing men die for, and it is not a thing that can be disguised under phrases or whittled by imagination.'[2]

A few weeks later, Robert Barton, out of prison but on the run, introduced Erskine to Michael Collins, who, taking an instant liking to him, in turn introduced him to de Valera. To both men Erskine made clear his burning desire to involve himself in the activities of Sinn Fein. He considered that he had a great deal to offer the movement; but both men were understandably cautious and non-committal. At the end of April, considering himself well again, he returned home to Chelsea. The report for the Air Ministry at last completed, he used his experiences in Belgium to write occasional pieces for magazines and newspapers. It was almost like old times. There was for instance his description of the U-boat pens at Bruges:

> The charm for us was partly due perhaps to the silence and solitude of the scene – the stupendous fabric of concrete stretching out echelon after echelon into a deserted basin, its vistas of graceful columns dimly recalling the submerged ruins of the temples and palaces of Luxor or the mythical stories, immortalised by Turner's brush, of the building of Dido's Carthage.[3]

At the end of May, he was delighted to receive a letter from Sinn Fein, inviting him for urgent talks in Dublin. Barely able to contain his excitement, he caught the first train to Holyhead, and so to Ireland. But his reception, and the offer subsequently made to him, left him bewildered and disappointed. As so often in his life, his hopes were dashed by other people's caution. Upon arrival at Sinn Fein's headquarters he was met by Collins, then interviewed, it might almost be said interrogated, by a series of Nationalist leaders, including Arthur Griffith, whom he now met for the first time. Erskine's character, in particular his transparent sincerity and honesty, usually ensured that people quickly took a liking to him. But Griffith, more than anyone in Sinn Fein, viewed him with deep suspicion almost from the start. The basic trouble was that, to Griffith, Erskine's whole bearing and accent cried out that he was English. Seen through Griffith's eyes, this meant that either Erskine was a British spy, or that he was plotting against his own country out of some personal spite. Either way he was obviously untrustworthy.

It quickly became apparent that, while Sinn Fein were prepared to make use of his talents, it would be only at arm's length and in a non-active capacity. What they wished him to do was to go to Paris as a member of a delegation to plead Ireland's case at the Peace Conference. If envoys from Albania and Lithuania were acceptable, then why not Ireland? It is likely that Erskine knew from the beginning that such an idea was naive and stood no real chance of success. He had spent enough time at Westminster to know how international politics operate. Nevertheless, if he wished to be accepted by Sinn Fein, he could hardly turn down the only chance they offered him.

He therefore went to Paris, where he joined Sean O'Kelly and Gavan Duffy early in July. His natural asceticism came to the fore almost at once, when he discovered the high living being enjoyed by his two new associates. With so many foreign delegations in Paris, all with access to the public purse and anxious to give good impressions of their respective countries, the city's hotels were all packed and expensive. The same could be said for the capital's many restaurants. Erskine tried to reduce the Irish delegation's spending to the minimum. In doing so, he is unlikely to have greatly endeared himself to his new comrades.

For the next month he did everything possible to bring the attention of the world's diplomats to Ireland's cause. He pestered them constantly, but made no impression whatever. And he had little more success with the French press. Inevitably the Irish were turned away unheard. Even the Americans refused to see them. The reasons for that failure are clear enough.

Seen from the British point of view, Lloyd George had no objection to Irish Home Rule, but he could not possibly allow the question to be raised at the Peace Conference. If the Americans were once permitted a say in the future of a part of the British Empire, there was no knowing where it would end. Other colonial powers, such as the French, saw things the same way and for the same reason. As for President Wilson, he had his own diplomatic agenda to worry about. The Americans were, as usual, thinking big. To Washington, the future of the whole world seemed to be at stake. Compared with such grandiose visions, Ireland was no more than a tiny dot on the map. And without the support of the British the United States could not hope to achieve anything. Returning from Paris on 4 August, unsuccessful but not surprised, Erskine took Molly for a holiday in Worthing.

Despite his failure in Paris, Erskine returned to Dublin feeling much happier. Molly had finally given in to his personal ambitions. In spite of all her misgivings, she had agreed to make her home in Ireland. She was not, however, prepared to give him a firm date, her refugee work still continuing unabated. In Molly's absence, Erskine became a guest of Alice Stopford Green at her house in Stephen's Green. When he went to Sinn Fein's headquarters to report on his diplomatic failure in Paris, it was Arthur Griffith who saw him. After hearing him out, Griffith thanked him for his efforts; then suggested that he went back to try again. Erskine promised to consider the idea, but saw no point in doing so and eventually turned the suggestion down.

For Erskine, the rest of that autumn was a depressing time. Everything seemed to be drifting, including his own life. Sinn Fein showed no inclination to employ him in any capacity that he considered worthwhile. Molly still remained in London. And he could not find the house that he wished to provide for her. The murder campaign against the police was inevitably leading to increasing lawlessness in Dublin. Prices were soaring. In the absence of effective civil courts landlords did as they liked. Tenants were evicted without notice, often leading to yet more lawlessness. The kind of house that Erskine wanted, in a pleasant neighbourhood, with a garden and a view of the Wicklow Hills, was becoming far beyond his means. In near despair he rented a furnished house in Wellington Road, hoping to find something better later. The one bright spot in his existence was that Molly promised to be with him by Christmas.

On 4 November 1919, a cabinet report to the British government advised, 'In view of the situation in Ireland itself, of public opinion in Great Britain and still more of public opinion in the Dominions and the USA, they cannot recommend the policy either of repealing or of postponing the Home Rule Act of 1914'. Taking that advice, which in any case agreed with his own inclinations, Lloyd George prepared to reintroduce the Home Rule Act to the House of Commons. Just forty-eight hours before the debate was scheduled to begin, while Erskine and Molly were being shown over their new home, the IRA made an attempt on the life of Viscount French, the Lord Lieutenant. He was completely unharmed, but the attack infuriated the security forces, who pressed strongly for something to be done, and for 'law and order' to be re-established. Until now, the 'war' had been entirely one-sided and low key, except for the unfortunate policemen. But the British authorities in Ireland could not be expected to ignore an attempt to kill the King's representative, especially when he was a war hero. There came a wave of police raids and the arrest of suspects. These were of course promptly denounced as heavy-handed and tyrannous.

The government in London was in a dilemma. The Royal Irish Constabulary was hard-pressed and increasingly demoralised; like most police forces, it was not really suited for dealing with terrorist organisations. At the same time the government was reluctant to commit the army, aware of the propaganda coup that would be for the IRA, especially in the United States. They were also dependent upon advice from their men on the spot, in Dublin Castle. They were led to believe what governments in their position like to believe, that they were dealing with only a handful of extremists without popular support. That had certainly been the position at the beginning, but it was no longer so. Throughout large areas of the country it was the IRA who were now in effective control, if only because they were seen to be more powerful and ruthless than the official government. Executions were commonplace. In some places farmers' sons were shot for refusing to dig trenches. Most people just wanted a quiet life, bowing to the prevailing wind, and by now there was no doubt which way the wind was blowing in Ireland.

For some time London continued to hold back, making use of the army only rarely and reluctantly 'in support of the civil authorities'. But when the situation continued to worsen they were compelled to do something. Torn between leaving it to the police or sending in the army, they dithered, and then came up with a compromise, the kind of compromise that satisfied nobody and led inevitably to disaster. Since the police badly needed the support of large numbers of men familiar with the use of weapons, the government began the recruitment within Britain of former soldiers, a policy that, for the government, had the additional merit of reducing the high level of unemployment. It was intended that the men would operate as police auxiliaries. Unfortunately many of those who volunteered were totally unsuited for the task. They had not been trained for police work, lacked discipline and had little but contempt for the people of Ireland; a contempt that they were not slow to exhibit. Within Ireland they quickly became known as Black and Tans and were soon deeply despised.

Erskine, anxious to exhibit his Republican credentials to his critics within Sinn Fein, became a judge in the Republican Court for County Wicklow. He also became a director, unpaid, of the recreated Land Bank, which had Robert Barton as its President. By now, although still refused the active part that he so earnestly desired, he was becoming more and more involved in the movement's important propaganda work. With his literary skill, journalistic contacts and well-known name, he soon began to show his worth. Between March and May 1920 he wrote eight articles for the *Daily News*; articles of immense propaganda value. Much of Erskine's skill at this task was that he never invented anything; if he wrote that such and such an event had happened, it had happened. But what he did do was to exaggerate, and of course his account of events was very selective, indeed totally one-sided. The result was that Sinn Fein propaganda became so effective and so widely spread that today it is almost impossible for biographer or historian to separate it from the truth, or to discover what really did happen in Ireland at that time.

One of Erskine's articles for the *Daily News*, published in April 1920, gave a brilliantly effective picture of a 'night raid' conducted by the security forces. It did not, of course, mention the nightly murders carried out by the IRA:

> Take a typical night in Dublin. As the citizens go to bed, the barracks spring to life. Lorries, tanks and armoured searchlight-cars muster in fleets, lists of 'objectives' are distributed and, when the midnight curfew order has emptied the streets – pitch dark streets – the weird cavalcades issue forth to the attack. Think of raiding a private house at dead of night, in a tank whose weird rumble and roar can be heard miles away. The procedure of the raid is in keeping, though the objectives are held for the most part by women and terrified children. A thunder of knocks; no time to dress (even for a woman alone) or the door will crash in. On opening, in charge the soldiers – literally charge – with fixed bayonets and in full war kit. No warrant shown on entering, no apology on leaving, if as in nine case out of ten suspicions prove to be groundless and the raid a mistake. In many recent instances even women occupants have been locked up under guard while their own property is ransacked. Imagine the moral effect of such a procedure on the young officers and men told off for this duty.[4]

Erskine knew his market, the readers of the English liberal press. He was always, in his articles for them, careful not to criticise the ordinary British soldier. Rather he expressed concern for them, especially for their 'moral welfare'. He pictured them as decent men being forced by a wicked government to perform disreputable acts. A picture, of course, all too close to the truth. He ended the last of his *Daily News* articles with a warning:

> I send with this one word of warning to the English readers of the *Daily News*. This Irish war, small as it may seem now, will if it is persisted in, corrupt and eventually ruin, not only your army, but your nation and your Empire itself. What right has England to torment and demoralise Ireland?

It is a shameful course, and the more shameful in that she professes to have fought five years for the liberty of oppressed nations. But her oppression of the Irish nation will react disastrously upon herself. The reaction has begun.[5]

Such articles were designed for British and international distribution. Within Ireland itself a completely different product was required. In the form of the mimeographed sheets of the *Irish Bulletin*, this set a very different tone, with no pretence of balance. In the *Bulletin* every Sinn Fein operation was a success, and always inflicted heavy casualties upon the enemy, receiving very few themselves. And they never, ever, retreated, or were driven back; always they withdrew successfully.

The May diary of Cork no. 3 Brigade shows that the enemy in that area are so afraid to stir out that it is difficult for our troops to get in touch with them at all. Most of the operations in that area consist in entering towns to search for enemy stragglers and attempt to draw the enemy out of barracks.
  These operations resulted in a loss to the enemy of one soldier and one RIC man killed and four Black and Tans wounded, one of whom has since died. The detailed reports gives a striking picture of enemy timidity and demoralisation in that area, the usual practice of the Black and Tans to run for barracks when they meet our troops.[6]

He also provided Sinn Fein with another useful service, his home in Wellington Road frequently providing shelter for men on the run. One such man was Robert Brennen, who had the opportunity to observe his host at his insouciant best. Learning that Brennen had been sleeping badly, Erskine recommended a hot bath before retiring for the night. Brennen took up the offer and was just getting out of the bath when there came a loud knocking on the door. Given the nature of the times, Erskine peeped through the curtains and was not surprised to see an army lorry parked outside. He called through the bathroom door:

'There's a lorry outside. Do you think they're after you?'
'More likely they're after you', replied Brennen.
'I don't think so', said Erskine. 'Would you think of slipping on some clothes and getting out through the back?'
'If they're after me, I'm sure they'll have the back covered'.

There came renewed hammering on the door. Erskine walked calmly downstairs to open it, saying to a maid, who had come into the hall:

'It's all right, Mary, I'll open the door.' More knocking, louder than ever. Erskine opened the door.

> 'What's the meaning of this?', he asked, in his English public-school accent.
> 'Who are you?', came the reply.
> 'I'm Major Erskine Childers, who are you?'
> 'Can you tell us where we will find no. 8 Victoria Road?'
> 'I'm sorry, I can't.'
> 'You mean you won't.'
> 'I said I'm sorry, I can't. Would you mind giving me your name and regiment. I intend making a complaint to the Commander in Chief about your conduct.' [7]

The soldier muttered something incomprehensible, backed away and shortly afterwards the lorry drove off. Erskine was often derided within the IRA for his accent, but it clearly had its uses.[8]

In June, at 12 Bushey Park Road, he finally found the house that he had been searching for. It offered the space required for him, for Molly, for the two boys when on holiday from school, and also for Molly's mother. She, recently widowed, had come to live with them. Having his mother-in-law living with them was not always an entirely happy arrangement. Quite apart from the traditional difficulties of the relationship, Molly's mother was strongly pro-British, continually referring to 'IRA murderers' and 'those poor policemen'. This at the same time that Erskine was passionately arguing that country policemen were instruments of oppression, whereas armed gangs who shot anyone who dared to disagree with them represented liberty. As for Molly herself, once settled in Ireland she was soon competing with her husband for the most extreme of positions.

Throughout 1920, for the British, the situation in Ireland went from bad to worse. On the night of 21 November, the IRA broke into houses in Dublin and shot eleven British officers in their beds, many in front of their wives. Even Erskine wrote 'poor devils' in his diary. The following afternoon, in reprisal, Black and Tans opened fire at a football match in Dublin, leaving twelve dead and many injured. And that was only the worst of a continuous wave of atrocities from both sides.

In December 1920 the Home Rule Bill finally received royal assent. In Belfast the new Northern Ireland regime quietly took over the province. But throughout the rest of Ireland the violence went on worse than ever. Collins had unleashed his army without specific war aims, other than the old dream of a united Ireland. The fact that such an objective was now impossible to achieve, and certainly not within the power of the British government to deliver, was ignored. By now the war was little more than pure insanity; just violence for violence's sake. The Irish continued to fight the British, determined to drive from Irish soil people who had already agreed to go, while the British continued to resist being forced to give up land they no longer wanted and couldn't wait to leave. Nevertheless, it took another six months of brutality and secret diplomacy to produce a ceasefire and the possibility of a negotiated peace.

Near the end of February 1921, Desmond Fitzgerald, the Minister of Propaganda, was arrested and imprisoned. Erskine was appointed to replace him, a decision that did not please everyone. Arthur Griffith in particular held that, while it was perfectly admissible to make use of 'a disgruntled Englishman' during their struggle, giving him an official position was another matter altogether and exceedingly dangerous. And not everyone was impressed by Erskine's ability either. At the same time that he was promoted, Piaras Beaslai was made Director of Publicity. The two men were expected to work closely together. It proved to be difficult, for they had little in common. As Beaslai later wrote:

> All information with regard to the IRA or military matters passed to him through my hands. This brought me into close daily association with him and gave me a good opportunity of observing his character and abilities. In view of Collins' high opinion of his capacity, I was amazed at the impression of fussy, feverish, futility he conveyed to me. He displayed the mind, outlook and ability of a capable British civil servant, but no adequate appreciation of the situation with which he was dealing. I formed the opinion, reluctantly, that he carried weight as an outsider, with an English-made reputation, which he could not have carried on his merits, had he been an Irishman in the movement for years and finding his own level.

Certainly the accusation that Erskine had little appreciation of the situation with which he was dealing had a great deal of truth in it. He was in charge of propaganda and was extremely good at disseminating it, especially through the British and American press. But he was also to some extent a victim of it himself. While he was very concerned to tell the world the truth of what was happening in Ireland, he was reliant entirely on the IRA and Sinn Fein for his information. And they would have been very curious organisations indeed if they always told him the truth and had never held anything back.

Early in February 1921, Mrs Lindsay, an elderly Protestant, was taken from her home by the IRA and shot for being an informer. Erskine knew that the IRA had seized her, but was not informed of her fate. They were aware that he could be curiously squeamish about the killing of women. Three months later, another woman, Kitty Carrol, was similarly shot for ignoring an IRA directive about distilling whiskey. Erskine sent a memo to Collins asking him for advice: 'Shall we say (a) that the execution of women is forbidden and that Kitty Carrol was not killed by the IRA or (b) that Kitty Carrol was killed in contravention of orders by the IRA and that (c) Mrs Lindsay is now in prison for giving information to the enemy?'[9] Collins chose not to answer. Only gradually, and some time later, did Erskine learn what really happened to the two women.

In April the British authorities allowed new elections to take place. Why and what they expected to happen is something of a mystery. In fact 128 candidates were returned unopposed. Apart from four representatives from Trinity College, all were Sinn Fein. Given the lawless state of Ireland at the time, only an idiot would have stood against them. Erskine was elected as Member for Wicklow West. On the day Parliament was due to meet, only the Trinity College Members turned up. Since they failed to provide a quorum they promptly went home again. That was the beginning and end of the Parliament.

On the evening of 9 May, Erskine was working at his home, with his assistant Frank Gallaher, when there came a great hammering on the front door. That it was being made by one of the security forces was self-evident; the only question was which one? This was a question of more than academic interest, since it could decide how well or how badly they would behave. A list of names, the only genuinely secret document in the house, was given to Molly, to hide about her person. A few moments later auxiliaries crowded into the room, which they began to search, looking for incriminating evidence. Molly remained, stretched out on her couch, mocking them as they ransacked her husband's desk. Erskine had been working on papers relating to the Land Bank. These were immediately confiscated and the two men arrested:

We were both taken to the Castle. From there Frank was sent to Wellington Barracks. I was put in an underground cell but, to my immense astonishment was called for in an hour, taken to an officer's sitting-room and given a cup of tea. After a long wait in another room, Arthur Cope (the Under Secretary) came and told me I was to be released. I insisted that Frank Gallaher must be released too and this he agreed to and sent officers to get him out. The disgust of the officers at the whole business was amusing, but Cope was adamant. When the Colonel eventually reported that Frank had been released, I left the Castle myself, Cope effusive in his manner and actually carrying my valise out of the gate for me.[10]

This sequence of events, especially the carrying of his case by Arthur Cope, was to acquire an immense significance for those in Ireland always on the lookout for conspiracies. For them the implications were, and in some cases still are, obvious. Childers was a British agent. In fact the answer to the strange behaviour of the authorities was simple enough. At the very time that Erskine was being arrested, secret talks were being held in an attempt to end the conflict. They were at a delicate stage. The last thing the British wanted was to give Sinn Fein an excuse to break off negotiations. Hence the two men were released. A truce was announced that same night.

By this time Erskine's opinions were more extreme than most members of Sinn Fein. He was strongly opposed to any talks with the British that did not promise complete independence for the whole of Ireland under a Dublin government. That such a demand bore no resemblance to reality, being far beyond the ability of the British government to deliver, he resolutely refused to believe. It has been argued that Erskine deliberately adopted an extreme position because, with his Anglo-Irish origins, to be accepted by Sinn Fein he had to be more Irish than the Irish. But that is to completely ignore everything that went before. The fact is that Erskine Childers went to extremes with everything he did. He went to extremes as a yachtsman. He went to extremes as a writer. He went to extremes as a soldier. With him it was moderation that was impossible to maintain.

On 12 July De Valera set off for talks in London with Lloyd George. He took with him his Vice-President, Arthur Griffith, Austin Stack, Robert Barton and Erskine Childers. It must have been at this time that Basil Williams met Erskine for the last time. Basil, one of the few old friends that Erskine still had left, was living a peaceful life with his wife and family, clear of political involvement. He was shocked and saddened by what he saw:

> Erskine was persuaded to come and dine quietly with us one evening. He was a very changed Erskine from the one we had known. Physically he looked almost a wreck; thin and deadly pale and with quite white hair. His mind was as alert and bright as ever, but it seemed a hectic brightness, with almost all his old sense of humour and proportion vanished, at least when he spoke of Ireland.
>
> I say almost, for when we got him for a few odd moments to talk of the old loved things, or of joys we had shared in former days, then the old Erskine seemed to flash out with that dear smile of his. But it was not for long, for he could not keep off Ireland for many minutes, and when he spoke of her, he would accept no compromise and could not for a moment see that the substance, for example, of Dominion status might mean all and perhaps more than all that the name of republic would give. And when it came to means of achieving his end, he had become almost ferocious and pitiless.[11]

Erskine's visit to London with an Irish delegation also enabled Tom Jones, a senior British civil servant, to meet him for the first time. He wrote his impressions to Bonar Law: 'Barton I found a reasonable man – educated at Oxford, landowner, Protestant, joined up in the war, and lost two brothers in it. Erskine Childers I thought to be on the edge of a breakdown and very overwrought and "logical".' [12]

De Valera and Lloyd George had four meetings together. The two men did not take to one another; they had nothing in common. Lloyd George was always the practical politician, looking for solutions and not too bothered about abstract principles. He was also quickly bored by long tirades about Oliver Cromwell. De Valera he found impossible to pin down. As he commented after one of their meetings: 'It's like sitting on a merry-go-round and trying to catch up with the swing in front.' De Valera habitually distrusted everyone and hated to say what he really thought about anything. He found Lloyd George completely lacking in principle and much too clever. From then on he avoided meeting Lloyd George, just as, some years later, he always refused to meet Churchill. He simply could not bear the fact that there were men cleverer or more popular than he was. Which was, of course, the reason he disliked Collins so much and why he took the first opportunity to destroy him.

The talks ended with the Irish taking away British proposals amounting to Dominion status; terms which the Irish could have had several years earlier without fighting at all. The proposals served their purpose very well from Lloyd George's point of view, in that they split the Irish leadership from top to bottom. Some were in favour of acceptance, some against, some preferred not to say. In the end the terms were rejected, but that didn't bother Lloyd George; they had never been intended as more than an opening gambit. For the next two months letters flowed in a steady stream from London to Dublin and back again. There were numerous complications to overcome, not least the Irish claim to be already an independent republic. It was not something that the British could admit before the talks even began. But gradually, bit by bit, Lloyd George chipped away at the Irish conditions. Eventually the Irish offered to attend a conference in London, which they would attend 'without prejudice'. Lloyd George promptly pounced on the offer; it was what he had wanted all along.

The conference began on 11 October at 10 Downing Street. From the beginning the British had distinct advantages. For one thing, they were playing at home, with the entire Imperial Civil Service at their beck and call. The talks were taking place in impressive and historic surroundings. Everywhere were paintings of famous British statesmen of the past – Cecil, Pitt, Palmerston, Gladstone. And pictures of battles won – the Spanish Armada, Blenheim, Waterloo. The Irish would have been less than human if they had not been impressed; perhaps even a little overawed. But the British also had more tangible reasons for being confident. The team they were putting up was a formidable one: Lloyd George, Churchill, Austen Chamberlain and Lord Birkenhead. And, above all, they had the advantage that came of being united, of knowing precisely what they wanted and of how they could achieve it.

The Irish had none of these assets. They were in no sense a team, but a collection of individuals, suspicious and distrustful of one another. This sorry state of affairs did not come about by accident but by careful design. Their President, De Valera, had not come himself but had remained in Ireland, watching from a distance, safe from criticism, positioned either to take the credit or deny responsibility, whichever way the cards fell.

The delegates who did go were Collins, Griffith, Barton, Duffy and

Duggan, with Erskine Childers as secretary. Of those, Collins and Griffith were the only ones with genuine political talent. But their approaches to the negotiations were very different. Collins wanted an agreement, but was determined to squeeze every possible concession out of the British in obtaining it. Griffith was even more anxious for a settlement. But his negotiating position was weakened by his hatred of bloodshed and his willingness to concede almost anything to avoid it. As to the other delegates, Eamon Duggan, 'a sober, resolute man' according to Churchill, was a solicitor from humble origins, and probably the delegate most in touch with ordinary members of the Republican movement. A moderate, Gavan Duffy was also a lawyer, but from a privileged background. He had a much more rigid, legalistic mind, not unlike Erskine; indeed the two men often conspired together in attempts to block agreements that failed to satisfy their hard-line position. As for Barton, he was, according to Lloyd George, 'a pipsqueak of a man, who I would not make a private secretary to an under-secretary'. An opinion that was by no means confined to Lloyd George.

As for Erskine himself, he was not originally intended to go at all, and for a very good reason. His position on independence was now so extreme and uncompromising that, short of a total British surrender, it was unlikely that he would accept any offer made, however generous. De Valera, however, for reasons of his own, chose Erskine as secretary to the delegation. Even this proposal was met with strong opposition from other members of the government. There was a determined attempt to squeeze him out by ruling that only Irish speakers should be included, but De Valera was insistent. So Erskine went, but isolated and distrusted by his colleagues.

Lloyd George and Michael Collins took to one another almost immediately. They were both born politicians, concerned solely with practicalities and believers in the art of the possible. Each recognised the other as 'a man I can do business with'. If it had been entirely up to them the conference would have reached a successful conclusion much more quickly than it in fact did. But it was not up to them; any agreement they reached had to be sold to others, especially to men sitting well away from the conference room, only waiting for the opportunity to criticise and condemn. Lloyd George had to convince the House of Commons, which could be difficult but was not potentially fatal. Collins on the other hand was playing for much higher stakes. He could not for one moment forget that, if he got it wrong, he would pay with his life.

Amongst the advisers to the British delegation was the ubiquitous Eddie Marsh. It is from him that we learn of Erskine's state of mind at the beginning of that crucial conference:

> I had a painful moment when I first saw Erskine Childers sitting at the council table. We had been great friends at Trinity and later, and I knew him for one of the sweetest natures in the world; but now, when our eyes met, in his there was no recognition.[13]

Even sadder is the fact that Erskine's snub of Marsh was not accidental. It was not caused by forgetfulness, or through having his mind on other things, but was deliberate and premeditated. It was completely out of character for the Erskine Childers of old. There can be no clearer illustration of his deteriorating mental state; of the extent to which his mind was now entirely controlled by a single obsession.

The first two weeks of negotiations saw the two sides feeling each other out, discovering where agreement was possible and where the major sticking points were likely to be. They were also getting to know each other as individuals, in some cases learning mutual respect, in others mutual antipathy. The British were not slow to discover the fault lines that lay within the Irish delegation. They were equally quick to spot their most determined adversary. On 26 October, their members agreed that copies of the next set of British proposals should be shown 'in advance' to Griffith and Collins, so that agreement could be secured before they got into the hands of Childers.

For already Erskine was beginning to irritate not just the British but the Irish as well. The rigidity of his mind, together with the unrelenting obsessional manner in which he did his drafting work, was becoming intolerable to Collins and Griffith alike. Collins, as usual, managed to hide his irritation behind his natural affability. But Griffith, a man already feeling the pressure of the task upon which he was engaged, found it difficult to disguise his contempt. There was also another reason for their distrust of Erskine; the suspicion that he was secretly sending reports back to De Valera. He seems to hae been fated always to be suspected of spying for someone. Whether in this case there were any grounds for suspicion there is no way of knowing. It is certainly possible. Not that he would have regarded it as spying. To his legalistic mind De Valera was President of the Republic and therefore his boss. He seems never to have understood the complex underlying cross-currents of Irish politics.

A curious feature of the treaty negotiations is that those points which might be thought the most important, and therefore the most difficult to resolve, in fact gave little real trouble. Defence facilities, especially the use of Irish ports by British warships in time of war, were conceded by the Irish without much argument. The intractable problem of Ulster, while the cause of early difficulties, was dealt with by a Lloyd George fudge. The real problems arose from disputes over issues that were entirely symbolic. There was the question of allegiance to the Crown, of an oath to the King, and therefore to the very existence of a republic. Although symbolic, these were issues that aroused deep passions in Ireland, passions so strong that they were to be eventually responsible, directly or indirectly, for the deaths of three members of the Irish negotiating team.

As the weeks passed, the negotiations slowly progressed, with each side submitting proposals to the other; who, in turn considered them and then submitted their own counter-proposals. While the constant drafting and redrafting of the proposals was taking place, relationships within the Irish delegation became ever more strained. Barton and Duffy, primed by Erskine, continually adopted hard-line positions, intended to block the more conciliatory plans of Griffith and Duggan. Only the quiet but determined efforts of Collins, who invariably supported Griffith, prevented a major rupture from occurring.

On the all important question of sovereignty, the British pressed the case for Dominion status, always endeavouring to calm Irish doubts by pointing to the example of Canada. Erskine, who had once been a strong supporter of precisely that solution, but was now violently against it, produced a memorandum devised to strengthen Irish opposition. He argued that, while it was perfectly true that Britain did not interfere in Canadian affairs, Canada was a long way from Britain and therefore there was little opportunity to interfere. Ireland, on the other hand, was on England's doorstep. The temptations for British governments to meddle in Irish domestic affairs would be ever-present. For a while this remained a major stumbling-block, much to Erskine's satisfaction. Until the British suddenly offered to allow the Irish 'to insert into the Treaty any phrase they liked which would ensure that the position of the Crown in Ireland should be no more in practice than it was in Canada or in any other Dominion'. The Childers obstacle was overcome. By the end of November the British produced their 'final draft' of the treaty. Over the next few days minor amendments were accepted and incorporated in the documents which were handed to Griffith early on the morning of Friday 2 December. Within a few hours he was on his way to Dublin. Erskine, together with Collins and Duffy, followed on the night train from Euston.

It proved an eventful and tiring journey. Erskine was working until half-past two in the morning, at which time he took to his bunk for a few hours sleep. He was awoken an hour later when the ship collided with a schooner. Only four members of the sailing-ship's crew were picked up by the mail-boat which returned with them to Holyhead. It was a quarter past ten before the Irish delegation finally landed at Kingstown, in no real state to face a cabinet meeting that began less than an hour later, and which lasted for seven contentious hours.

Questioned by hard-line members of the government, by Cathal Brugha, Stack and by De Valera himself, the delegation immediately split down the middle. Griffith pressed for acceptance, arguing that the terms offered were the best that they could hope to get. Barton strongly disagreed, claiming that a better offer could be obtained and that the terms should be rejected. Duffy supported him. He believed that the British were bluffing; that everything the Irish wanted could be obtained; it was only necessary that they held firm. Duggan, predictably, gave his support to Griffith. Collins was unusually quiet, probably conscious of the hostility of Cathal Brugha and Stack, his rivals for power within the army. Nevertheless, he agreed with Griffith that the terms should be accepted. Erskine, when asked for his opinion, was of course opposed to accepting, describing the terms as humiliating. The only effect of the meeting was to further accentuate the deep divisions within the government and the delegation. A situation not helped by delphic utterances from De Valera which could be, and were, interpreted differently by the two sides. When the time came to return to London, Collins and Griffith travelled on one boat, Barton, Duffy and Childers on another.

And what was the ostensible cause of all this disagreement? It was the precise wording of the Oath of Allegiance; something that could easily have been dropped once the British were gone. It should surely have been obvious to everyone that, once it had been withdrawn from Ireland, it would be politically almost impossible to send the British Army back again. Certainly not because of an Oath of Allegiance. But then the real cause of the conflict had little to do with the terms of the treaty. The problem was one of distrust and petty jealousy. The closer Collins came to success, the more De Valera and Cathal Brugha disliked him. They feared him as an Irish Caesar.

The final stages of the negotiations saw Lloyd George performing every political stunt in the book. There was the 'breakdown of the talks' act, which saw the whole British delegation suddenly collect up their papers and leave the room, perhaps never to return. There was the 'two envelope trick', one of which meant peace, the other war. Which was he to send? And there were theatrical cries of horror at the possibility of Irish 'breach of faith'. But, gradually, clause by clause, by one means or another, the genius of Lloyd George produced a treaty document.

And always, in the wings, performing the part of evil genius, lurked Erskine Childers; forever trying to manipulate the Irish delegates into uncompromising positions, but becoming more and more isolated, ignored and distrusted by representatives of both sides. His relationship with Griffith, who by now was clearly almost as overwrought as Erskine himself, was now worse than ever.

> AG insolent to me about altering drafts. Attacks me about *Riddle of the Sands*. Says I caused the European War and now I want to cause another. I said I stood on the strategic case in both instances … I protested and virtually threatened resignation. He climbed down.[14]

Almost the last act of the drama occurred as the Irish delegation argued whether or not to sign the finished treaty. Collins, Griffith and Duggan pressed for acceptance. Barton and Duffy, propped up by Erskine, held out against signing. Collins, losing patience, asked Barton, 'How many young men do you want slaughtered in another war?' Duggan, close to tears, declared, 'Barton, you will be hanged from a lamp-post in Dublin if your refusal to sign causes a new war in Ireland'. Ironically, it was Erskine who finally swung the argument, but not in the way he intended. In urging Barton not to sign, he added, 'I feel Molly is with us'. Now Molly had long had a low opinion of Barton and of his influence over her husband. And she had never made any secret of it. The two had barely been on speaking terms for years. The idea that Molly had any say in the matter was enough to drive Barton in the opposite direction. He gave in and signed. Duffy, now completely isolated, had no choice but to surrender. In his account of the official signing ceremony, Lloyd George wrote:

> Outside in the lobby, sat a man who had used all the resources of an ingenious and well-trained mind, backed by a tenacious will, to wreck every endeavour to reach agreement – Mr Erskine Childers. A man whose slight figure, whose kindly, refined, and intellectual countenance, whose calm and courteous demeanour offered no clue to the fierce passions which raged inside him.
>
> At every crucial point in the negotiations he played a sinister part. He was clearly De Valera's emissary, and faithfully did he fulfill the trust in him by that visionary. Every draft that emanated from his pen – and all the first drafts were written by him – challenged every fundamental position to which the British delegates were irrevocably committed. He was one of those men who by temperament are incapable of compromise. Brave and resolute he undoubtedly was, but, unhappily for himself, he was also rigid and fanatical.
>
> When we walked out of the room where we had sat for hours together, worn with toil and anxious labour, but all happy that our great task of reconciliation had been achieved, we met Mr Erskine Childers outside, sullen with disappointment and compressed wrath at what he conceived to be the surrender of principles he had fought for.[15]

After Birkenhead had put his own signature to the document, he turned to Collins, commenting, 'I may have signed my political death warrant tonight'. To which Collins quietly replied, 'I may have signed my actual death warrant'. Both men were right.

12

Civil War

News of the signing of the Anglo-Irish Treaty received immediate world-wide acclaim, producing a flood of congratulations to both London and Dublin. The ordinary people of Ireland and England alike quietly rejoiced that the killings were over at last. For the Irish especially it seemed an opportunity for a new beginning, a chance for a quiet life without fear of guns or midnight knocks on the door. But inevitably there were men who did not welcome peace, who did not look forward to returning to their previous dull existence on the farm or going back to being a nonentity in a Dublin slum. They had had a taste of power, the power to frighten other, socially superior men; and they had had, and used, a licence to kill and maim as they thought fit. Such men did not relish becoming, what they had been before, nothing. Nevertheless, wise politicians could have ensured that such men did become reasonably law-abiding citizens. Unfortunately wisdom was in short supply and those who had it were not listened to.

Eamon Duggan was the first member of the Irish delegation to arrive back in Dublin. He it was who reported to De Valera. He found the President in a ferocious rage over the treaty, even though he had not yet seen it, or been informed of its contents. But that, of course, was the reason for his anger; it was not his treaty. When Duggan gave him a copy, suggesting that he read it, De Valera threw it to one side, remarking, 'Why should I read it?' Why indeed. The contents were unimportant. He had already decided to reject it, regardless of its terms or the consequences of his action.

The following morning he called a cabinet meeting, which he opened by announcing his intention of forcing the resignation of Collins, Griffith and Barton, all of whom were absent, not yet having returned from England. Other members were more cautious, suggesting that the three men should be given the chance to offer their own explanations before any drastic decisions were made. Fearing himself outvoted, De Valera grudgingly gave way. He insisted, however, upon issuing a press release which hinted at his personal rejection of the treaty. This was the first indication, to a contented people, that the peace they were celebrating might yet be dashed from their hands.

When a full cabinet meeting was held, De Valera attacked the delegates for accepting the British terms; for throwing everything away without even trying. He declared that had he been there it would have been very different, that he would have held out, would have obtained the Republic, would have achieved all their objectives. Barton had the temerity to point out that De Valera had been given every opportunity to go to London and had always refused, adding that his instructions to them had been confused and contradictory.

De Valera asked whether they had signed under duress. Collins replied that in negotiations between a small nation and a great empire there were limits to what the small nation could hope to achieve. Only in that sense were they intimidated. At the end of the discussion the treaty was narrowly approved. De Valera immediately issued a statement to the press repudiating it:

> The terms of this agreement are in violent conflict with the wishes of the majority of this nation as expressed in successive elections during the past three years. I feel it my duty to inform you immediately that I cannot recommend the acceptance of this treaty ... In this attitude I am supported by Ministers of Home Affairs and Defence.[1]

The following day, De Valera met Erskine Childers, Gavan Duffy and Robert Barton, the three delegates who continued to oppose the treaty. Barton having argued that he had signed under duress, De Valera told them he intended following a policy designed to attract the extremists in the party rather than the moderates. Erskine was amazed, but delighted. He was, after all, an extremist himself. He said that he considered De Valera to be 'certain of winning', with a policy that would be 'productive of real peace'. From then on it is impossible to say whether Erskine was a bad influence on De Valera, or De Valera a bad influence on Erskine. Probably it worked both ways, each of them encouraging the other to adopt an uncompromising position. It is equally difficult to say which of them had less contact with reality. The next day Griffith issued a statement of his own: 'I believe that this treaty will lay the foundations of peace and friendship between the two nations. What I have signed I will stand by, in the belief that the end of the conflict of centuries is at hand.' The same day fifteen Irish bishops gave their own influential support to the treaty.

The Irish Parliament began to debate the treaty on 14 December; a debate which continued, apart from the Christmas break, until 7 January. The two sides of the argument were basically simple. Those for the treaty argued that half a loaf was better than none, and that they could always ask for more later. While those against the treaty claimed that any kind of compromise was a betrayal. They advocated a war against the British until they achieved everything they desired, however long it took and regardless of the cost in human lives. When Griffith faced the assembly, he made no apologies for his part in the negotiations. He was proud of their achievements:

> We have brought back the flag; we have brought back the evacuation of Ireland after 700 years by British troops and the formation of an Irish army. I signed the treaty not as an ideal thing, but fully believing, as I believe now, it is a treaty honourable to Ireland, and safeguards the vital interests of Ireland.[2]

De Valera, as was his custom, posed as a moderate while advocating extremism: 'I am against this treaty, not because I am a man of war, but a man of peace. I am against this treaty because it will not end centuries of conflict between the two nations.' It was Collins who put the case for the treaty at its clearest: 'In my opinion it gives us freedom, not the ultimate freedom that all nations desire and develop to, but the freedom to achieve it.' To those like Erskine, who argued that under the terms of the treaty Britain still held effective control over Irish affairs, he gave a military answer. He said that the only hold that Britain had over Ireland was the presence of their army: 'I maintain that the disappearance of that military strength gives us the chief proof that our national liberties are established.' As for the treaty's recognition of partition, he once more relied on cold logic:

> What was the use of talking big phrases about not agreeing to the partition of our country. Surely we recognise that the North-East corner does exist,

and surely our intention was that we should take such steps as would lead to mutual understanding.[3]

Yet, at the very time he was talking about mutual understanding, Collins was organising acts of terrorism against the Ulster Protestants; acts which inevitably led to reprisal attacks upon Catholics, hardening opinions and making unification even more unlikely. It was not only De Valera who never let his right hand know what his left hand was doing. When Erskine's time came to speak, he did so in the apocalyptic terms that were now becoming usual with him: 'This treaty is a step backward, and I, for my part, would be inclined to say he would be a bold man who would dare set a boundary to the backward march of a nation which of its own free will had deliberately relinquished its own independence.' Griffith summed up the debate in a mood of hope and reconciliation that reflected the feelings of the vast majority of the people outside the chamber: 'It does not forever bind us not to ask for more. England is going beyond where she is at present ... and in the meantime we can move on in comfort and peace to the ultimate goal.'

At the end of the debate the treaty was ratified, if only narrowly, by sixty-four votes to fifty-seven. The treaty had now been approved by both government and Parliament. Under normal democratic procedure that should have settled the matter and have given Ireland the peace it longed for and deserved. But De Valera was not a normal democrat. Immediately after the result was announced he declared his intention of resigning the presidency. From another man, that might have been an honourable act, the admission of defeat; the handing over of power to someone with opinions more acceptable to the assembly. But not from De Valera. From him it was a refusal to admit defeat; a declaration of political war. Collins appealed to his defeated opponent to assist in maintaining order in a country rapidly being torn into warring factions. His appeal was ignored.

Three days later De Valera's resignation led to another debate on the treaty. All the same arguments were repeated, but with increased bitterness. Erskine played a prominent part, making few friends and many enemies in the process. He repeatedly clashed with Griffith:

Griffith: 'I will not reply to any Englishman in this Dail.'
Childers: 'My nationality is a matter for myself and for the constituents who

sent me here.'

'Your constituents did not know what your nationality was.'

'They have known me since my boyhood days.'

'I will not reply to any damned Englishman in this assembly.' [4]

At another stage of the debate Griffith resumed his attack by charging Erskine of having 'spent his life in the English Secret Service'. During his own speech, which showed that same fault of long-windedness that had irritated his friends at the Magpie and Stump so many years before, Erskine tried to warn the assembly:

> Don't you see every act and deed of the Irish Parliament is going to be jealously watched from over the water and that every act of legislation done by Ireland will be read in the light of that inflexible condition that Ireland is virtually a protectorate of England, for under this treaty she is nothing more.[5]

Considering the number of years he had been employed in the House of Commons, Erskine seems to have been remarkably ignorant of British political realities. The British electorate was sick and tired of Ireland; they couldn't wait to have their troops withdrawn and would punish severely any government who attempted to send them back again. And most British politicians heartily agreed with them. But it was not necessary for anyone in England to answer Erskine's warnings and demands. Kevin O'Higgins, who by now disliked him even more than Griffith, replied in scathing words:

> We would all desire better terms and what we have to decide is whether we are going to take our chances of securing them if we reject these. Deputy Childers has taken a lot of unnecessary time and trouble in explaining how much nicer it would be to get better terms than these. He did not tell us, as an authority on military and naval matters, how we are going to break the British Army and Navy and get these better terms.[6]

Voting at the end of the debate was even closer than it had been before. Sixty votes to fifty-eight. De Valera and his supporters marched out in protest. Griffith was elected President in his place. Outside the chamber the country drifted towards civil war. Men began to clean their revolvers and check their ammunition. Collins himself had taught them how to deal with political opponents – with a bullet in the back. Now they were prepared to put his lessons into practice.

With the treaty ratified by both governments, British soldiers began to withdraw. As they left, their barracks were occupied by Irish troops, sometimes by units supporting the treaty, sometimes by those who opposed it. Minor skirmishes took place between the two sides. While the politicians argued and dithered, putting their egos before their country, the army was splitting apart, taking up key positions, seizing arms and ammunition for their own use. As one of the British troopships was sailing from Dublin, a group of Irishmen watched the ship depart. One of them called out: 'Goodbye and good riddance. Now we can fight our own battles in peace.' At the time it no doubt raised a laugh. But given the situation the British were leaving behind, it was ominous for the future. A trail of promises that could not be kept; and mutual cries of treachery; angry men and confused organisations like the IRA. All were taking the new country towards disaster. Ireland had achieved a revolution, now it was to pay the price; the revolution would devour its young. Erskine made his contribution to the gathering storm by once more taking up his pen for propaganda purposes. On 9 April, Collins declared, with a mixture of shame and indignation: 'Our country is now in a more lawless and chaotic state than it was during the Black and Tan regime. Could there be a more staggering blow to our national pride and our fair national hopes.'

As if taking Collins's complaint as a challenge, five days later Republican forces, led by Cathal Brugha, seized control of the Four Courts, Ireland's judicial centre. It had more than symbolic significance; the rule of law had been overthrown. They turned the building into a military headquarters. De Valera, that man of peace, responded by throwing petrol on to the flames: 'Young men and young women of Ireland, the goal is at last in sight. Steady all together; forward. Ireland is yours for the taking. Take it.'

The implications were obvious enough. The movement towards civil war continued, steadily gaining momentum day by day. Outbreaks of firing between the two sections of the army occurred with increasing frequency. Collins struggled to hold the country together. In May, in an attempt to find common ground, he arranged talks between army officers of both sides. The talks failed. On 22 May an American journalist, Elizabeth Lazenby, met Erskine for the first time. He was not what she had expected:

The photographs I have seen of Erskine Childers have little prepared me for the shock which runs over me as I turn towards him. Thin almost to emaciation, he looks ill, and unhappy to the point of death. I can only liken his face to a mask, to which the eyes alone give life. Restless they show him, and haunted, as if he is driven by an inner soul-consuming fire. However courteous, he is aloof, and seems hardly aware of what is taking place about him. One emotion only lightens the intensity of his eyes – his very real devotion to his wife.[7]

Collins, refusing to be provoked by the seizure of the Four Courts, approached De Valera, offering an alliance. De Valera, belatedly realising the nature of the forces that he had unleashed, was not unsympathetic. Between them they thrashed out a deal: they would reopen talks with the British and hold new elections. Whether he planned it that way or not, events went Collins's way. Talks with the British were soon aborted; so far as London was concerned a treaty had been agreed and ratified. They had no intention of going beyond it.

But Collins got his elections, which were held on 22 June. At last the ordinary people of Ireland were given the chance to express their own opinions on the treaty. The result was clear-cut. Pro-treaty candidates were returned with a large majority. In the constituency of Kildare and Wicklow, Erskine Childers lost his seat, placed bottom of the poll, no doubt to Griffith's delight. The other side of St George's Channel the result was seen with satisfaction. The *Times* commented, 'Erskine Childers who, as many think, is the chief brain of the Republican movement, has been defeated in his constituency'.

That same day, in London, two members of the IRA shot and killed Field Marshal Sir Henry Wilson on his doorstep in Eaton Square. They then fled, pursued by unarmed policemen and ordinary members of the public. Despite repeatedly firing at their pursuers, both men were soon caught, one after having been struck on the head by a milk-bottle thrown by an angry Londoner. The motive for the murder was obvious. The IRA wished to draw Britain back into the Irish shambles. An action that, they thought, would unite all Irishmen against the invaders and lead to the destruction of the treaty. As usual, they completely mis-understood the mood of the British people and government. If the popular view in Ireland was, 'Now we can fight our own battles in peace', the English response was the equally dismissive, 'Let them stew in their own juice'. Official British pressure upon the new government in Ireland did, however, become intense. Lloyd George urged Collins to act: 'You call yourselves a Government, who do you govern? You have handed over the government of Ireland to an Englishman, to Erskine Childers.'

On 28 June, Free State artillery, using field guns borrowed from the British Army, began a bombardment of the Four Courts. The attack continued without pause for eight days, by which time the buildings were engulfed in flames. Cathal Brugha died in the ruins. Meanwhile civil war erupted all over the country. The day that the sound of 18-pounder guns first began to rattle windows throughout Dublin, Erskine left his home to take up a post as staff captain with the Southern Brigade of the IRA. Once again he was soon disappointed; his wish for action was denied and his extensive knowledge of military strategy ignored. Instead he was ordered to produce a weekly edition of *War News*, the Republican propaganda organ, for distribution in Cork and Kerry.

Producing *War News* was a difficult and largely thankless job. The brigade was continually on the move, dodging army columns, while Erskine tagged along behind with his portable printing press and other essential equipment. Paper was in short supply, distribution of the finished product erratic. The days of acting virtually as a special correspondent of influential British and American newspapers was gone. As for content, it varied little beyond the constant demand for a united Ireland and the rejection of the Dominion status he had once pressed for so strongly. Of military successes there was little to report beyond the occasional acts of pointless sabotage, burned houses and blown-up bridges. Fierce fighting took place throughout July as rebel forces were slowly pushed back westward. By the end of the month the only parts of the country still in rebel hands were Cork and Kerry.

August saw the deaths of the only men in the government who were both moderate and influential. On 12 August Griffith, seeing everything that he had dreaded and fought against coming to pass, had a heart attack and died. Ten days later Collins was shot and killed in a skirmish in County Cork. The Irish government, now dominated by O'Higgins and Cosgrave, increasingly portrayed Erskine as the instigator of the war and leader of the rebel forces. The habit of blaming the English for every evil in the world was deeply ingrained in the Irish mind. It was, in any case, a useful propaganda tool and the easiest way of discrediting their opponents. His skilled hand was seen behind every incident; he blew up a bridge in one place and the very next day conducted an ambush in another place miles away. In this way he acquired a reputation of De Wet proportions. Amongst the wanted men on the government's list, none was more wanted than Erskine Childers. O'Higgins, in a speech after the death of Collins, said:

> I do know that the able Erskine Childers, who is leading those who are opposed to this government, has his eye quite definitely on one objective, and that is the complete breakdown of the economic and social fabric, so that this thing that is trying so hard to become an Irish nation will go down in chaos, anarchy and futility.

Erskine himself, meanwhile, was continuing quietly to produce his news-sheet in Cork. Frank O'Connor met him at the Victoria Hotel:

> A small, slight, grey-haired man in tweeds, with a tweed cap pulled down over his eyes, wearing a light mackintosh stuffed with papers and carrying another coat over his arm. Apart from his accent, which would have identified him anywhere, there was something peculiarly English about him; something that nowadays reminds me of some old parson or public-school teacher I have known, conscientous to a fault and over-burdened with minor cares. His thin, grey face, shrunk almost to its mould of bone, had a coldness as though life had contracted behind it to its narrowest span, the brows were puckered in a triangle of obsessive thought like pain, and the eyes were clear, pale and tragic.

By the middle of August most of the south west also came under government control. Driven out of Cork, the rebels withdrew into the mountains. By now they no longer constituted an army, being little more than band of outlaws, conducting hit-and-run attacks, brutal murders and acts of sabotage of no military value. By far the largest and most dangerous concentration of rebel forces, numbering five or six hundred men, was centred around two villages, Ballyvourney and Ballymakeera, on the south-west slopes of the Derrynasaggart Mountains. It was here that Erskine spent the summer, engaged in the thankless task of producing his propaganda sheet; his morale not helped by occasional discoveries of bundles of his news-sheets lying undistributed in the corners of disused barns and similar convenient hiding places. He was further depressed when, during one of his sudden moves, dodging army sweeps, he lost part of his printing press in a bog.

One of the few bright spots in his life at this difficult time was the presence amongst the rebels of an old friend, first met during school holidays. This was David Robinson, a former British cavalry officer, tank commander and holder of the Croix de Guerre. Despite all the government propaganda it was Robinson, not Erskine, who was the most active leader of rebel forces in the south west. He was a good friend in more ways than one. In a letter to Molly, he wrote:

> I need hardly say very few of us have either his mania for work, his power of concentration or the capacity to accomplish things. And so we are not always so sympathetic to him as we ought to be since we still retain a liking for food and sleep which apparently don't count with him.

This was more kindness and consideration for Molly than the true situation. The fact was that, apart from Robinson, Erskine was surrounded by young men who knew little about him and cared less. To them he was just an elderly and fussy Englishman whose opinions counted for nothing. And the attitude of their officers was worse. Robinson, aware of government propaganda and concerned at Erskine's fate should he be caught, attempted to arrange for his escape to England. The local rebel commander told him that, should Erskine try to leave, he would be shot. That was the reality of Erskine's position compared with the very different picture seen from outside. To quote the *Times:*

> Erskine Childers was stated officially to have commanded the expedition which set out to cut the Atlantic cables at Valentia. He is also known to have been involved in the destruction of railway bridges and signal boxes. (7 September) [8]

> Erskine Childers is said to be leading the Irregulars in the district of Kenmare. (19 September) [9]

Even normally well-informed Irishmen, like Bernard Shaw, greatly overestimated Erskine's power to control events:

> Mr De Valera and Mr Childers have attempted to subdue the country by armed force and coerce it to become an independent little republic, whether it likes it or not. But, having no war chest and apparently no programme

beyond calling Ireland a Republic, they have been forced to tell their troops on pay day that they must live on their country, which means that the leaders are to be Republicans contending for a principle and their troops are to be brigands. This is an impossible situation.

On 18 September, eight members of the government forces, including a colonel and a captain, were killed by a booby-trapped landmine planted on a bridge near Macroon. In reaction, on the 22nd, the cabinet abdicated responsibility by conferring emergency powers on the National Army. In future captured rebels would be tried by court martial. Severe penalties, including death, could be passed for trivial offences, such as the possession of firearms without proper authority. A few weeks later an official statement was issued declaring: 'If prisoners are taken they must not be released until they are incapable of further harm. If executions are necessary, they must be carried out with no fear of the chimera of popular reaction.'

In late October Erskine, deeply depressed both by the parlous state of the rebel cause and of his own inability to do anything about it, was cheered by a summons from De Valera. With David Robinson as a companion, he set off on 25 October for Dublin, by way of Waterford, Wexford and Wicklow, areas all tightly held by pro-treaty troops. They travelled mostly on foot or by farm cart, sleeping under the stars or in the houses of complete strangers, who might or might not be trustworthy. On 10 November the two men slipped through one of the gaps in the Wicklow Hills to the valley of Avondale. By midnight they had reached the friendly sanctuary of Glendalough. Robert Barton was once more in prison, but had given strict instructions to his staff that if Erskine turned up he was to be hidden in the dark cellar-like space beneath the dining-room floor. But Erskine would have none of it, going instead to his old bedroom on the first floor.

He was soon betrayed. Only a short time later, a detachment of soldiers, smashing their way through the front door with rifle-butts, charged up the stairs. Erskine, who had been writing in his room, met them at the top, holding in his hand the small, pearl-handled revolver given to him by Michael Collins as a keepsake. As the first of the soldiers approached him, Erskine raised his gun. A maid immediately threw herself between him and the soldiers, calling out, 'Don't you dare touch Mr Childers'. Curiously suspicious behaviour. If they didn't know his identity before, they certainly did now. It also prevented him from defending himself. He was quickly overpowered and taken away.

At this time it did not apparently occur to him that his capture in possession of a revolver would rank as a capital offence or that the military court would be bound to find him guilty, whether or not he chose to recognise its legality. But when he was told that he was to be tried by court martial, did he not remember what he himself had written for the *Daily News* about British courts martial procedure only eighteen months before?

> This branch of a soldier's work in Ireland should be, and for all I know, is, intolerably odious to just and honourable men. Soldiers have no business with the law; they are not trained for it; they could not do impartial justice if they would.
>
> I have seen some of these courts martial. They deliver savage sentences for the most trivial offences, while giving no impression of active bias. A kind of listless fatalism. The prisoner, refusing to recognise the court, does not plead or cross-examine. So nobody cross-examines or seeks to elicit the truth. If a nice point of law arises it is expounded by legal officers in Khaki; the case proceeds and ends like the march of destiny.

In London, Erskine's importance as a leading member of the rebels continued to be exaggerated. Once more from the *Times*: 'Erskine Childers is of course a trained soldier, as well as a man of remarkable intelligence, and his loss will be felt very seriously by the Republicans.' Shortly after his capture, it was announced that Erskine was to be tried 'for his life'. In London, Churchill seized the chance to express his own opinion on the man who had been involved in so many of his pet schemes:

> I have seen with satisfaction that the mischief-making murderous renegade, Erskine Childers, has been captured. No man has done more harm or shown more genuine malice, or endevoured to bring a greater curse upon the common people of Ireland, than this strange being, actuated by a deadly and malignant hatred for the land of his birth. Such as he is may all who hate us be.

The Republicans, who had consistently refused to allow Erskine to make any real contribution to the war, and had always viewed him with the deepest suspicion, now saw the opportunity to make propaganda use of his plight. On the day of his trial young women patrolled the streets of Dublin bearing placards declaring that Erskine Childers was to be executed 'by order of the British government'.

On 17 November Erskine, his face marked by signs of a beating given to him after his arrest, was brought before a military tribunal in Portobello Barracks. The proceedings were conducted much as he had described in the *Daily News*, except that there was no question this time of lack of bias. This court had been set up with the specific intention of finding him guilty, and its members could barely wait to do so. Without speaking, he presented the presiding officer with a statement drawn up by his legal adviser:

> He recognises the authority only of the Irish Republican Government. He has been taken prisoner in war. He is an officer of the Irish Republican Army and he claims that if he be detained at all by an enemy whose legality he repudiates, he should receive the treatment of a prisoner of war. His own Government, the Irish Republican Government, has accorded to the troops of the Provisional Government, while not recognising its authority, belligerent rights, and he demands reciprocity on behalf of himself and his fellow prisoners.[10]

Having read his statement, the presiding officer ordered his removal from the court. So ended the accused man's one and only appearance before his judges. All further deliberations were held in secret. Erskine, meanwhile, was taken by armoured car to Beggar's Bush Barracks, which also served as the army headquarters. His new warders, unlike their predecessors, were consistently kind and considerate to him. That same evening, he read in a newspaper that four unnamed IRA prisoners had all been shot for being in possession of weapons. Only then did he realise the seriousness of his position.

That same evening, O'Higgins told Parliament that he thought it better for the first executions to be average cases: 'If we took, as our first case, some man who was outstandingly active and outstandingly wicked in his activities, the unfortunate dupes, throughout the country, might say that he was killed because he was a leader, because he was an Englishman or because he combined with others to commit raids.' That he was referring to Erskine Childers could not have been more obvious. Equally obvious was the verdict and sentence intended for him. Even so, several days passed before the miltary tribunal announced that it had reached a guilty verdict and passed a death sentence upon him.

Erskine's eldest son and namesake was given compassionate leave from his English public school to visit his father. Erskine asked permission to see his son for the last time after his request to see Molly had been turned down. Probably they were aware of the extent to which she was also involved in the Republican cause. They were presumably unaware that the boy had, on numerous occasions, been used by his father to carry messages for the IRA. When father and fifteen-year-old son met in the condemned cell, Erskine asked the boy to promise him two things:

> The first is this. I want you to shake the hands of every Minister in the Provisional Government who's responsible for my death. I forgive them and so must you. The second will apply if you ever go into Irish politics. You must not speak of my execution in public.[11]

It had been Erskine's intention to maintain his refusal to recognise the authority of the court. He was forced to change his mind, not in an attempt to save his own life but with the hope of saving the lives of others. His lawyers told him that eight other men faced the same fate, and for the same reason. They wished to use Erskine as a test case. Despite the establishment of the Irish Free State, some vestiges of British law still remained, at any rate in theory. His lawyers wanted to issue a writ of Habeas Corpus. In the circumstances he reluctantly gave his approval.

At about five o'clock on the afternoon of 20 November, the officer of the guard entered Erskine's cell to inform him that he was to executed at dawn the following morning. The prisoner thanked him and asked for more paper upon which to write. He then began a last letter to Molly:

> Beloved wife, I am told that I am to be shot tomorrow at 7. I am fully prepared. I think it's best so, viewing it from the best standpoint, and perhaps you will agree. To have followed those other brave lads is a great thing for a good cause. I have belief in the beneficial shaping of our destiny – yours and mine – and I believe God means this for the best; for us, Ireland and humanity. So in the midst of anguish at leaving you, and in mortal solicitude for you, beloved of my heart, I triumph and I know you triumph with me. It is such

a simple thing too, a soldier's death, what millions risk and incur, what so many in our cause face and suffer daily. There is this, too, that living I was weighted with a load of prejudice, unjust but so heavy that it may be I was even harming our cause. Dead I shall have a better chance of being understood and of helping the cause. I am, as I sit here, the happiest of men. I have had nineteen years of happiness with you. No man ever could claim so precious a blessing as that.

I die at peace with all men, asking all to forgive me for wrongs I have done, and in my turn bearing ill-will to no one. Personal things merge in something much bigger. I see big forces rending and at the same time moulding our people in affection. I pity and hope without bitterness and I die full of intense love for Ireland. I hope one day my good name will be cleared in England. I felt what Churchill said about my 'hatred' and 'malice' against England. Don't we know it isn't true and what line I ever spoke or wrote justifies that charge. I die loving England and passionately praying that she may change completely and finally towards Ireland.[12]

At this point his writing was interrupted by another visit from the officer of the guard with the news that the execution had been postponed. His solicitor's application for a writ of Habeas Corpus had gone to the Master of the Rolls for his consideration. He had ordered that no sentence passed by the military court should be carried out until he had given his ruling. Counsel for the government argued that Erskine had taken up the position of an Englishman coming into an English colony, while at the same time claiming treatment as a prisoner of war. Three days later the Master of the Rolls washed his hands on the case: Erskine was doomed. Once more he wrote to Molly:

The guard was relieved at eight and the men going off all said 'Goodbye and God bless you' and I to them. They wanted souvenirs but I have very few – the books you sent and some signatures. It will be the same with the present lot in case I am not able to record it; all privately and infinitely considerate. So we 'Children of the Universal Mother' touch hands and go our ways in the very midst of this way of brothers. This is all disjointed but you will not mind. I can only say, thank God I am dying, thank God. I never sought not to, and now I leap to it.

It is 6 a.m. You would be pleased to see how imperturbably normal and tranquil I have been this night and a.m. It all seems perfectly simple and inevitable like lying down after a long day's walk. I enclose a lock of hair. Smile now. It must be washed!

Now I am going. Coming to you, heart's beloved, sweetheart, comrade, wife. I shall fall asleep in your arms, God blessing us – all four of us. Erskine.[13]

As his last request, Erskine asked for the execution to be delayed for a short time so that he could see the sunrise. A request that was granted, if reluctantly.

When the time came to face the firing-squad, he limped out into the prison courtyard, followed by his escort. The soldiers were already lined up, waiting for him. He paused for a moment to speak quietly to the officer in charge, who nodded his compliance. Erskine walked over to the firing-squad and strolled down the line, as if conducting an inspection. He shook hands with each man in turn. Only then did he go to the appointed spot and stand facing the soldiers. The officer approached him with the bandage for his eyes. He tried to refuse. But the officer insisted, by now more concerned for the morale of his men than the fate of the prisoner.

Erskine then spoke his last words:

Take a step or two forwards, lads. It will be easier that way.[14]

He gave a prearranged signal, there was a crash of gunfire and he fell. The firing-squad turned and marched away, some of the men brushing tears from their eyes.

Official. Mr Erskine Childers was tried by a military court at Portobello Barracks, Dublin, on 17 November 1922, and charged with having possession, without proper authority, of an automatic pistol, when apprehended by a party of National Forces on 10 November 1922 at Annamoe House, County Wicklow. The accused was found guilty and sentenced to death. The finding and sentence were duly confirmed and the execution was carried out this morning at seven o'clock.

In the short time available between sentence and execution, a few friends and admirers, from both sides of the Atlantic, did try to save his life. A petition raised in England was signed by, amongst others, Captain Wedgwood Benn, Sir Arthur Marshall, John Masefield, Gilbert Murray, Arthur Ponsonby, Sir John Simon and Josiah Wedgwood. No official attempts were made to help him. To the British he was a traitor; to the Irish a spy. And so he died. A curious end for an honest man.

13

The Tragedy of Erskine Childers

The political reaction to Erskine's execution was very muted. In the House of Commons Keir Hardie asked the Prime Minister whether the government had made any representations to the Irish government on his behalf, and whether they would be making any representations to prevent further executions of 'prisoners of war'. In reply, Bonar Law said that the answer to both questions was 'No'. Other MPs remained silent. In the Irish Parliament reaction was almost as limited, but more lively. Gavan Duffy, a small quiet voice of reason in a country given over to hatred and violence, felt compelled to protest: 'Silence is not possible when an Irish government executes Erskine Childers for possessing a pistol in a dwelling-house without the authority of the Provisional Government, which is his political opponent.' He went on to describe Erskine as 'a great Irishman', who, he said, had been earmarked to be Irish Ambassador in Washington. There had, he declared, been an unscrupulous propaganda campaign to discredit him. Cosgrave's reply was Orwellian; typical of all too many official statements in the twentieth century. The military courts were secret, he said, 'for the purpose of sparing the public pain. The government had no defence to make, because there was no necessity for defence'. Kevin O'Higgins adopted an equally hardline position:

> Ireland is not a stage where neurotic women or megolomaniac men might cut their capers. We will see that any people coming here for adventure from other lands get it if they menace the life of the Irish nation, and if they menace the peace, the prosperity and the fundamental rights of Irish citizens.

Newspaper reactions were much more varied. In England Erskine was often still portrayed as the brilliant leader of a guerrilla army. This was especially the case with the *Daily Mail*:

> There is little doubt that Childers was the man who, during the recent fighting

in the south of Ireland, took an active part in the blowing up of the great railway viaduct across the Blackwater estuary at Mallow. Then it was he who, with a few followers, cut the American cables and when Michael Collins was killed in County Cork he was regarded as so culpable that a band of Free State officers swore to capture him and his chief De Valera and shoot them.

His loss to De Valera is probably immeasurable. It is said that no matter how black the outlook might be Childers never lost heart and was forever improving methods of warfare which came as a surprise to the Sinn Fein command. He was always just gone when the Regulars got there.[1]

The *Evening Standard* adopted a broader view of events, but still gave Erskine an importance that he never had:

> There is a feeling, which we must all have, of being in the presence of an historical event as profound in its significance as the execution of Robespierre. As long as the Government exists its enemies must be punished, but it is melancholy to think how much courage, how much real intellectual ability and what misdirected fervency of devotion went down with this misguided man.[2]

Strangely enough, the *Boston Post* was the only newspaper that actually understood the real weakness of Erskine's position in Ireland:

> The execution of Erskine Childers is a tragic blunder. It may not have its reaction in Ireland, where Childers, doubtless mistakenly, was looked upon with hostility and suspicion even in Republican circles. But, the world over, friends of Ireland will be dismayed that such sternness was invoked. Childers really counted for little in Ireland. He was an alien, full of contempt for democracy. Only two years ago he said that what Ireland really wanted was a king.[3]

It was also Boston that managed to discover an entirely new twist to theories of wicked English plots involving Erskine Childers and Ireland. Ireland itself already had several. There was the government view, that Erskine was an English agent sent over to destroy the new Irish state. There was the latest Republican view, that he had been executed in accordance with instructions from London. There was the Griffith view, that he was a double agent. Now, according to Republican supporters in Boston, it was the British government itself that had put out stories of his being a British spy, as a way of discrediting him. The sheer ingenuity of the British was boundless.

The *New York Times*, in commenting upon the behaviour of the Irish government, inadvertently raised an interesting question: 'A few days earlier it had executed four Irishmen for the same offence with which the Englishman was charged. If even-handed justice was to be measured out, he must meet the same fate as the others.' But let us look at this even-handedness and its implications. It is a curious fact that, until Erskine was arrested, no one had been executed for the possession of arms. On the very day of his trial four men were shot for that very offence. A week after his execution eight more men appeared before military courts charged with possession of arms. One man was acquitted. The other seven were all found guilty. None was shot. Instead they were given prison sentences ranging from eighteen months to five years. The implication is clear enough. Four young men were shot for trivial offences for no other reason than to provide a precedent for the execution of Erskine Childers.

But not every newspaper concerned itself with the intricities of Irish politics. Others preferred to consider Erskine as a man and to speculate upon those aspects of his character that led him to an early death. According to the *Daily Chronicle*:

> His end is tragic, not because he has died but because his talents, his intellect, his character, were such as might have led to a brilliant and honoured end. Through error and strange perversion of talent he was headed straight for his own doom. The Irish rebellion alone is not enough to account for this swift adopting of hatred of England. Was it his marriage with a woman who was herself the prey of fanatical loathing for this country?[4]

The *Daily Mail* said:

> Those of us who knew him will say this; that he was utterly sincere and that if he fought hard, he fought clean. Apart from his politics, he was a charming man, courteous, witty and a man of his word. But he was quite ruthless.[5]

In the eyes of the *Daily News*:

> with a troubled look under a wrinkled brow, he seemed during the last year or two to be wasting away, as if he were being burnt up by some fire within. His face had grown thin and drawn, his hair was prematurely white. He looked like a man who had suffered and not from selfish sufferings. Even when he laughed, the laughter did not drive out the look of suffering.[6]

Some of his friends also had their say, Basil Williams wrote:

We may think him wrong-headed and a fanatic, we may think of him as
'nourished by dreams', to quote a phrase of his own ... but of one thing all
those who knew him are convinced, that there was no particle of meanness
or treachery in his nature; and that whatever course of action he adopted –
however we may deplore the judgement – it was based on the prompting of
a conscience and sense of honour as sensitive and true as one may meet. He
is at rest now, that eager, loving soul, but the love he inspired remains as an
abiding treasure to those who knew him.

H. A. L. Fisher, in turn wrote:

I doubt whether the counsel of friends – and Erskine Childers had many
warm and devoted friends in England – could have saved him, for they
[Erskine and Molly] were impervious to advice and resolved to go their own
perilous way. All through history the miseries of mankind seem to me to
have been chiefly due not to a particularly low standard of behaviour but to
the vein of recklessness in human nature which is the substance of tragedy.
I suspect that element was an essential part of his character, but there may
be something too in an explanation given to me by one of his English friends,
that he was thrown off balance by the nervous strain of aviation in the war.

In the months that followed Erskine's death, the revolution continued
to consume its young. And with a growing appetite. Many of its
principal architects were already dead: Griffith by a heart attack; Collins
by assassination; others by the bullet or the bomb. Throughout the
country old friends gunned one another down without mercy. Erskine
was the fifth rebel prisoner to be executed; that after a court martial
which gave it at least some semblance of legitimacy. From then on
barely a day passed without someone facing a firing squad. In January
1923 alone thirty-four men were officially shot without even the pretence
of a trial.

Not that the government were alone in the killing frenzy; the rebels
were just as active and just as ruthless. There was also a religious element
to some of their activities. When the new Irish state had been established
about ten per cent of the population had been Protestant. Now many
of them were driven out, by guns and by arson, to a life of exile in
England. Men and women who had spent their lives campaigning for
an independent Ireland fled with what they could carry as their

homes were torched around them. Meanwhile, the Ulster Protestants watched and drew their own conclusions as to the desirability of a united Ireland.

The British government, watching with amazement and a certain grim satisfaction, handed over to their Dublin successors thousands of rifles and the two field-guns with which they had wrecked the General Post Office. With more men, better armed and professionally trained, and with public opinion predominately on their side, there was only one possible outcome to the war. Slowly but surely the rebels were driven back and then isolated. In May 1923 De Valera finally brought the blood-letting to a halt by ordering his men to lay down their arms. By then seventy-seven men had been executed and 13,000 imprisoned without trial. The total death toll was never calculated.

In the end, Erskine was proved wrong. The fire eventually burnt itself out, although not before many of the most honest and talented of Irishmen had been either murdered or driven into exile in England. Only a few years later, De Valera himself took the oath to the King, which had been the ostensible cause of the civil war. And despite Erskine's dire warnings, Britain did not continually meddle in Irish domestic affairs.

As Ireland slowly reverted to its normal peaceful self, the Childers family returned to Glendalough, the Bartons' old home in the Wicklow Hills. Molly had now dedicated herself to bringing up her two fatherless sons and to the restoration of her husband's reputation both in Ireland and in England. Glendalough had an important part to play in both of those objectives. Just as Erskine had once gone to school in England, returning home to Ireland during the holidays, his two sons now did the same. Their education was English, first at Gresham's School in Norfolk, then at Cambridge University. But their home, their real home, was to be Ireland. On that Molly was determined. As she saw it, Erskine had died for Ireland. Sooner or later, she believed, the Irish themselves would come to see that.

But if that were to happen, it would take longer than Molly could manage. There were too many old wounds barely healed; too many old scores unsettled. Only the passage of time and the arrival of new generations untainted by past events could bring calm re-evaluation and genuine reconciliation. As to his reputation in England, which caused him much concern during his last hours, he need not have worried. The English have very short historical memories and are not inclined to hold grudges. Within only a few years even Churchill, his anger cooled, felt able to write:

> Another man of distinction, ability and courage fell a victim. Erskine Childers, author of *The Riddle of the Sands*, who had shown daring and ardour against the Germans in the Cuxhaven Raid ... had espoused the Irish cause with even more than Irish irreconcilability. He, too, was shot for rebellion against the Free State.

In the English mind Erskine reverted to being the man who wrote *The Riddle of the Sands*, as patriotic a book as you could wish to read. His involvement with Ireland was not considered important and was rapidly forgotten.

When, shortly before his execution, Erskine spoke to his eldest son, Erskine Hamilton Childers, about him possibly, one day, entering Irish politics, he could not have dreamt what the future held in store for the boy. Young Erskine went first into business. Whilst still in his mid twenties he chose to widen his experience by becoming the European manager for an American travel company. In 1931 he returned to Ireland to become advertising manager of the recently formed *Irish Press*. Later he became Secretary of the Federation of Irish Manufacturers. In 1938 he turned to politics by being elected Fianna Fail Member of Parliament for Athlone-Longford. He soon made himself noticed and in 1944 was appointed Parliamentary Secretary to the Minister for Local Government and Public Health. His inclination was always for liberalisation. In 1951 he had his chance to make a name for himself by being made Minister for Posts and Telegraphs, in which position he was responsible for turning Radio Eirann from a government department into an independent organisation similar to the BBC.

Slowly but steadily he climbed the political ladder: Minister for Lands; Minister for Transport; Deputy Prime Minister. In 1973, so close to the top of Irish politics, his luck seemed to desert him when his party lost the election and he was once more just an ordinary Member of Parliament. But it was no more than a pause before the greatest prize of all came his way. Later that year he was opposition candidate in the presidential election, which he won by 635,867 votes to 587,771. Erskine Childers, President of the Irish Republic: how proud his parents would have been. Only eighteen months later he died of a heart attack. Throughout his long parliamentary career he had kept the promise made to his father never to mention the execution.

One event which would have pleased the elder Erskine occurred in 1961, when his yacht, *Asgard*, once more sailed into the harbour of Howth. This time she had no arms on board and was in no danger of arrest. Instead she was formally handed over to the Irish Republic as a sail-training ship, a function that she continued to perform until 1975, at which date she went into honourable retirement in a Dublin museum.

As for Erskine himself, there still remain some aspects of his life and character that require examination, even if the evidence available is only circumstantial or even non-existent. To deal with the easiest question first, there is the accusation, still believed by some in Ireland, that he was some form of British agent. A suspicion that still denies him credit for the efforts he made on Ireland's behalf. Let us endeavour to finally put that idea to rest. That he was suspected of being a spy is, given the curious conditions that existed in Ireland between 1910 and 1922, perfectly understandable. It is known, from British official documents, that the Ulster Volunteer Force was deeply infiltrated by the British secret service. It is only to be expected that they also had agents or informers within the Irish nationalist movement.

The first doubts as to Erskine's loyalty to the Nationalist cause must naturally have arisen from the fact that he was English. That his mother had been Irish and that he had been brought up in Ireland would not have convinced anyone. Erskine was not only English, he was almost excessively English. His accent was English; his very bearing was English. But the real suspicions arose from that telegram from Admiralty Intelligence in 1914. The leaders of the Irish Volunteers would have been less than human if they had not wondered about the significance of that. The seed once planted was almost bound to grow and flourish, watered by political events and the paranoia they produced.

But was he a British agent? No, of course he was not. For one thing, he was far too honest, on occasions too honest for his own good. If he

had been a little less honest, a little less forthright in his views, he would
not have made so many enemies and would perhaps have lived longer.
Judging by his behaviour during the planning of the gun-running he
seems to have had no concept of secrecy. To tell two serving British
army officers not only that he intended smuggling guns into Ireland,
but also the precise way in which he intended to do it, was an act of
lunacy. He had a concept of honour that made deceit impossible. A
man less suited to be a double agent is difficult to imagine.

If we are to end suspicions once and for all, however, we must look
closer at those events in Ireland which, it is alleged, show Erskine
involved in espionage. It is perfectly possible that there was a British
agent involved in the Howth gun-running. Royal Navy knowledge of
the plot would explain many curious aspects of the voyage; not least
their astonishing inability, after the event, to find a large white yacht in
the narrow confines of the Irish Sea, especially when it anchored, for
all the world to see, in Holyhead harbour. But there would be no need
for Admiralty Intelligence to recruit Erskine for the task. As we have
seen, Gordon Shephard had been working for them for years.

In the autumn and winter of 1914, the new Director of Naval Intelligence, Reginald Hall, conducted an operation against Sinn Fein. A
chartered American yacht, *Sayonara*, roamed the coasts of Ireland.
Manned by a Royal Navy crew, its ostensibly American 'owner' sought
out and befriended Sinn Fein activists. Irish historians have, for some
reason, usually mocked the operation as being foolishly conceived and
a complete failure. But that ignores the fact that the Easter Rising did
not spread much beyond Dublin because the security forces arrested
almost all Sinn Fein leaders in the west and south of the country before
they could make a move. Inevitably, since a yacht was used, an Erskine
Childers involvement has been suspected. But throughout the whole of
the time that the operation was being conceived and carried out he was
busy elsewhere, on HMS *Engadine* in the North Sea.

In March 1916, shortly before the rebellion, Erskine returned to London, according to some accounts to 'take up a post in Admiralty
Intelligence'. That for the next nine months he said very little of his
Admiralty work and wrote nothing about it at all has been seen by some
as a clear indication that he was up to no good; engaged in secret activities
– naturally against Ireland. But the truth is much simpler: he neither

spoke nor wrote about his work at that time because there was nothing in it to interest anyone, not even him. He spent the whole nine months sitting at a desk in the Air Department 'moving pieces of paper about'.

For the rest of the First World War his activities are well documented. Apart from his efforts at the Irish Convention he had no opportunity to indulge in Irish affairs, being kept busy either on or above the North Sea. As for his activities after 1918, any idea that he was working on behalf of the British government is frankly ludicrous. The truth of the matter is that not only did he not 'work all his life for the British Secret Service', he never did work for them, ever.

We must now turn our attention to a much more interesting and difficult question. To the question of Erskine's character; to what an earlier biographer has rightly called, 'The Riddle of Erskine Childers'. But not to the obvious riddle, not to the question of how the man who wrote an English spy classic came to be involved in the IRA. As we have seen, that was simply the culminating point of a long political slide leftwards that lasted most of his life. There are much more fascinating aspects to his character than his politics. Perhaps the most surprising thing about him is not that he died at the comparatively early age of fifty-two, but that he lived so long. It is not difficult to see why other, more level-headed men thought him a crackpot. Few men have sought danger to the extent that Erskine did and fewer still have survived it for so long.

It is not just that he was adventurous; Henry was equally adventurous. But there was an essential difference between the two brothers: Henry sought adventure, Erskine was driven to it. To see that process in action, we need to look no further than the outbreak of the Boer War. When Basil Williams sent Erskine a message advising him of the need to volunteer, he expected his friend to be keen to take part, just as he was himself. But Basil was astonished at the vehemence of Erskine's reaction. He was not just eager to go, he was desperate to go, almost begging his friend to press his case with the HAC. And it is that desperation which surfaces again and again throughout his life. As if the only way that life could be made bearable was a constant flow of adrenalin. One author has commented that during that last year of his life Erskine seemed to be seeking death. But that was nothing new: he was always like that, right back to that long walk in the Irish rain and his negligence in changing his wet clothes. And to that great reluctance of his to take his yacht into the safety of harbour, preferring to ride out storms in the most dangerous of places, anchored against a lee shore, as if daring the elements to destroy him. That was why he was thought a crackpot.

He was of course a romantic, that strange aspect of the English character that threads an uneasy line between the heroic and the preposterous. And like all such men there are times when he seems to be playing a part, like a small boy imagining himself as King Arthur. In Erskine's case that was never more so than in that final scene before the firing-squad, when one almost expects him to declare, 'It is a far, far, better thing ...' But, for good or ill, we live in a much more cynical age than he did.

It is interesting to compare Erskine with that other, even odder, romantic T. E. Lawrence. There are curious similarities betrween the two men: the same fondness for bleak, lonely, inhospitable places; the same asceticism; the same search for danger and love of speed. The same adoption of a nationalist cause that was not their own. And both men seem to have been haunted by an inner demon that denied them rest.

But that does not mean that the two men were both driven by the same ghost. There is not the slightest reason for supposing that Erskine was anything but heterosexual. He certainly spent a great deal of his time with young men, but given his passion for danger that was inescapable. His best friends, like Basil Williams, married and lived normal family lives. His closest and dearest male companion, Gordon Shephard, was attractive to and attracted by women. And above all, of course, his love for Molly was deep and lasting. It is surely not a coincidence that the only period of his life when he seemed content with a normal quiet existence was in the ten years that followed his marriage. The love he found for Molly kept the old ghosts at bay. What brought them back with renewed vigour? Probably the war, which both separated him from Molly and placed him under great physical and mental stress.

As for the precise nature of the devils that haunted him, we can never be sure, but it is safe to assume that they had their origins in those events at the age of six that so devastated his childhood. It was the combination of those childhood scars together with his obsessive nature that led him to involvement in Ireland's tragic divisions and his own destruction.

Erskine's favourite poet was Tennyson; his favourite poem, 'Ulysses'.
For him it makes a curiously apt epitaph:

> I cannot rest from travel; I will drink
> Life to the lees: all times I have enjoy'd
> Greatly. I have suffer'd greatly, both with those
> That loved me, and alone: on shore and when
> Thro' scudding drifts the rainy Hyades
> Vext the dim sea; I am become a name;
> For always roaming with a hungry heart
> Much have I seen and known; cities of men
> And manners, climates, councils, governments.
> Myself not least, but honour'd of them all;
> And drunk delight of battle with my peers,
> Far on the ringing plains of Troy.

Notes

Notes to Chapter 1: Young Erskine

1. *Dictionary of National Biography.*
2. *Cambridge Review,* 10 March 1892.

Notes to Chapter 2: Sea Fever

1. *Times,* 11 May 1909.
2. *Times,* 11 May 1909.
3. *Times,* 11 May 1909.
4. *Times,* 11 May 1909.
5. *Times,* 6 July 1909.
6. *Cruising Club Journal* (1895).
7. *Cruising Club Journal* (1895).
8. *Cruising Club Journal* (1897).
9. *Cruising Club Journal* (1897).
10. *Cruising Club Journal* (1897).
11. *Cruising Club Journal* (1897).
12. *Cruising Club Journal* (1897).
13. *Cruising Club Journal* (1897).
14. Erskine Childers, *The Riddle of the Sands,* p. 29.
15. Childers, *The Riddle of the Sands,* 43.
16. Childers, *The Riddle of the Sands,* p. 43.
17. Childers, *The Riddle of the Sands,* p. 35.
18. *Times,* 28 June 1910.
19. *Times,* 12 May 1908.
20. *Times,* 12 May 1908.
21. *Times,* 12 May 1908.

Notes to Chapter 3: Soldier

1. *Evening Standard,* 3 February 1900.
2. Erskine Childers, *In the Ranks of the CIV* (London, 1900), p. 3
3. Childers, *In the Ranks of the CIV,* p. 8.
4. Childers, *In the Ranks of the CIV,* p. 49.
5. Childers, *In the Ranks of the CIV,* p. 63.
6. Childers, *In the Ranks of the CIV,* p. 69.
7. Childers, *In the Ranks of the CIV,* p. 87.
8. Childers, *In the Ranks of the CIV,* p. 93.
9. Childers, *In the Ranks of the CIV,* p. 114.
10. Childers, *In the Ranks of the CIV,* p. 133.
11. Childers, *In the Ranks of the CIV,* p. 127.
12. Childers, *In the Ranks of the CIV,* p. 141.
13. Childers, *In the Ranks of the CIV,* p. 152.
14. Arthur F. B. Williams, *Erskine Childers.*
15. Childers, *In the Ranks of the CIV.*
16. Childers, *In the Ranks of the CIV.*
17. Childers, *In the Ranks of the CIV.*
18. Childers, *In the Ranks of the CIV.*
19. Childers, *In the Ranks of the CIV.*
20. Childers, *In the Ranks of the CIV.*
21. Childers, *In the Ranks of the CIV.*
22. Childers, *In the Ranks of the CIV.*
23. Childers, *In the Ranks of the CIV.*
24. Childers, *In the Ranks of the CIV.*
25. Childers, *In the Ranks of the CIV.*
26. Childers, *In the Ranks of the CIV.*
27. Childers, *In the Ranks of the CIV.*
28. Childers, *In the Ranks of the CIV.*
29. Childers, *In the Ranks of the CIV.*

Notes to Chapter 4: Author

1. Andrew Boyle, *The Riddle of Erskine Childers* (London, 1977).
2. Erskine Childers, *The HAC in South Africa* (London, 1903), p. 94.
3. Erskine Childers, *The Riddle of the Sands* (London, 1903), p. 25.
4. Childers, *The Riddle of the Sands,* p. 36.
5. Childers, *The Riddle of the Sands,* p. 59.
6. Childers, *The Riddle of the Sands,* p. 59.

7. Childers, *The Riddle of the Sands*, p. 167.
8. Peter Padfield, *The Great Naval Race*.
9. A. F. B. Williams, *Erskine Childers*, p. 11.
10. Boyle, *The Riddle of Erskine Childers*.
11. Padfield, *The Great Naval Race*.
12. PRO, ADM 116, 940B.
13. Childers, *The Riddle of the Sands*, p. 95.
14. Childers, *The Riddle of the Sands*, p. 95.
15. *Times Literary Supplement*, 14 August 1903.
16. *Times*, 13 June 1903.
17. *Boston Post*.

Notes to Chapter 5: Marriage

1. Burke Williams, *The Zeal of the Convert* (Gerrards Cross, 1978).
2. *Boston Post*.
3. *Boston Post*.
4. Andrew Boyle, *The Riddle of Erskine Childers* (London, 1977).
5. Boyle, *The Riddle of Erskine Childers*.
6. *Boston Post*.
7. Boyle, *The Riddle of Erskine Childers*, p. 135.
8. Boyle, *The Riddle of Erskine Childers*, p. 138.
9. Hugh and Diana Popham, *A Thirst for the Sea* (London, 1979).
10. Boyle, *The Riddle of Erskine Childers*.
11. Leo Amery, *My Political Life*, p. 93.
12. Erskine Childers, *The Times History of the War in South Africa* (London, 1907).
13. *Times*, 13 June 1907.
14. Popham, *A Thirst for the Sea*, p. 125.
15. Popham, *A Thirst for the Sea*, p. 131.
16. *Times*, 11 September 1908.
17. Boyle, *The Riddle of Erskine Childers*.

Notes to Chapter 6: New Interests

1. Shane Leslie, *Memoirs of Brigadier-General Gordon Shephard* (privately printed, London, 1924), p. 9.
2. *Times*, 16 November 1910.
3. Erskine Childers, *The Framework of Home Rule* (London, 1911), p. 182.
4. Erskine Childers, *The Form and Purpose of Home Rule* (London, 1912), p. 11.
5. Childers, *The Form and Purpose of Home Rule*, p. 14.

6. Childers, *The Form and Purpose of Home Rule*, p. 14.
7. Andrew Boyle, *The Riddle of Erskine Childers* (London, 1977), p. 176.
8. Leslie, *Memoirs of Brigadier-General Gordon Shephard*.
9. Hugh and Diana Popham, *A Thirst for the Sea* (London, 1979).
10. Leslie, *Memoirs of Brigadier-General Gordon Shephard*.
11. Popham, *A Thirst for the Sea*.
12. Popham, *A Thirst for the Sea*.

Notes to Chapter 7: Gun-Runner

1. F. X. Martin, *The Howth Gun-Running* (Dublin, 1964). See J. Ring, *Erskine Childers* (London, 1996), pp. 140–47.
2. Martin, *The Howth Gun-Running*, p. 71.
3. Martin, *The Howth Gun-Running*, p. 73.
4. Martin, *The Howth Gun-Running*, p. 75.
5. Martin, *The Howth Gun-Running*, p. 67.
6. Martin, *The Howth Gun-Running*, p. 77.
7. Martin, *The Howth Gun-Running*, p. 77.
8. Martin, *The Howth Gun-Running*, p. 79.
9. Martin, *The Howth Gun-Running*, p. 81.
10. Martin, *The Howth Gun-Running*, p. 82.
11. Martin, *The Howth Gun-Running*, p. 86.
12. Martin, *The Howth Gun-Running*, p. 87.
13. Martin, *The Howth Gun-Running*, p. 90.
14. Martin, *The Howth Gun-Running*, p. 92.
15. Martin, *The Howth Gun-Running*, p. 93.

Notes to Chapter 8: The Cuxhaven Raid

1. PRO, ADM137, 452.
2. PRO, ADM137, 552.
3. Andrew Boyle, *The Riddle of Erskine Childers* (London, 1977).
4. Paul G. Halpern, *A Naval History of World War I*, p. 103.
5. Arthur Marder, *Portrait of an Admiral*.
6. Roger Keyes, *Naval Memoirs*.
7. Halpern, *A Naval History of World War I*, p. 43.
8. PRO, ADM116, 1352.
9. PRO, ADM116, 1352.
10. PRO, ADM116, 1352.
11. PRO, AIR1, 148/15/88.

Notes to Chapter 9: The Dardanelles

1. Roger Keyes, *Naval Memoirs*.
2. PRO, AIR1, 625/17/12.
3. Sir Frederick Sykes, *From Many Angles* (London, 1942).
4. PRO, AIR1, 665/17/122/714.
5. Peter Liddle, *Men of Gallipoli*, p. 242.
6. PRO, AIR1, 361/15/228/17.
7. Richard Hough, *The Great War at Sea*.
8. PRO, ADM1, 8432/263.
9. Liddle, *Men of Gallipoli*, p. 242.
10. Sykes, *From Many Angles*, p. 174.
11. Charles Samson, *Flights and Fights*, p. 273.
12. PRO, AIR1, 649/17/122/420.
13. Sykes, *From Many Angles*, p. 176.
14. Andrew Boyle, *The Riddle of Erskine Childers* (London, 1977), p. 217.
15. Boyle, *The Riddle of Erskine Childers*, p. 218.
16. Boyle, *The Riddle of Erskine Childers*.
17. PRO, AIR1, 1707/204/123/68.
18. PRO, AIR1, 1707/204/123/68.
19. Boyle, *The Riddle of Erskine Childers*.

Notes to Chapter 10: Sea and Sky

1. PRO, AIR1, 185/15/226/2.
2. Andrew Boyle, *The Riddle of Erskine Childers* (London, 1977).
3. Reginald Bacon, *The Dover Patrol*, p. 466.
4. Shane Leslie, *Memoirs of Brigadier-General Gordon Shephard* (privately printed, London, 1924), p. 28.
5. Leslie, *Memoirs of Brigadier-General Gordon Shephard*, p. 29.
6. Boyle, *The Riddle of Erskine Childers*.
7. Boyle, *The Riddle of Erskine Childers*.
8. Boyle, *The Riddle of Erskine Childers*.
9. Boyle, *The Riddle of Erskine Childers*.
10. Boyle, *The Riddle of Erskine Childers*.
11. Boyle, *The Riddle of Erskine Childers*.

Notes to Chapter 11: Sinn Fein

1. Calton Younger, *Ireland's Civil War*, p. 214.

2. Andrew Boyle, *The Riddle of Erskine Childers* (London, 1977), p. 249.
3. *Times.*
4. *Daily News,* April 1920.
5. *Daily News,* April 1920.
6. *Irish Bulletin.*
7. Boyle, *The Riddle of Erskine Childers,* p. 269.
8. Boyle, *The Riddle of Erskine Childers.*
9. Boyle, *The Riddle of Erskine Childers.*
10. Boyle, *The Riddle of Erskine Childers,* p. 272.
11. Boyle, *The Riddle of Erskine Childers.*
12. Tom Jones, *Whitehall Diary,* p. 112.
13. Eddie Marsh, *A Number of People.*
14. Boyle, *The Riddle of Erskine Childers,* p. 288.
15. *Daily Telegraph,* 23 December 1922.

Notes to Chapter 12: Civil War

1. T. P. Coogan, *Michael Collins,* p. 296.
2. Newspaper report of speeches in Irish Parliament.
3. Ibid.
4. Ibid.
5. Ibid.
6. Ibid.
7. Elizabeth Lazenby, *Ireland: A Catspaw,* p. 110.
8. *Times,* 7 September 1922.
9. *Times,* 19 September 1922.
10. Andrew Boyle, *The Riddle of Erskine Childers* (London, 1977), p. 17.
11. Boyle, *The Riddle of Erskine Childers,* p. 16.
12. Boyle, *The Riddle of Erskine Childers,* p. 23.
13. Boyle, *The Riddle of Erskine Childers,* p. 25.
14. Boyle, *The Riddle of Erskine Childers,* p. 25.

Notes to Chapter 13: The Tragedy of Erskine Childers

1. *Daily Mail,* obituary of Erskine Childers.
2. *Evening Standard,* obituary of Erskine Childers.
3. *Boston Post,* obituary of Erskine Childers.
4. *Daily Chronicle,* obituary of Erskine Childers.
5. *Daily Mail,* obituary of Erskine Childers.
6. *Daily News,* obituary of Erskine Childers.

Bibliography

Primary Sources

The main body of material on and by Erskine Childers is held by Trinity College Dublin. There is also a collection of Childers material at Trinity College, Cambridge. His war diary is held at the Imperial War Museum. The sources for his service in the First World War can be found in Public Record Office classes ADM1, ADM53, ADM116, ADM137 and AIR1.

Works by Erskine Childers

In the Ranks of the CIV (London, 1900).
The HAC in South Africa (London, 1903).
The Riddle of the Sands (London, 1903).
The Times History of the War in South Africa (London, 1907).
War and the Arme Blanche (London, 1910).
The German Influence on British Cavalry (London, 1911).
The Framework of Home Rule (London, 1911).
The Form and Purpose of Home Rule (London, 1912).
Military Rule in Ireland (London, 1920).
Who Burnt Cork City? (London, 1921).

Yachting Journalism

Royal Cruising Club Journal.
The Times.

Other Works

Andrew Boyle, *The Riddle of Erskine Childers* (London, 1970).
Richard Bennett, *The Black and Tans* (London, 1970).

Mary C. Bromage, *De Valera* (London, 1956).

Padriac Colum, *Arthur Griffith* (Dublin, 1959).

Tim Pat Coogan, *De Valera* (London, 1993).

—, *Michael Collins* (London 1901).

Spencer Childers, *Life and Correspondence of the Rt Hon. Hugh Culling Eardley Childers* (London, 1901).

Darrell Figgis, *Recollections of the Irish War* (London, 1927).

Margery Forester, *Michael Collins: The Lost Leader* (London, 1972).

R. F. Foster, *Modern Ireland* (London, 1988).

Brian Inglis, *Roger Casement* (London, 1973).

Robert Kee, *The Green Flag* (London, 1972).

Helen Landreth, *The Mind and Heart of Mary Childers* (privately printed, 1965).

Elizabeth Lazenby, *Ireland: A Catspaw* (London, 1968).

Shane Leslie, *Memoirs of Brigadier-General Gordon Shephard* (privately printed, London, 1924).

Longford, Earl of, and T. P. O'Neill, *Eamon de Valera* (London, 1970).

F. S. L. Lyons, *Ireland since the Famine* (London, 1971)

Michael McInerney, *The Riddle of Erskine Childers* (Dublin, 1971).

Jim Ring, *Erskine Childers* (London, 1996)

Sir Frederick Sykes, *From Many Angles* (London, 1942).

Terence de Vere White, *Kevin O'Higgins* (London, 1948).

Burke Wilkinson, *The Zeal of the Convert* (Gerrards Cross, 1978)

Basil Williams, *Erskine Childers: A Sketch* (privately printed, 1926).

Calton Younger, *Ireland's Civil War* (London, 1968).

—, *A State of Disunion* (London, 1972).

Index

REC = Robert Erskine Childers

Admiral de Horsey Silver Cup 28
Admiralty Intelligence 116, 119, 137, 140, 237, 238
Air Department of the Admiralty 172, 173, 239
aircraft 153, 158, 161, 188
    types of 148, 155, 166, 181, 190
aircraft-carriers 142, 150, 154, 167
    Anne 167
    Ark Royal 158, 159
    Ben-My-Chree 154, 155, 157–70
    Raven II 167
    see also Engadine, HMS
America, *see* United States of America
Amery, Leo 77, 78, 92
Ancient and Honourable Artillery Company, Massachusetts (Boston Ancients) 79, 82
Anglo-Irish Protestants 123
Anglo-Irish Treaty 208, 208–14, 215–20
Anne (aircraft-carrier) 167
Archer, Colin 90
Arethusa (cruiser) 147
Ark Royal (aircraft-carrier) 158, 159
arms dealers 123, 124
Asgard (REC's yacht) 90–91, 93–94, 117–20, 133
    gun-running 124, 126, 127–37
    mystery 95

retires to a Dublin museum 237
Ashbourne, Edward Gibson, Lord 123
Asquith, Herbert H. 113, 139
Aston, Major-General Sir George 139
Aurania (passenger ship) 57
Australian troops 163
Austria 136, 194
Autigny, France 188

Bacon, Vice-Admiral 179, 180, 182, 183
Baring, Maurice 18
Bartels, Captain 31, 68
Barton, Anna Henrietta, *see* Childers, Anna Henrietta
Barton, Captain Robert (grandfather of REC) 5, 177
Barton, Charles (uncle of REC) 6, 8, 15
Barton family 6, 34
Barton, Robert (cousin of REC) 88, 97, 200, 206, 214
    and Anglo-Irish Treaty 212
    arrested 196
    and De Valera 215, 216
    influence on REC 186, 187
    in prison 225
    on the run 196
Basutoland, South Africa 47
Bayly, Rear-Admiral 139

Beaslai, Piaras 204
Beggar's Bush Barracks 227
Belfast, Northern Ireland 110, 116
Belgian refugees 29, 153, 184, 186, 196
Belgium 180, 181, 184, 196, 197
Ben-My-Chree (aircraft-carrier) 154, 155, 157–70
Bengeo school, Hertfordshire 10, 69
Benn, Captain Wedgwood Benn 230
Bennett, Arnold 72, 178
Berlin 190, 191
Berliner Neueste Nachtrichten 105
Bernhardi, General von 103
Bethlehem, South Africa 48, 50
Bircham Newton, Norfolk 188, 189
Black and Tans 200, 203
Bloemfontein, South Africa 42, 43
boats (1890s) 20
Boer people 34, 35, 44, 50, 64
Boer War 34, 36–37, 42–55, 239
    cavalry in 101
    REC's letters on 62
    the welcome home 57–59
    see also South Africa
bomb sights 164
bombers 164, 189, 190
Bonar Law, Andrew 113, 121, 207, 231
Borkum 139, 141, 154
Boston Ancients 79, 82
Boston, Massachusetts 79, 81–85, 86, 232
    see also United States of America
Boston Post 83, 88, 232
Boston Sunday Post 84
Brandon, Lieutenant Vivian 105, 106, 107
Brandon and Trench spying charges 105, 106, 107, 116

Brennen, Robert 202
Bridges, Robert 99
British army 176, 200, 201, 213, 217, 220
    in Boer War 42
British Secret Service 237
Bruges, Belgium 197
Brugha, Cathal 194, 212, 220, 222
Brunning, Commander von 68
Buchan, John 99
Budworth, Major, VC 82
Bulgaria 165
Buller, Sir Redvers 36, 44

Cambridge Review 16, 70
Cambridge University 13, 14–17, 21, 235
Canada 85–86
Carrol, Kitty 205
Carson, Sir Edward 112, 121, 124
Casement, Roger 116, 123, 174, 175, 178
casualties
    in Boer War 53
    in Dardanelles 161
    in Easter Rising 175, 176
    in Irish Civil War 235
    on Southland 164
cavalry 101, 102, 103, 176
censorship 143
Ceylon 1, 3–4
Chamberlain, Austen 208
Chamberlain, Joseph 35
Channel Tunnel 14–15
Chesterton, G. K. 178
Chicago (US warship) 83
Childers, Agnes 6, 15
Childers, Anna Henrietta (née Barton) (mother of REC) 1, 2, 4–5, 7–8, 89

Childers, Charles (grandfather of REC) 3, 13, 15, 28

Childers, Constance (sister of REC) 1, 32

Childers, Dulcibella (sister of REC) 1, 32, 67

Childers, Erskine Hamilton (first son of REC) 91, 101, 228, 236, 237

Childers family 3, 8, 34, 235

Childers, Henry (brother of REC) 1, 9, 13, 97–98
  character 21, 63, 239
  education 10
  sea voyages with REC 21–24, 27, 29, 31
  visits REC in Pretoria hospital 56

Childers, Hugh (first cousin of REC) 3, 6–7, 12, 18, 28

Childers, John 3

Childers, Leonard (racehorse breeder 1721) 3

Childers, Mary Alden (Molly) (née Osgood) 90, 91, 186, 198, 228, 240
  awarded MBE 187
  and Belgian refugees 153, 184, 186
  on gun-running voyage 126, 127, 130, 134, 135
  health 87, 94, 100
  letters, see letters
  marriage to REC 87, 88, 185–86

Childers, Mildred (later Walbanke) 3

Childers, Robert Caesar (father of REC) 1–2, 3–4, 5, 7–8

Childers, Robert Erskine
  birth 1
  career
    in Admiralty Air Department 172, 173
    as an author 72–73, 76
    and Anglo-Irish treaty 212, 213, 218–19
    in Coastal Motor Boat Squadron 179, 180
    in Honourable Artillery Company 37, 46, 47, 64, 81, 90
    in House of Commons 18, 19–20, 79, 104
    legal 18, 200
    political 114, 115, 116, 205
    in Royal Air Force 187
    in the Royal Naval Volunteer Reserve 140, 142, 152, 153, 159
    as a soldier 39–59 passim
  character 10, 63, 160, 239–40
    fanaticism 104
    obsession 11, 89, 195
      with Ireland 97, 104, 108, 115, 210
    sexuality 240
    teetotalism 64, 79
  children
    Erskine Hamilton (first son of REC,) 91, 101, 228, 236–37
    Henry (second son) 94, 100
    Robert Alden (third son) 101
  education 10, 12, 15
    at Bengeo prep school 10, 69
    at Cambridge 13, 18, 21, 69
    at Haileybury 11, 69
  friends, see friends of REC
  health 10, 13, 55, 195, 196
    mental deterioration 210
  homes
    after marriage 88–89
    in Ireland 199, 203
    Glendalough House, Ireland 5, 225
    London 1, 2, 5, 19, 32

honours (DSO) 183
marriage 87, 88, 185–86
sports and pastimes 12, 39
  Asgard 90–91
  Mad Agnes (Marguerite) 24, 25,
    27, 28
  Shulah 22, 23, 24
  Sunbeam 66, 79, 90
  Vixen 28, 29, 30, 31, 32, 35
  walking 10, 11, 13, 99, 239
works
  Daily News articles 200, 201
  In the Ranks of the CIV 63, 95
  published articles 95–96, 197
  The Form and Purpose of Home
    Rule (lecture) 113–14
  The Framework of Home Rule
    110–12
  The HAC in South Africa 66
  The Riddle of the Sands, see The
    Riddle of the Sands
  Times articles 63
  War News 222
death 230, 231, 233, 234
obituaries 231–34
Childers, Sybil (sister of REC) 1, 32
Churchill, Winston 77, 139, 140, 141,
  143
forced from office (1915) 157
on REC 226, 236
City Imperial Volunteers 37, 65
Clarke, Sir George 90
Coastal Motor Boat Squadron 179–83
coastguards 134, 136
Coffey, Diarmid 185
Collins, Michael 22, 196, 197, 218,
  219, 220
and Anglo-Irish Treaty 208–17
his army 194, 195, 204
death 222, 234

communications 44, 50, 147, 161
Connolly, James 174
Conservative Party 108, 113
cooperative societies 97
Cope, Arthur 206
Cornwall, HMS (training ship) 107
Cosgrave, William T. 222, 231
cruisers 20, 145, 146, 147, 151, 155
Cruising Club Journal 26, 67, 95
Cruising Club, The 21, 25, 28
Cuxhaven Raid 139–55

Dacre, Flight-Lieutenant 162, 166
Daily Chronicle 233
Daily Mail 231, 233
Daily News 105–6, 200, 201, 226,
  233
Dardanelles campaign 155, 157–72
Darley, Major (pilot) 190
Davidson, Colonel 188
De Havilland 4 reconnaissance
  aircraft 181
De Robeck, Admiral 162
De Valera, Eamon 193, 208, 212,
  221, 235
and Anglo-Irish Treaty 215, 216,
  217
in meetings with Lloyd George
  206, 207, 208
and REC 196, 209, 225
resignation as President of the
  Irish Republic 218, 219
De Wet, Christiaan R. 45, 47, 50, 52,
  53, 55
Denbigh, Lady 82
Denbigh, Lord 64, 65, 72, 81, 82
in Boston 83, 85
Denmark 139
Dennis, A. H. 66, 79, 90
Derbyshire Regiment 45

destroyers 145, 180–81, 182, 183
Devonport, Devon 114, 115, 116
diaries
    of Mary Spring Rice 128–34
        passim
    of REC 41, 61, 190
Dictionary of National Biography 99
Digby, Major (pilot) 190
Dominion status 207, 208, 211
Doyle, Sir Arthur Conan 70, 178
Dublin 110, 122, 126, 135, 175, 237
Duffy, Gavan 197, 216, 231
    and Anglo-Irish Treaty 208, 211,
        212, 213
Duggan, Eamon (solicitor) 209, 211,
    212, 213, 215

Earles, Bob 25
East Indies and Egypt Seaplane
    Squadron 167, 171
Easter Rising 174–78, 238
Edmonds, Flight Lieutenant 153,
    160, 162, 166, 169–70
Edward VII, King of Great Britain
    and Ireland 73, 109
Egypt 169
Eighth Submarine Flotilla 145
elections 109, 110, 205, 221
Empiricism 34
Empress, HMS (aircraft carrier) 142,
    147, 151, 167
Engadine, HMS (aircraft-carrier) 144,
    145, 147, 153, 154, 155
    Churchill and Jellicoe visit 143
    REC joins 142
Erskine, Thomas (eighteenth
    century) 1
Evening Standard 232
Evil in the Universe (translation by
    Anna Childers) 2

Faith (sloop) 33
fashion, ladies 88
'fatigues' 62–63
Fearless, HMS (cruiser) 146, 151
Felixstowe, Suffolk 187
Fellowes, Squadron Leader 181
Figgis, Darrell 123, 124–25, 129,
    131
First World War 139, 191, 193, 239
Fisher, H. A. L. 234
Fitzgerald, Desmond 204
Flanders 157, 184
Four Courts attack 220, 222
Fouriesburg, S. Africa 49, 52
Fram (Nansen's boat) 90
Free State artillery bombard Four
    Courts 222
French, Sir John, Field-Marshal, Earl
    of Ypres 103, 104, 199
friends of REC 17–18, 66, 69, 90,
    100, 234
    Le Fanu 32
    Lloyd-Jones 15
    Marsh 15
    Robinson 224
    Runciman 15, 68
    Shephard 100
    Trevelyan 15
    Williams, *see* Williams, Basil
Frisian Islands 70, 105, 116, 139
    plans to attack 139, 141, 154
Fry, Roger 99

Gallaher, Frank 205–6
Gallipoli 160, 164–65, 167
Galsworthy, John 72, 178
general elections 109, 110
George V, King of Great Britain and
    Ireland 109
German Navy 149–50, 152, 173

Germany 73, 75, 105, 140, 152, 174
    bombards east coast of England
        146
    submarines 158, 169, 173
    Zeppelin sheds 145
gin palace boats 20
Gladstone, William E. 108
Glendalough House 5–6, 8, 9, 235
    REC betrayed at 225
    REC holidays at 12, 37, 97
    REC recuperates at 196
Green, Alice Stopford 122, 198
Green, Sir Graham 183
Gresham's School, Norfolk 235
Griffith, Arthur 198, 204, 206, 212,
    215
    and Anglo-Irish Treaty 212, 217,
        218–19
    as President of Irish Republic 219
    and REC 197
    death 222, 234
gun-running 122–23, 124, 126,
    127–37, 238
guns, artillery 41, 42, 43, 48, 51, 176,
    235
    REC's duties with 46–47
guns, rifles 101, 103, 122, 124, 174,
    235
    REC and Figgis search for 123,
        124–25

Habeas Corpus 228, 229
Haileybury school, Hertfordshire 11,
    69
Hall, Captain Reginald ('Reggie')
    107, 238
Hamilton-Gordon, George 16, 17
Handley-Page aircraft 188, 190
Hardie, Keir 231
Harrer, General 140

Hartlepool, Durham 144, 146
'Harwich Force' (fleet) 145, 146
Helga (fishery-protection vessel) 176
Henri Farman aircraft 166
Hobson, Bulmer 125
Holland 139
Holmes, Oliver Wendell 91
Honourable Artillery Company 37,
    39, 46, 79
    in action 46, 47
    American tour 85–86
    in Boston, Massachusetts 81–85,
        86
    Canadian tour 85–86
    REC training with 64, 81, 90
House of Commons 69, 231
    REC's career in 18, 19–20, 79, 104
House of Lords 108, 109, 112, 121
Howe, General William 82
Howth Bay, Dublin 126, 135, 136,
    238
Hungary 194
Hunter, General 48, 49, 51, 52

Ilbert, Sir Courtney 114
Illustrated London News 58
In the Ranks of the CIV 63, 95
influenza epidemic 195
IRA 194, 200, 201, 203, 205, 220
    assassinate Field Marshal Sir
        Henry Wilson 221
Ireland 110, 115, 184, 193, 194
    opinions of 198, 219, 221–22
    at peace 235
Irish Bulletin 202
Irish Civil War 215–30, 235
Irish Convention 184, 186, 187, 239
Irish government 222, 233
Irish Home Rule 108, 110, 115
    Liberal Party support for 108

Irish Home Rule Bill 109, 112, 121, 174, 193, 199
  receives royal assent 203
Irish Parliament 193, 217, 231
Irish Press 236
Irish Rebellion, *see* Easter Rising
Irish Republic, Presidents of 218, 219, 237
Irish Republican Army, *see* IRA
Irish Volunteers 125, 133, 135, 136, 173, 174
  asked for knowledge of REC's whereabouts 137, 140, 237
  created 122
  renamed Irish Republican Army (IRA) 194
Irish Yeomanry 45

James, Henry 90
Jameson Raid 34
Jellicoe, Admiral Sir John 142, 143
Jermome, Jerome K. 178
Johannes (ketch) 31
Jones, Tom 207
Journal of the Royal Asiatic Society 2
Juler, Mrs (landlady) 14

Kelpie (yacht) 123–24, 127, 129, 130
Keyes, Commodore Sir Roger 142, 145, 153, 158
Keynes, John Maynard 99
Khuddaka Patha (translated by Robert Caesar Childers) 2
Kilmer, Flying Officer 144, 148, 149, 151
  mentioned in despatches 152, 153
Kimberley, South Africa 36, 42, 44
Kitchener, Horatio H., first Earl Kitchener of Khartoum 42

Kroonstadt, South Africa 45
Kruger, Paul 35

Ladysmith, South Africa 36–37, 42, 44
Lansdowne, Henry Charles, Lord 36
Law, Andrew Bonar *see* Bonar Law, Andrew
Lawrence, Sir Alexander 123
Lawrence, T. E. 240
Lazenby, Elizabeth 220
Le Fanu, William 32, 36, 66, 79, 90
Le Strange Malone, Squadron Commander C. 158
letters
  between Molly Childers and Robert Barton 187
  David Robinson to Molly Childers 224
  Molly Childers to Gordon Shephard's mother 185
  REC on the Boer War 62
  REC on rebels 177–78
  REC to aunt 71
  REC to Basil Williams 71, 79, 85, 86, 97
  REC to the *Daily News* on Brandon and Trench spying charges 105–6
  REC to home 40
  REC to Molly 89, 116, 127, 196
  REC to Gordon Shephard's mother 185
  REC to Sir Frederick Sykes 188
  REC to sisters 41, 61, 64
  REC's last, to Molly Childers 228–29, 229–30
  REC's, offer to publish 61, 62
Leveson, Rear-Admiral 139

Liberal Party 108, 109, 113
    REC in 107, 114, 115, 116
Lindley, South Africa 46, 47
Lindsay, Mrs (IRA victim) 205
Lloyd George, David 77, 97, 108,
    184, 194
    and Anglo-Irish treaty 213, 214
    and Home Rule Bill 199
    in talks with De Valera 206, 207,
    208
Lloyd-Jones, Ivor 15, 25, 91
    voyages with REC 25, 28, 29, 30,
    79, 93
Lowe, General 176
Lurcher, HMS 147, 151

M19 (monitor ship) 160, 161
MacLysaght, Edward 185, 186, 187
MacNeill, Eoin (John) 122, 124, 125,
    174, 175
Mafeking, South Africa 36, 42, 44
Magpie and Stump Debating Society,
    Cambridge 14–17
Maitland, F. W. 99, 100, 119
Malone, Lieutenant-Commander
    152, 153, 154, 163
Maritza river bridge, Bulgaria 165–67
marriages 240
    Charles Barton to Agnes Childers
    6
    Colonel John Childers to daughter
    of Lord Eardley 3
    Mildred Childers to William
    Walbanke 3
    RES to Molly Osgood 87, 88,
    185–86
Marsh, Eddie 15, 17, 18, 77, 210
Marshall, Sir Arthur 230
Masefield, John 230
Maxwell, General Sir John 176, 177

Mayflower (Dominion Line ship) 81,
    83
Milner, Alfred, first Viscount 34, 35,
    92
monitor ships 160, 161, 162, 164, 165
Montfort, SS (embarkation ship) 40, 81
Moritz Magnus (arms dealers) 124
Morning Post 74
Mulock, Colonel (Bircham's station
    commander) 190
Murray, Gilbert 230

Nansen, Fridtjof 90
National Army 225
Naville, Ernest 2
New York Times 233
Norderney island 150
Norway 91
novels 72
Nowell, Robert 117

Oath of Allegiance 213, 235
O'Brien, Conor 123, 126, 128, 130,
    131
observers 147, 148
O'Connor, Frank 223
O'Higgins, Kevin 219, 222, 223, 227,
    231
O'Kelly, Sean 197
Oliver, Sir Henry 140
Ollivant, Major Alfred 100, 119, 120,
    196
Orange Free State annexed to the
    British Crown 43–44
Osgood, Dr Hamilton (Molly
    Childers's father) 87, 90, 95
Osgood, Mary Alden (Molly) (later
    Childers) 87–88, 185–86
Osgood, Mrs (Molly Childers's
    mother) 203

Paget, General 47, 48, 49, 50, 51
Paris Peace Conference 197–98
Parnell, Charles Stewart 6, 14
partition, Irish 217–18
Passchendaele, Belgium 184
Payne, Commodore 184
Peace Conference, Paris 197–98
Pearse, Patrick 174, 175, 176
Pierce, Samuel 117
Pipon, Colonel Robert 125, 126
Piquetberg, South Africa 42
Plunkett, Sir Horace 97, 110, 185
policemen 195, 199
Pollock, Sir Frederick 91
Ponsonby, Arthur 230
Pretoria, South Africa 54, 56
prisoners of war 45, 53
propaganda 200, 201, 204, 220, 222,
    223, 226–27
Protestants 121, 123, 218, 234, 235

racing yachts 20
Racoon, HMS 164
Radford, Basil 71
radio communication 147, 161
Rainsford, Laurie 91
Ratief's Nek, South Africa 51
Raven II (aircraft-carrier) 167
reconnaissance 164, 165, 168
    REC on 168, 169, 170–71, 181
red tape 52
Redmond, John 122
religion 6, 12, 97, 171
Republicans 220, 222, 226–27
    in Boston, Massachusetts 232
Retribution, HMS (warship) 83, 86
Rhodes, Cecil 34
Richmond, Captain 141, 142, 179
Riviera, HMS (aircraft-carrier) 142,
    146, 147, 155

Roberts, Frederick Sleigh, first Earl
    42, 44, 45, 54, 64, 65
    preface to War and the Arme
        Blanche 102, 104
Roberts (monitor ship) 160, 161
Robertson, Lieutenant Commander
    147, 151, 153
Robinson, David 224, 225
Roman Catholicism 110, 218
Roodewal railway station, South
    Africa 45
Rosebery, Archibald, fifth Earl of
    75, 76
Rothenstein, William 99
Royal Air Force 187, 188, 190
Royal Flying corps 140, 187
Royal Irish Constabulary 195,
    199
Royal Naval Volunteer Reserve
    (RNVR) 140, 142, 152, 153,
    159
Royal Navy 73, 74, 147, 178, 238
Royal Navy Volunteer Force 74
Runciman, Walter 15, 21, 68, 107
Rundle, General 51–52
Russell, Bertrand 17
Russia 184

sabre versus rifle 101
Salonika, Macedonia 165
Samson, Commander C. R. 158,
    166
Santa Cruz (fishing smack) 123
Sargent, John 90
Sayonara (yacht) 238
Scarborough, Yorkshire 146
Schillig Roads, Germany 149–50
Schlesinger, Barthol 117
Scoones, Mr (tutor) 18
scorched-earth policy 50

seaplane-carriers *see* aircraft-carriers
seaplanes 143, 147, 148, 150, 155, 158
    action in Dardanelles 162
    'East Indies and Egypt Seaplane
        Squadron' 167, 171
    mystery of the unidentified
        seaplane 149
    number 136 150, 151
    Short seaplane 158, 162, 166,
        181
Selborne, William, second Earl of
    75
Senussi tribesmen 168, 169
Serbia 136, 165
Shaw, Bernard 224–25
Shephard, Gordon 100, 116, 117,
    118, 119, 240
    and Admiralty Intelligence 238
    gun-running 125, 126, 127, 129,
        132
        leaves *Asgard* 133
        meets *Asgard* at Howth 136
    joins Royal Flying Corps 140
    death 185
Shephard, Jack 118
Sherlock Holmes stories 70
Short seaplane 158, 162, 166, 181
Simon, Sir John 99, 230
Sinn Fein 184, 185, 187, 193, 205,
    206
    declares a republic 193
    and elections 205
    and intelligence services 238
    as reported in the press 202
Slabbert's Nek, South Africa 47–48,
    50, 51
Smalldeel, South Africa 53–54
Smith, Elders publishers 71, 72
Smith, Reginald 61, 71, 72
smuggling, *see* gun-running

social reform 97, 108
Sopwith Schneider aircraft 15, 155
South Africa 34, 40–41
    see also Boer War
Southland casualties 164
sovereignty 211
Spring Rice, Mary 123, 126, 127, 135
    diary on gun-running 128–34
        passim
spy stories 70, 71
spying 139, 232, 237
    Brandon and Trench spying
        charges 105, 106, 107, 116
Stack, Austin 206, 212
Stephens, Leslie 99
Strachey, Lytton 18
Strand Magazine 70
submarines, British 145, 146, 147,
    153
submarines, German 158, 169, 173
Sueter, Captain Murray 153
Suez Canal 168, 170
suffrage 97
Sunbeam (yacht) 79
'Sunday Tramps' 99–100
Sykes, Colonel F. H. (later Chief of
    Air Staff) 159, 160, 165, 188

Tel Aviv 171
Tennyson, Alfred, Lord 241
The Form and Purpose of Home Rule
    (lecture) 113–14
The Framework of Home Rule 110–12
*The German Influence on British
    Cavalry* 103–4
The HAC in South Africa 66
The Lady Vanishes 71
The Riddle of the Sands 28–29, 66–78,
    93, 95, 114
    critics of 75–76

as evidence in Brandon and
  Trench spy trial 106
film of 107
further editions and popularity of
  104–5, 107
postscript 74
published (1903) 72
see also spying
Thompson, Mrs (family friend) 61
Times History of the War in South
  Africa, The 77, 89, 91–93
Times Literary Supplement 75, 112
Times, The 28, 36, 63, 95, 221
  on REC 224, 226
Tirpitz, Alfred von 73
torpedoes 162, 179–80, 183
Trench, Captain Bernard 105, 106,
  107
Trenchard, Hugh M. (RFC) 188, 189,
  190, 191
Trevelyan, Charles 15, 99
Trevelyan, George 99
Trude (French warship) 83
Turkey 157, 165, 194
Tyrwhitt, Commodore 145, 147, 152,
  153

Ulster 122
Ulster Protestants 121, 218, 235
Ulster Volunteer Force 113, 122, 237
Undaunted (cruiser) 147
uniforms 81, 82, 83, 84
United Irish League 113
United States of America 85–86, 184,
  198, 199–200
  see also Boston

Victoria, Queen of Great Britain and
  Ireland 37, 73
Von Brunning, Commander 68

Walbanke, William 3
Wales 17–18
War and the Arme Blanche 101–3
War News 222
Waterwitch (Runciman's yacht) 68
Wayne, Naughton 71
weather 146, 148, 154, 163, 191
Wedgwood, Josiah 230
Wellman, Lieutenant-Commander
  181, 182
West Indian (tramp steamer) 32
Westminster Gazette 76
Whitby, Yorkshire 146
Wilhelm II, Kaiser 73, 76
Williams, Basil 37, 54, 77, 100
  and Boer War 239
  and Honourable Artillery
    Company 37
  letters from REC 71, 79, 85, 86, 97
Williams, Basil (continued)
  married 240
  obituary on REC 234
  on REC 50, 185, 207
  REC campaigns for 110
  REC dines with 206–7
Wilson, Field-Marshal Sir Henry 221
Wilson, President Woodrow 198
Woodhead, R. C. 119
Woodhead, Robert 100
Woolf, Leonard 99
World War I 139, 191, 193, 239

yachts 20, 68, 238
  see also Asgard; Kelpie
Yeomanry Hospital, Pretoria 56
Young, Sir George and Lady 123

Zeebrugge, Belgium 180, 181
Zeppelin airships 144, 145, 149, 151,
  154–55